How To Analyze A Bank Statement

Seventh Edition

F.L. Garcia, M.A., J.D., L.L.M

Bankers Publishing Company   Boston

Library of Congress Cataloging in Publication Data

Garcia, F. L. (Ferdinand Lawrence), 1909–
  How to analyze a bank statement.
  Bibliography: p.
  1. Banks and banking—Accounting   2. Banks and
banking—United States   I. Title.
HG1708.G3   1984   657′.833   84-18490
ISBN 0–87267–050–3

Printed in the United States of America

BANKERS PUBLISHING COMPANY
210 South Street
Boston, MA 02111

Executive Editor: Robert M. Roen
Managing Editor: Nancy Long Coleman

Jacket/cover design: William Samatis

Contents

Preface

As a result of the Federal Financial Institutions Examination Council's development of the Uniform Bank Performance Report (UBPR) for all commercial banks analysis of bank statements has become very important.

The Call Reports of Condition and Income along with their supporting schedules have been made uniform for all commercial banks; their accounting has been standardized for comparability; and their data have been subjected to detailed ratio analysis for computerization for the individual bank, for its peer group, and for state averages.

Bank holding company statements, however, have not been made similarly uniform, and it seems unlikely to occur for at least some time. Since bank holding companies control commercial banks with about 84 percent of the total assets of commercial banks and some 67 percent of all banking offices in the U.S., there is still a need for a review of analytical ratios and techniques to use in analysis of bank holding company statements, both consolidated and unconsolidated.

In this edition of *How to Analyze a Bank Statement*, I have given particular attention to the Securities and Exchange Commission's newly revised reporting requirements for publicly financed bank holding companies which provide the data for annual reports to stockholders, for the official Form 10-K, and for other reports submitted to the SEC.

I have also gone into detail of the Federal Reserve System's basic reporting forms for registered bank holding companies. If the recommendations of the Bush Task Force are adopted, these reporting forms will probably be revised in the not too distant future. The task force recommends that the large multinational and other bank holding companies remain in the jurisdiction of the Federal Reserve System but that the rest of the bank holding company population be reassigned to the jurisdiction of the proposed new Federal Banking Agency. Moreover, legislation considered as of early 1984 in Congress, such as the Depository Institutions Holding Company Act Amendments, if passed, would add to or result in changes in the content and detail of the bank holding company reporting forms.

The coverage of analysis techniques of bank holding company consolidated reports is illustrated by specific examples drawn from the annual reports of Citicorp which are responsive to the reporting requirements of the Securities and Exchange Commission. It should be understood, however, that neither Citicorp nor Citibank, N.A. is sponsoring this publication, and that the annual report data are included for illustrative purposes only.

I wish to express my appreciation for the numerous courtesies extended by the supervisory banking agencies, members of the staffs of the Securities and Exchange Commission, firms specializing in bank stocks, and fellow analysts and academic colleagues.

Part 1

Bank Holding Company Financial Statements

Chapter 1

Securities Laws Regulation and Reporting

SECURITIES LAWS AND REGULATIONS

Bank holding companies are chartered as business corporations under the laws of their home state of incorporation, and are subject to special banking regulation and reporting requirements in addition to the usual reporting requirements under the securities laws. Both types of requirements—for banking regulatory purposes and for compliance with securities laws and regulations—continue to undergo changes designed to provide additional detail and disclosure. We review first the updated requirements under the securities laws and regulations.

On September 2, 1980, the Securities and Exchange Commission (SEC) announced the first of a series of revisions and proposals intended to improve disclosure, reduce disclosure burdens, and facilitate the integration of the disclosure systems under the Securities Act of 1933 and the Securities Exchange Act of 1934.

These changes have included, among others, final rules relating to the following:

1. Amendment to the annual report form, Form 10-K, required to be filed by most publicly-owned companies, including bank holding companies. Bank holding companies also file quarterly reports on Form 10-Q.

2. Amendment to related forms, rules, regulations and guides, including the Industry Guides 3, Disclosure by Bank Holding Companies. These guides pertain to filings under the Securities Act of 1933 (Securities Act Industry Guide 3), and under the Securities Exchange Act of 1934 (Securities Exchange Act of 1934 Guide also numbered Guide 3).

> These guides were formerly Guide 61 (pertaining to preparation for filing of registration statements under the Securities Act of 1933); and Guide 3 (pertaining to preparation for filing of reports and proxy and registration statements under the Securities Exchange Act of 1934). On March 3, 1982 the SEC numbered each guide, Guide 3 under each respective Act.[1]

3. Amendment of Regulation S-X, the accounting rules regulation, which together with the Accounting Series releases of the SEC sets forth the form and content of and requirements for financial statements required to be filed. Article 9 of Regulation S-X pertains to consolidated financial statements to be filed by bank holding companies and to financial statements of banks. In addition, Article 9 of Regulation S-X also specifies, with modifications, the applicability of Article 5 of Regulation S-X to unconsolidated financial statements filed by bank holding companies.

Amendment of Article 9

On March 7, 1983 the SEC announced the adoption of final amendment of Article 9 of Regulation S-X regarding financial statements for bank holding companies, effective for fiscal years ending on or after December 31, 1983 (although earlier application of the amended rules in their entirety was permitted).[2]

The SEC explained that the amendment of Article 9 was being adopted to eliminate rules which were duplicative of generally accepted accounting principles (GAAP); integrate and simplify the rules; reflect current accounting practices; and to improve financial reporting generally.

The SEC also amended its proxy rules to eliminate the interim rule that required only substantial compliance with Article 9 in annual reports to stockholders. Consequently, bank holding companies that are required to comply with the SEC's proxy rules will be required to include in annual reports to shareholders financial statements prepared in accordance with the amended requirements of Regulation S-X.

Exhibit A in the Appendix reproduces Article 9 as amended in full. For background and fuller understanding, the SEC's discussion of changes in the Income Statement are of particular interest.

Investment securities gains or losses. The SEC's change in the format of the Income Statement for reporting realized gains or losses on investment securities, as a separate component of income before income tax expense, rather than as a separate item less its applicable income tax expense, after the caption entitled "Income before securities gains or losses," has been adopted despite the fact that a majority of the invited comments that the SEC received in response to its proposals[3] opposed the proposed change.

> The SEC reported that objection to its proposal and to its finally adopted one-step approach was based primarily on the view that the two-step reporting format had been the customary presentation which banks had used for many years; that the inclusion of the effect of investment securities transactions as a part of income from banking operations is inappropriate; and will result in a less useful presentation.
>
> Other objections indicated that banks should have the ability to restructure their investment portfolio without penalizing current operating income with any related losses; and that the proposed change would increase the potential to manage or smooth reported earnings through the timing and selection of securities transactions.

On the other hand, the SEC reported that a significant number of commentators strongly endorsed the change.

> Proponents indicated that a uniform net income approach was long overdue; that conforming the reporting format used by bank holding companies to that used by virtually all other entities would eliminate much of the confusion surrounding a bank holding company's actual

earnings; that in general agreement with the SEC there is no conceptual basis for reporting investment transactions in a manner that implies that the gains or losses thereon represent something other than operating earnings; and that the two-step reporting was inconsistent in that security losses are excluded from operations, while the interest on the replacement security, "which generally exceeds the interest on the previous security" (sic), is included in operating income. On this point, it was mentioned that the sale of securities generally has the same objective as the sale of mortgage loans and should be classified similarly.

The SEC answered the objections to the one-step format with the following points:

1. The two-step Income Statement format promoted the misconception that securities transactions are not part of normal banking operations, and such format detracts from the importance of Net Income, which should be of primary importance to investors. Our comment:

> Since the "bottom-line" of the two-step Income Statement had been *Net* Income, and the intermediate caption had been merely *Income* before securities gains or losses (after income tax expense), the above allegation of deemphasis of Net Income appears to be argumentative.
>
> On the contrary, the break-out separately of securities gains or losses with their related tax effect was welcomed by bank stock analysts (including ourselves) as conducive to greater disclosure regarding the extent if any to which the Net Income figure was affected by "management" of such realized gains or losses on the securities portfolio. Thus in very good income years, the taking of losses on sale of securities might serve to save on taxes while still keeping Net Income at good levels (and replacing the bonds sold at prevailing higher yields for the future). On the other hand, in poor income years, the taking of profits on sale of securities might serve to "window-dress" Net Income in such years.

2. In response to the objection that there would be increased potentiality in the one-step format for "management" of earnings, the Commission emphasized the responsibility of bank holding companies as well as all other registrants to identify clearly and explain in the Management's Discussion and Analysis (required in the complete reports) the nature and impact of all special, discretionary, or nonrecurring items (such as investment

securities gains or losses) having a material effect on reported financial condition, changes in financial condition, and results of operations. Our comment:

> However, the complete reports containing the Management's Disclosure and Analysis appear with a time lag, and may or may not be sufficiently objective.

3. The Commission wished to emphasize its belief that the revised one-step reporting format should not have a bearing on conduct and restructuring of the investment portfolio or prudent decision making; and that existing disclosure requirements call for detail about the content of the investment securities portfolio and the yields thereon. Our comment:

> Carrying values and market values in *aggregates* are required to be shown in *aggregates* for classifications as to totals for (1) U.S. Treasury and other Government agencies and corporations; (2) states of the U.S. and political subdivisions; and (3) other securities (see Exhibit A). However, listing of individual issues held, with cost and market value of each issue held, is not required, so that it would be impossible to check the turnover of individual issues and the profit or loss thereon.

For the above reasons, and "because of the potential for inappropriate reporting of certain transactions as security gains or losses," the SEC adopted the one-step format for the Income Statement for bank holding companies as it proposed, with one change.

> The change in the final revision calls for the presentation of investment securities gains or losses, in their entirety regardless of size, as a separate subcategory (see 13(h) in Exhibit A) in other income, with disclosure of the related income taxes.
>
> However, the SEC fell back on encouragement to the Financial Accounting Standards Board (FASB) to pursue "aggressively" the FASB's project on its agenda, as part of its conceptual framework to explore display issues in reporting earnings.[4] Thus the Commission "stands ready to reconsider the adopted provisions of Article 9's one-step income statement, as well as other provisions of Regulation S-X governing the form and content of financial statements, based on its evaluation of the results of the FASB project."

Short-term investments. The rules adopted for interest-bearing deposits in other banks have been revised in the new Article 9 in response to the comments received. Under the proposal, these deposits would have been presented in a new short-term investment category. Commentators stated that these deposits can have maturities longer than one year and that their risk characteristics differ from those of other short-term investments.

The SEC agreed, and accordingly the final rules require that interest-bearing deposits in other banks be included as a separate line item, following cash and due from banks. In addition, the final rules require that federal funds sold and securities purchased under resale agreements be shown as a separate caption, with all other short-term investments presented separately.

> This presentation is consistent with the new Bank Audit Guide which has been approved for issuance by the American Institute of Certified Public Accountants.[5]

Cash and due from banks. Title of this caption appears to be narrower than the previous caption in Article 9, ''Cash and Due from Depository Institutions,'' but purports to continue the same scope, with the specification however of disclosure of any withdrawal and usage restrictions (including requirements of the Federal Reserve to maintain ''certain *average*'' reserve balances) or compensating balance requirements.

Acceptances of the bank. (Bank acceptances outstanding) This is the liability item for the aggregate of unmatured drafts and bills of exchange accepted by a bank subsidiary, or by some bank as its agent, less the amount of such acceptances acquired by the bank subsidiary through discount or purchase.

The contra asset item is due from customers on acceptances, which includes the amounts receivable from customers in unmatured drafts and bills of exchange that have been accepted by a bank subsidiary or by other banks for the account of a subsidiary and that are oustanding (not held by a subsidiary bank) on the reporting date. If held by a bank subsidiary, they are to be reported as part of loans.

> The preceding has been the customary method of reporting activity in acceptances of banks, and is affirmed in the Bank Audit Guide newly

TABLE 1 Bank Holding Companies

Comparative Format for Income Statements Before and After Revision of Article 9, Regulation S-X, March 7, 1983

Before (Two-Step Format)	After (One-Step Format)
Total Interest Income (itemized)	Total Interest Income (itemized)
Total Interest Expense (itemized)	Total Interest Expense (itemized)
Net Interest Income	Net Interest Income
Provision for Loan Losses	Provision for Loan Losses
Net Interest Income after Provision for Loan Losses	Net Interest Income after Provision for Loan Losses
Other Income (itemized)	Other Income (itemized) (Investment Securities Gains or Losses shall be shown separately here regardless of size)
Other Expense (itemized)	Other Expense (itemized)
Income or Loss before Income Tax Expense, Securities Gains or Losses, and Appropriate Items below	Income or Loss before Income Tax Expense, and Appropriate Items below
Income Tax Expense	Income Tax Expense
Income before Securities Gains or Losses	
Investment Securities Gains or Losses, Less Applicable Tax	
Income or Losses before Extraordinary Items	Income or Losses before Extraordinary Items
Extraordinary Items, less Applicable Tax	Extraordinary Items, less Applicable Tax
Cumulative Effects of Changes in Accounting Principles	Cumulative Effects of Changes in Accounting Principles
Net Income or Loss	Net Income or Loss
Earnings Per Share Data	Earnings Per Share Data

Source: SEC, Regulation S-X, Article 9.

issued by the American Institute of Certified Public Accountants.[6] The SEC, however, reported that some responding commentators maintained that acceptances are best characterized as contingent liabilities, while others stated their belief that the prevailing practice is appropriate, and a significant number of commentators suggested that this issue should be left to the private sector for resolution.

The SEC determined that it will not take any further action at this time, in the absence of a consensus as to the most appropriate accounting in this area. Instead, the Commission "encourages industry and accounting groups to continue to consider this issue, and if deemed necessary, to refer the matter to the FASB."

> In our judgment, there is nothing contingent about either the asset or liability involved: (1) the customer signs a customers' liability agreement to reimburse the accepting bank upon its payment at maturity of the acceptance, and such liability is often secured; (2) the acceptance of the bank is a negotiable instrument with a definite maturity calling for payment on the due date by the accepting bank.

Parent company financial information. In its proposing release, the SEC requested comments on the need for parent company financial information when consolidated financial statements are presented for bank holding companies.

> The SEC reported that the response to this inquiry indicated that many users and preparers of bank holding company financial statements strongly believe that information provided by separate financial statements of the parent company are necessary for informed decisions, since intercompany loans, advances, and cash dividends by bank subsidiaries are subject to substantial regulatory restrictions. The Commission believes that these views are valid, and that the parent company information should be widely available to assist in making informed investment decisions.

Commentary. We thoroughly agree that separate financial statements of the parent company, supported by detail with respect to subsidiaries, be provided. But the final rules provide that the condensed parent only financial information previously provided in Schedule III be presented in the notes to the consolidated financial statements. And the requirement to provide information in a schedule about investments in and indebtedness of and to bank subsidiaries, and cash dividends paid by bank subsidiaries was rescinded by Accounting Series Release (ASR) 302 in Securities Act Release 6359, November 6, 1981 (46 FR 56171), which is now found in detail in section 213 of the SEC's Codification of Financial Policies, April 15, 1982.

ASR 302, among other things, provides commentary by the SEC itself pertaining to the degree and extent of additional financial disclosure: (1) with respect to consolidated subsidiaries engaged in diverse financial activities: the Commission's decision to delete all requirements for additional financial information for consolidated finance-type subsidiaries in Commission filings was significantly influenced by its conclusion that the disclosures required provide adequate information on these activities "to most investors," and by the views of commentators that the marginal utility of additional information may not be cost-justified, considering the burdens associated with the presentation of such information; (2) with respect to unconsolidated subsidiaries and fifty percent or less owned persons, by raising the level of the percentage tests for "significant subsidiary" in providing audited separate financial statements in Commission filings from ten to twenty percent, greater reliance is being placed on summarized financial information. To improve consistency in reporting this information, rules were adopted to establish standards for the content of summarized financial information. Since separate financial statements of unconsolidated subsidiaries and fifty percent or less owned persons are only considered necessary to satisfy the "informational needs of sophisticated users," they are required in registration and reporting forms filed with the Commission, but not in annual reports to security holders.

CITICORP's significant subsidiaries (as defined by Regulation S-X of the SEC) and their place of incorporation or organization include:

Citibank, N.A.	United States
Citibank (South Dakota), N.A.	United States
Citicorp Banking Corporation	Delaware

Other subsidiaries of Citicorp and their place of incorporation or organization include:

Citibank (Delaware)   Delaware
Citibank (New York State), N.A.   United States
Citicorp International Group, Inc.   Delaware

Although as noted above there are three significant CITICORP subsidiaries, as reported in CITICORP's 1983 Annual Report only a Consolidated Balance Sheet (no Statement of Income) is separately included for Citibank, N.A. and its subsidiaries, and none for the other two significant Citicorp subsidiaries. It will be noted from the exhibit of Citicorp's 1983 Annual Report that all of the $272 million in dividends from bank subsidiaries (none in dividends from other subsidiaries) of Citicorp for 1983 came from the $272 million in dividends declared of Citibank, N.A. (See Exhibit C in the Appendix.) This compared with Citicorp's own cash dividends declared for 1983 of $271 million.

Citicorp's annual report and Form 10-K incorporate the requirements of the accounting profession and the Securities and Exchange Commission into a single document, including a comprehensive explanation of annual results. However, these official requirements provide only generalized references to financial relationships between the parent holding company and its bank and non-bank subsidiaries, without identification of the separate units involved. Such detail would provide meaningful insights for specific analysis.

Loans to Related Parties

The SEC continues to believe that specific information about loans to related parties (Schedule I, Indebtedness to Related Parties) is material information for investors and shareholders.

However, the Commission did modify its original proposals for amendment, which called for inclusion of loans to distant relatives, to provide for lesser degree of relationship: (1) the final rules apply to members of the immediate family only[7], which still encompasses more relatives than the former rule for this schedule; (2) the Commission deleted the originally proposed requirement that the amount of related party loans include loans to any corporation or organization of which an executive officer, director, or principal shareholder of the registrant or any of its significant subsidiaries is an officer, although not a principal shareholder.

Also excluded from the related party loans required to be reported was the amount of all indebtedness of this type which did not exceed $60,000 during the latest fiscal year. The SEC's original proposal for amendment also called for computation of the weighted average amount of related party loans outstanding during the year, and in some cases to discuss individual transactions when such weighted average amount significantly exceeded the amount of related party loans at the balance sheet date. The final rules call for an analysis of the amount of aggregate loans to related parties from the beginning to the end of the period for the latest fiscal year.

Nonperforming Loans

In its final amendments to Article 9, the SEC adopted related amendments to the Guides for Statistical Disclosure by Bank Holding Companies (Securities Act Industry Guide 3 and Securities Exchange Act Industry Guide 3) to incorporate a number of disclosures which have been eliminated from Article 9.

The most significant of these include information about short-term borrowings, disclosure of investment concentrations, and certain details about foreign activities. The SEC concluded that these disclosures are ''primarily analytical in nature and thus are similiar in character to the other types of disclosures called for by Guide 3.''

Subsequent separate amendment of Guide 3 deleted the term ''Nonperforming Loans'' and established a new section—''Risk Elements''—for four new categories of disclosure on problem loans (see section on *Guide 3*).

Commentary. Since each of these Guides is part of Regulation S-K (Items 801 and 802 of Regulation S-K, 17 CFR 229), they are to be officially followed in the filing of financial statement portions of registration statements under each Act as well as annual and quarterly reports to the SEC.

Our analytical preference is for the former complete content of Article 9 of Regulation S-X, so that it might serve as the repository of the full accounting requirements for bank holding companies, instead of further reference to the Guides required for full information, and to Regulation S-K.

The Guides are discussed in a separate section.

Other Changes in Article 9

Other substantive changes made in the final rules in Article 9 included the following:

1. The instructions in Article 9 concerning disclosure of the valuation of trading account assets were deleted, since generally accepted accounting principles (GAAP) call for such assets to be carried at market value.

2. Provision was added to Rule 9-03(7) of Article 9 allowing the registrant to use different loan categories than those specified if it results in a more meaningful presentation.

AMENDMENT OF GUIDE 3

As of early 1984, problem loans of domestic and foreign banks continued to be a concern of the SEC (primarily interested in disclosure for investors) and to the federal and state banking regulatory agencies.

As of August 11, 1983 the SEC authorized "final" amendments to its guidelines concerning disclosure by bank holding companies with respect to information about nonaccrual, past due and restructured loans, potential problem loans, foreign outstandings, and loan concentrations.

These final amendments are reproduced in Exhibit B in the Appendix. It is probable, however, that the SEC might further amend its disclosure requirements to keep pace with either legislated or voluntary additional disclosure by the banking agencies. Of the two, the SEC historically has prescribed more disclosure than necessary for public dissemination by the banking regulatory agencies, which have been more restrictive in disclosure policy lest the identification of problem banks aggravate their marginal situation.

Background on SEC disclosure requirements. The SEC points out that disclosure of nonperforming loans has been formally required in filings since the Commission implemented the Industry Guides for Disclosure by Bank Holding Companies in August 1976 (Securities Act Release 5735, August 31, 1976 (41 FR 39007)).

The Commission authorized amendments to the Guides in July 1980, which among other things refined the definition of nonperforming loans set forth in the 1976 release (Securities Act Release 6221, July 8, 1980 (45 FR 47138)).

The principal revisions to the definition of nonperforming loans in that release included an expansion of the criteria to include non-accrual loans; an increase in the time period for accruing loans contractually past due from 60 to 90 days before such loans would be classified as nonperforming; and deletion of the requirement to disclose (1) the amount of interest reflected in income on any nonperforming loans during the period, and (2) the gross amount of interest income which would have been recorded on all such loans during the period if they had been current (in accordance with their original terms) and outstanding throughout the period or since their origination, whichever was shorter.

Commentary. Certainly these milder disclosure requirements at a time of economic recession attest to an SEC "rule of reason" in its disclosure policy.

The provisions in effect in Guide 3 before its latest (1983) amendments called for the aggregate amount of loans in each of the following categories to be separately disclosed: (Item III. C)

1. Loans accounted for on a non-accrual basis
2. Loans which are contractually past due 90 days or more as to principal or interest payments

3. Loans whose terms have been renegotiated to provide a reduction or deferral of interest or in principal because of a deterioration in the financial position of the borrower

4. Current loans where there are serious doubts about the ability of the borrower to comply with present loan repayment terms.

As will be noted by reference to Exhibit B of the Appendix, the new III C of Guide 3 establishes a new section, "Risk Elements," in place of the former "Nonperforming Loans", which calls for four categories of disclosure: Nonaccrual, past due and restructured loans; potential problem loans; foreign outstandings, and loan concentrations.

I. Nonaccrual, past due and, restructured loans, with separate totals for loans accounted for on a nonaccrual basis; accruing loans which are contractually past due 90 days or more as to principal *or* interest payments; and loans not included in the above which are "troubled debt structurings" as defined in Statement of Financial Accounting Standards No. 15 ("FAS 15"), "Accounting for Debtors and Creditors for Troubled Debt Restructurings." The instructions for these items include the following:

a. The information required shall be provided separately for domestic *and for foreign loans* for each reported period.

b. As of the most recent reported period, stating separately *as to foreign* and domestic loans included in I above the following information:

(i.) The gross interest income that would have been recorded in the period then ended if the loans had been current in accordance with their original terms and had been outstanding throughout the period or since origination, if held for part of the period.

(ii.) The amount of interest income on those loans that was included in net income for the period.

c. A discussion of the registrant's policy for placing loans on nonaccrual status should be provided.

d. No loans shall be excluded from the amounts presented. Supplemental disclosures may be made to facilitate understanding of the aggregate amounts reported. These disclosures may include information as to the nature of the loans, any guarantees, the extent of collateral, or amounts in process of collection.

Commentary. These are quite detailed disclosure requirements. However Paragraph 40a of FAS 15 provides that a receivable whose terms have been modified need not be included in that disclosure (as a troubled debt restructuring) if subsequent to its restructuring, its effective interest rate . . . has been equal to or greater than the rate that the creditor was willing to accept for a new receivable with comparable risk.

There is no limitation specified as to the length of the "supplemental disclosures" which may be given under Guide 3 in explanation of the underlying protections to the lender on a troubled loan; compared with a 100-word limitation on the "narrative comment" which a bank may choose to include (beginning with the June 30, 1983 Supervisory Supplement No. 1 to bank call reports—and regardless of the number of words, not in excess of 750 characters (sic)).

II. Potential Problem Loans. As of the end of the most recent reported period, disclosure is called for describing the nature and extent of any loans which are not now disclosed pursuant to Item III. C. 1., but where known information about possible credit problems of borrowers (which are not related to transfer risk inherent in cross-border lending activities) "causes management to have serious doubts as to the ability of such borrowers to comply with the present loan repayment terms and which may result in disclosure of such loans pursuant to Item III. C. 1."

Commentary. This is in essence a "seriously doubtful" category of loans, which does not have an exact parallel in the classification of problem loans by the banking agencies. "Transfer risk" is defined by the banking agencies as indicating the possibility that a borrower may not be able to maintain debt service in the currency in which the debt is to be paid because of a lack of foreign exchange.

III. Foreign Outstandings. This part of Guide 3 is a main thrust of the SEC's disclosure program, in view of the sensitive status of large outstandings as of early 1984 with certain countries experiencing difficulties in continuing to service the loans. The required disclosure is that as of the end of *each of the last three reported periods,* there shall be stated the name of the country and aggregate amount of cross-border outstandings to borrowers *in each foreign country* where such outstandings exceed 1 percent of total assets.

Eight specifications of instructions for disclosure of foreign outstandings call for the following detail:

1. "Cross-border" outstandings are defined as loans (including accrued interest); acceptances; interest-bearing deposits with other banks; other interest-bearing investments and any other monetary assets which are denominated in dollars or other non-local currency. To the extent that material local currency outstandings are not hedged or are not funded by local currency borrowings, such amounts should be included in cross-border outstandings.

   Commitments such as irrevocable letters of credit should not be included in outstandings; however, where such items are material, the amounts should be separately disclosed.

2. Disclosure separately of the amounts of cross-border outstandings by type of foreign borrower as set forth in Item III. A. (of Guide 3).

   Note: Item III. A. of Guide 3, which was left undisturbed by Guide 3's August 11, 1983 amendments reproduced as Exhibit B of the Appendix, calls for the following categories:

Loan Portfolio:

Types of loans. As of the end of each reported period, present separately the amount of loans in each category listed below. Also show the total amount of all loans for each reported period; the amounts should be the same as those shown on the balance sheets.

Domestic:

1. Commercial, financial and agricultural
2. Real estate—construction
3. Real estate—mortgage
4. Installment loans to individuals
5. Lease financing

Foreign:

6. Governments and official institutions
7. Banks and other financial institutions
8. Commercial and industrial
9. Other loans

Instructions: A series of categories other than those specified above may be used to present details of loans if considered a more appropriate presentation.

(*End of Note on Item III. A. of Guide 3*)

Continuing Guide 3's Instructions for disclosures of Foreign Outstandings as amended by Guide 3's August 11, 1983 revision:

3. If a material amount of the outstandings to any foreign country disclosed herein is included in the amounts disclosed pursuant to Item III. C. 1. or 2., identify each such country and the related amounts disclosed pursuant to those items.
4. Amounts of any legally enforceable, written guarantees of principal or interest by domestic or other non-local third parties may be netted against cross-border outstandings of a country. If such a guarantee is made by a foreign guarantor, the guarantee amount shall be reflected as an outstanding of such guarantor. The value of any tangible, liquid col-

lateral may also be netted against cross-border outstandings of a country if it is held and realizable by the lender outside of the borrower's country.

Commentary. The banking agencies' Country Exposure Report (see end of this chapter) would be amended to include a disclosure section indicating on country exposures exceeding 1 percent of a bank total assets, profiles showing exposure on a gross basis and adjusted for third-country guarantees; and by sector and maturities.

5. For purposes of determining the amount of outstandings to be reported, loans made to, or deposits placed with a branch of a foreign bank located outside the foreign bank's home country should be considered as loans to, or deposits with, the foreign bank.

6. Where current conditions in a foreign country give rise to liquidity problems which are expected to have a material impact on the timely payment of interest or principal on that country's private or public sector debt, disclosure of the nature and impact of such developments should be made.

7. For countries whose outstandings are between .75 percent and 1 percent of total assets, disclosure shall be made of the names of the countries and the aggregate amount of outstandings attributable to all such countries.

8. Finally, the SEC's cautionary admonition that the disclosure threshold set forth in this item is for disclosure guidance and is not intended as an indicator of a prudent level of lending to any one country by an individual bank.

Commentary. Under proposed revisions in examination procedures to strengthen supervision of country risk in foreign loans, the banking agencies would expect bank management to make systematic reports to their boards of directors on country exposures and country conditions.

IV. Loan Concentrations. As of the end of the most recent reported period, Guide 3 calls for the description of any concentration of loans exceeding 10 percent of total loans which are not otherwise disclosed as a category of loans pursuant to Item III. A. of Guide 3, *supra*.

In the SEC's view, loan concentrations are considered to exist when there are amounts loaned to a multiple number of borrowers engaged in similar activities which would cause them to be similarly impacted by economic or other conditions.

Commentary. It will be noted that Item III. A. of Guide 3 calls for a conventional classification of domestic and foreign loans by types of loans. "Similarly impacted by economic or other conditions" would be a classification as to borrowers that would call for economic analysis of their varying sensitivity to general as well as specific developments in their lines of activity. Such an analytical type of classification of borrowers would indeed be of value to analysts and investors in judging concentrations in loans.

The SEC's *Instructions* as to loan concentrations call for the following:

1. If a material amount of the loan concentrations thus disclosed or pursuant to Item III. A. is included in the amounts disclosed pursuant to Item III. C. 1. or 2., that fact should be discussed.

> Items included in Item III. C. 1. or 2. of the Guide refer to Nonaccrual, Past Due and Restructured Loans (C. 1.) and to Potential Problem Loans (C. 2.).

2. The SEC points out again that the disclosure threshold in this item is for disclosure guidance and is not intended as an indicator of a prudent level of banking.

In its last listed item of disclosure in the August 11, 1983 revision of Guide 3, the SEC goes beyond Risk Elements in loans, as follows:

Other interest bearing assets. As of the end of the most recent reported period, disclose the nature and amounts of any other interest bearing assets that would be required to be disclosed under Item III. C. 1. or 2., if such assets were loans.

> Since the other principal classification of interest bearing assets is Investments, this specification would call for disclosure of any such Investments in a Nonaccrual, Past Due, and Restructured status, or Potential Problem Investments.

Note: The August 11, 1983 revision of Guide 3 by the SEC left undisturbed III. B. section of the previous Guide 3. It is reproduced here for completeness.

Maturities and Sensitivity to Changes in Interest Rates. As of the end of the latest fiscal year reported on, present separately the amount of loans in each category listed in paragraph A. (of Item III.), (except that this information need not be presented for categories 3, 4 and 5, and categories 6 through 9 may be aggregated) which are:

1. Due in one year or less
2. Due after one year through five years
3. Due after five years.

In addition, present separately the total amount of all such loans due after one year which: have predetermined interest rates, and have floating or adjustable interest rates.

Instructions. (1) Scheduled repayments should be reported in the maturity category in which the payment is due; (2) Demand loans, loans having no stated schedule of repayments and no stated maturity, and overdrafts should be reported as due in one year or less; (3) Determinations of maturities should be based upon contract terms. However, such terms may vary due to the registrant's "rollover policy," in which case the maturity should be revised as appropriate and the rollover policy should be briefly discussed.

End of Note on III. B. of Guide 3

Commentary on III. B. of Guide 3: The specified schedules of maturities and thus sensitivity of loans to changes in interest rates has been of particular interest to analysts and investors in recent past years of upturns in the level of interest rates, and for such upturns in the future. The shorter the maturities of outstanding loans, and the larger the proportion of floating or adjustable interest rates on such loans, the lower the sensitivity to changes in interest rates. We would respectfully disagree with the SEC in its exemption from maturity classifications of Category 3 (of Item III. A. 3.), which calls for listing aggregate Real Estate Mortgage Loans. These are typically long-term loans, which if fixed rate in terms and market interest rates subsequently rise above the fixed rates on outstanding mortgages, will recreate the crunch on earnings and values of the mortgage portfolio experienced by fixed rate-lending institutions in the recent past of upturns in interest rates.

SUMMARY OF SEC REPORTING REQUIREMENTS FOR BANK HOLDING COMPANIES

As indicated in the preceding review of the amendments to Article 9 of Regulation S-X and to the Industry Guides Nos. 3, in its program begun in 1980 the SEC has among other things increased the scope and detail of financial disclosure by bank holding companies under the Securities Act of 1933 and Securities Exchange Act of 1934, as well as in their annual reports to security holders prepared in accordance with the Commission's proxy rules.

Antedating the SEC's revision of Industry Guides Nos. 3, the gist of the later official criteria for disclosure of foreign loan concentrations of bank holding companies in countries experiencing liquidity problems were first indicated in the SEC's Staff Accounting Bulletin No. 49 (October 26, 1982). This SAB 49 expressed the staff's views with regard to the appropriate minimum information necessary in Securities Act or Securities Exchange Act filings to inform investors about the possible impact of cross border lending on registrants.

In a critique reminiscent of the domestic flap in 1975 over the SEC staff's Accounting Series Release (ASR) 166 call for disclosure of nonperforming loans by banks to real estate investment trusts (REIT's), a leading private banker characterized the disclosure requirements in SAB 49 as ''arbitrary accounting criteria that can create a cloud of concern which might shake confidence in the American banking system,'' and that ''paradoxically could create grave risks for the entire banking system.''[8]

Actually, the SEC's latest Industry Guides Nos. 3, which made official the SEC Staff's point of view on foreign lending disclosures, were specified to be effective December 31, 1983 (although registrants were encouraged to comply before then). In November 1983, Congress passes the *Domestic Housing and International Recovery and Financial Stability Act,* which relieved the situation by authorizing an increase of $8.4 billion in the U.S.A.'s contribution to the International Monetary Fund. This increase and increased contributions of other member nations' measurably enhanced the IMF's ability to assist needy debtor countries and justified rescheduled and new loans by private banking lenders.

This timely legislation thus perhaps avoided a showdown between the "tell it as it is" policy of the SEC on foreign loan disclosure, and the traditionally more protective minimum disclosure policy of the banking regulatory agencies.

However, as a seeming *quid pro quo* for passing the legislation, Congress imposed supervisory requirements far more rigorous than the SEC's requirements upon the Federal banking agencies in supervising foreign lending by banks. A summary of the Act's requirements follows.

Title IX, *International Lending Supervision,* of the *Domestic Housing and International Recovery and Financial Stability Act,* contains among others the following general directives to the Federal banking agencies:

1. Authorization to the banking agencies to require more frequent and complete reports from banking institutions with respect to foreign country exposure in loans—reports no fewer than four times a year, versus present semi-annual frequency. (Sec. 907 (a)).

> "Each appropriate Federal banking agency shall require, by regulation, banking institutions to disclose to the public information regarding material foreign country exposure in relation to assets and to capital." (Sec. 907 (b)).

2. Directive to each appropriate banking agency to require its banks to establish and maintain a special reserve against foreign loans that in its judgment are of protracted impaired quality. (Sec. 905 (a (1)(A)).

> "Such reserves shall be charged against current income and shall not be considered as part of capital and surplus or allowances for possible loan losses for regulatory, supervisory, or disclosure purposes." (Sec. 905 (a)(a)(2)).

3. Directive to each appropriate banking agency to require the establishment and maintenance of minimum levels of adequate capital by its banking institutions. (Sec. 908 (a)(1)).

> "Failure of a banking institution to maintain capital at or above its minimum level as established pursuant to subsection (a) may be deemed by the appropriate Federal banking agency, in its discretion, to constitute an unsafe and unsound practice within the meaning of section 8 of the Federal Deposit Insurance Act." (Sec. 908 (b)(1)).

4. Directive to each appropriate banking agency to establish rules for accounting treatment of the fees charged by banks in connection with their international loans, including agency, commitment, management and other fees charged. (Sec. 906 (b)(1)).

> "In order to avoid excessive debt service burdens on debtor countries, no banking institution shall charge, in connection with the restructuring of an international loan, any fee exceeding the administrative cost of the restructuring unless it amortizes such fee over the effective life of each such loan." (Sec. 906 (a)(1)).

In the view of the president of the American Bankers Association, "the new regulatory requirements are stringent. But they will give regulators the flexibility to judge loans on a case-by-case basis."

Country exposure report. The federal banking agencies point out that since 1977 U.S. banks have been required to file a Country Exposure Report for federal supervisory purposes. This report, which is published in the aggregate, has proved to be very useful for both the bank supervisors and the banks themselves. Other countries have used it as a model for their own consolidated reporting systems for the country exposure of their banks. The growth of international lending and the increased number of short-term international liquidity problems suggested the advisability of more frequent reporting for supervisory purposes. Accordingly, the federal banking agencies quickened the frequency of requiring U.S. banks to file the Country Exposure Report from semi-annually to quarterly, and on a tighter time schedule than formerly required.

TABLE 2 Country Exposure Information Report

Part A. Information on exposures to any country that exceed 1 percent of total assets or 20 percent of primary capital, whichever is less.

			Adjusted Cross-Border and Foreign Office Non-Local Currency Claims				
Country	Claims Outstanding After Mandated Adjustments for Transfer of Exposure (1)	Amount of Net Local Currency Claims Included In Column (1) (2)	Total Column 1 minus 2 (3)	To Banks (4)	To Public Sector Entities (5)	To Other (6)	Amount Maturing in Less than 1 year (7)	More than 1 year (8)

Part B. Information on exposures to a country that are between 0.75 and 1 percent of total assets or between 15 and 20 percent of primary capital, whichever is less.

List of Countries where Exposure is within these Limits

Total Amount of Exposure to all Countries Listed

The Country Exposure Report (FFIEC Form 009) was amended to include a disclosure section which the federal banking agencies make available on request. The disclosure section indicates concentrations of country risk. This new Country Exposure Information Report, which is filed as a supplement to the quarterly Country Exposure Report (see Table 2) will be made available to the public.

Concentrations of country risk are indicated by the Country Exposure Information Report. Country exposures exceeding one percent of a bank's total assets would be profiled to detail risk. The profile would show exposure on a gross basis and adjusted for third-country guarantees, and show the exposure by sector and maturities. Country exposures between three-quarters of 1 percent and 1 percent of a bank's total assets would also be indicated, but not profiled.

Allocated transfer risk reserve (ATRR). Sec. 905(a) of the Domestic Housing and International Recovery and Financial Stability Act (*supra*) requires banking institutions to maintain special reserves, provided *out of current income* against the risks present in designated international loans or other international assets, when the federal banking agencies (Board of Governors of the Federal Reserve System, Comptroller of the Currency, and Federal Deposit Insurance Corporation) determine that such reserves are necessary.

The principal elements of these rules, as announced by the Board of Governors of the Federal Reserve System, are the following:

1. A banking institution shall establish an Allocated Transfer Risk Reserve (ATRR) for specified international assets (principally loans) when required under these rules.
2. At least annually, the agencies shall jointly determine which international assets are subject to risks warranting establishment of an ATRR; the size of the ATRR; whether an already established ATRR may be reduced.

The rules also set forth the criteria to be used in determining whether an ATRR is required under two headings: (1) whether the quality of international assets has been impaired by protracted inability of borrowers to make payments on their obligations; and (2) whether there are no definite prospects for restoring orderly debt service.

When required, the initial year's ATRR normally will be 10 percent of the principal amount of the asset on which reserves must be kept, or more or less, as determined by the federal banking agencies, and when required for subsequent years, normally will be 15 percent, or more or less, as the federal banking agencies determine. The rules specify the factors according to which of these amounts will be determined.

The Board of Governors of the Federal Reserve System will notify each banking institution it supervises of the amount of any ATRR and if an ATRR may be reduced. A banking institution may write down an asset in lieu of establishing an ATRR. If an institution does so, it must replenish its allowance for possible loan losses to the extent necessary to provide adequately for estimated losses on its loan portfolio. An institution may at any time reduce an ATRR to the extent of any write-down on its books of the value of the relevant asset.

The Board of Governors also adopted a rule setting forth the framework for requiring Country Exposure Reports by banking institutions (under section 907 of the referenced Act). This rule provides that the Board of Governors will prescribe jointly with the other federal banking agencies, the format, content, and reporting and filing date of the reports. For this purpose, the federal banking agencies have initiated modifications in the Country Exposure Report form (FFIEC-009).

Commentary. Any provision for the ATRR ''out of current income'' would be in addition to and separate from the general allowance for possible loan losses, and will not be included as part of the bank's capital funds. Moreover, as indicated in their April 7, 1983 letter to Senator Garn (chairman of the Senate's Committe on Banking, Housing and Urban Affairs), the three federal banking agencies called for any payment of interest on credits subjected to the ATRR provision, to be applied to reduce principal of the debts or credited to the ATRR, and not credited to income. No ATRR provision, however, would be required if the bank has already written down the designated credits by the requisite amount.

However, a particular country's debt subjected to such "reservable" category by the federal banking agencies would have to be practically hopeless near-term, based on: (a) full interest payments on indebtedness to banks had not been made for more than six months; (b) the terms of restructured indebtedness had not been met for over one year; (c) International Monetary Fund (IMF) or other suitable adjustment programs had not been complied with and there is no immediate prospect for such compliance; or (d) no definite prospects exist for the orderly restoration of debt service in the near future.

Chapter 2

Federal Banking Agency Regulation and Reporting

On January 31, 1984 the Task Group on Regulation of Financial Services, chaired by Vice President George Bush, with Treasury Secretary Donald Regan as Vice Chairman, unanimously endorsed a proposal to reorganize substantially the federal agencies which regulate bank holding companies and commercial banks.

> None of the existing agencies would be eliminated, but the proposal would importantly revise the allocation of authority among the agencies and complement the legislation proposed by the Administration concerning broadened powers and services for holding companies of depository institutions and simplified procedures under the Bank Holding Company Act.

Specifically, the Task Group's recommendations call for the creation of a new agency, the *Federal Banking Agency (FBA)*, within the Treasury Department, with the current office of the Comptroller of the Currency as its nucleus, to: (1) regulate all national banks; (2) assume the authority from the Federal Reserve Board (FRB) to regulate the holding companies of all national banks, except some 35 holding companies of the largest institutions which would remain under FRB supervision, as would other "international class" holding companies having significant international activities and impact; (3) take over entirely from the FRB the FRB's current authority to define permissible non-banking activities for all bank holding companies in the U.S., subject only to disapproval by two-thirds vote of the FRB of any permitted activities "likely to undermine the stability of the entire U.S. banking system or have a seriously adverse effect on safe and sound financial practices."

It also established a new "certification program" under which federal agencies would be required to defer to state agencies in the supervision of state-chartered banks and their holding companies, "where state programs are judged to be equivalently reliable to those at the federal level": (1) to the extent certified, federal supervision of non-troubled banks would be largely eliminated, subject only to residual regulatory authority or oversight by the FRB and the deposit insurance authority of the Federal Deposit Insurance Corporation (FDIC); (2) standards for certification would be established by a committee of the FBA, FRB, and FDIC, with the FRB acting on individual state applications.

Commentary. The above and other recommendations of the Task Group on Regulation of Financial Services will if adopted relieve the FRB of much of the considerable operational detail in regulation which has grown in recent years, especially in the push by holding companies, banks, and non-banks into the burgeoning fields of permissible non-bank activities and interestate operations, while keeping a measure of control over excesses in these areas.

The new FBA, therefore, would substantially revise the procedures and range of permissible non-banking activities of bank holding companies, and these changes will be reflected in revision of the required reports and their detail. We repeat the historical background of the legislation and Regulation Y of the FRB to indicate the contrasts in legislation and regulation that are to come.

LEGISLATIVE AND REGULATORY BACKGROUND

The Bank Holding Company Act Amendments of 1970 (P.L. 91-607, approved December 31, 1970) expanded the coverage of the Bank Holding Company Act of 1956 (12 U.S.C. 1841(a)) to require also the registration of one-bank holding companies. Such companies that control only one bank had been theretofore exempt from registration and regulation. The amended Act now requires registration and regulation of all bank holding companies, one-bank as well as multi-bank holding companies, coming under the purview of the Act, by the Board of Governors of the Federal Reserve System.

The Financial Institutions Regulatory and Interest Rate Control Act (P.L. 95–630, November 10, 1978) gave the Board of Governors of the Federal Reserve System additional powers over bank holding companies with regard to divestment or termination of non-bank subsidiaries and procedural actions, and repealed the original Bank Holding Company Act's exemption for labor, agricultural, or horticultural organizations (also keeping the "grandfather clause" of existing such organizations).

Regulation Y was promulgated by the FRB under authority of the Bank Holding Company Act. Primarily, the regulation sets forth procedures for determining control and for obtaining the board's approval for the acquisition of voting shares or assets of banks or nonbank companies. Regulation Y also specifies those nonbank activities that are "closely related to banking" and therefore within the scope of activities permissible for bank holding companies as congenerics in their diversification of holdings. Foreign activities of domestic bank holding companies and permissible activities for foreign bank holding companies are separately dealt with in the Regulation.

Section 225.5 of Regulation Y of the FRB requires each bank holding company to file a registration statement with its district Federal Reserve Bank and to furnish the Board of Governors of the Federal Reserve System with a report of the company's operations for the fiscal year in which it becomes a bank holding company, and for each fiscal year thereafter until it ceases to be a bank holding company. These annual reports are to be filed with the appropriate district Federal Reserve Bank. A bank holding company and its subsidiaries are subject to examination by the Board of Governors. These reports are: the Y-6 Annual Report of Domestic Bank Holding Companies; the Y-9 Bank Holding Company Financial Supplement; and the Y-7 Annual Report of Foreign Banking Organizations.

Y-6 Annual Report

The Annual Report (F.R. Y-6) must be filed by any domestic company that is covered by the definition of "bank holding company" under the Bank Holding Company Act of 1956 as amended.

A single report may be filed by tiered bank holding companies. (A tiered bank holding company occurs when a bank holding company indirectly controls a subsidiary bank through another bank holding company which owns, controls, or holds with power to vote 25 percent or more of any class of voting securities, or otherwise controls the subsidiary bank.)

Confidentiality. The submissions of this report are available to the public upon request on an individual respondent basis. However, if any bank holding company is of the opinion that disclosure of certain commercial or financial information contained in its submission would likely result in substantial harm to its competitive position or to the competitive position of its subsidiaries, or that disclosure of submitted information is of a personal nature that would result in a clearly unwarranted invasion of personal privacy, the bank holding company may request confidential treatment for such information.

The request for confidential treatment must be submitted in writing concurrently with the submission of the Annual Report, and must discuss in detail the justification for each reponse for which confidential treatment is requested. The bank holding company's reasons for requesting confidentiality should demonstrate the specific nature of the harm that would result from public release of the information; simply stating that the information would result in competitive harm or that it is personal in nature is not sufficient. Information for which confidential treatment is requested may subsequently be released by the Federal Reserve System, if the Board of

Governors determines that the disclosure of such information is in the public interest.

Substitution of information. Where completion of the requested information or strict compliance with the requirements of the Y-6 Report involves undue burden or expense to the bank holding company, the Board of Governors may, upon receipt of a written request—submitted through the district Federal Reserve Bank prior to the filing of the Y-6 Report—permit the substitution of appropriate information.

Additional information. The Federal Reserve System reserves the right to require the filing of additional statements and information if the request Y-6 Report's documents are not adequate to appraise the financial soundness of the bank holding company or to determine its compliance with applicable laws and regulations.

Report items. Consolidated and parent only 2-year comparative financial statements for the bank holding company shall be submitted which include:

1. Balance sheets
2. Income statements
3. Changes in capital accounts
4. Changes in financial position

All consolidated statements must be certified by an independent public accountant if the total assets of the bank holding company's bank subsidiaries are $100 million or more as determined by the subsidiary bank(s) total assets as reported on the Report of Condition. If the total assets of the bank holding company's bank subsidiaries are less than $100 million and the company's consolidated financial statements are not certified, then the statements should be prepared in accordance with generally accepted accounting principles.

All statements shall include as much detail as is necessary to disclose all material items, including any footnotes necessary to provide a complete and fair financial presentation. Requirements for this item may be satisfied by referring to individual statements submitted in Annual Reports to Stockholders and to the securities and exchange commission (Form 10-K), provided that the name and page number(s) of the appropriate report are given. Any one-bank holding company that has less than $100 million in total banking assets need not submit consolidated financial statements unless it normally prepares such statements.

Annual reports to stockholders and to the Securities and Exchange Commission. A copy of the following documents shall be submitted if prepared in the normal course of business:

1. The most recent Annual Stockholders Report of:
   a. the bank holding company
   b. any subsidiary of the bank holding company that prepares an annual report.
2. The most recent Annual Report, Form 10-K, filed with the SEC by:
   a. the bank holding company
   b. any subsidiary of the bank holding company that files Form 10-K.

Information on subsidiaries. Schedule A of the Y-6, entitled Information on Subsidiaries, shall be completed for each subsidiary (bank and nonbank, domestic and foreign) as defined in the Bank Holding Company Act as amended, excluding certain fiduciary holdings, which is directly or indirectly owned or controlled by the bank holding company. Grouping of subsidiaries engaged in consumer or sales financing, or mortgage banking, is permissible.

Organizational data include identification of the subsidiary; type of business engaged in; information on ownership of the subsidiary within the bank holding company's organization, including types and percentages of voting shares owned or controlled; number of offices and countries in which offices are operated. Although separate financial statements of each subsidiary are not called for, Schedule A does specify intra-company transactions (income from the subsidiary during the parent company's fiscal year, in the form of dividends paid or payable directly to the parent and interest, management, and service fees, etc. excluding the parent's equity in undistributed earnings of the subsidiary); and outstanding loans and advances from the parent holding company, including notes and debentures, from subsidiary banks of the bank holding company, and from other subsidiaries of the bank holding company, to the subsidiary reported on. (However, complete financial statements for each bank or nonbank subsidiary are not called for.)

Information on regulated investments. "Regulated investments" include a bank or nonbank organization in which the bank holding company directly or indirectly owns, controls, or has the power to vote more than 5 percent of any class of voting securities but not defined as a subsidiary owned 25 percent or more under the Act. Detail on such holdings includes ownership information; the three most important business activities of the investment and whether carried on in the U.S.; amount at which the investment is carried on the books of its owner(s) within the bank holding company organization, as well as its historic cost; and listing each organization within the bank holding company organization directly owning or controlling voting securities of the investment.

Activities of the parent bank holding company. List of business activities currently conducted by the parent company, whether conducted in the U.S.; listing of activities commenced or terminated by the parent company during the year; and number of existing offices compared (change) in number over the last fiscal year.

Information on terminations. Listing of each organization (subsidiary and regulated investment, bank and nonbank, domestic and foreign) that ceased being part of the bank holding company organization during the fiscal year; including those liquidated, divested, or merged out of existence, including name and address of each organization that absorbed a merged organization.

Organization chart. Chart showing the bank holding company's direct and indirect ownership or control of all of its bank and nonbank subsidiaries.

Shareholders. Listing of each shareholder of record that directly or indirectly owns, controls, or holds with power to vote 5 percent or more of any class of voting securities of the bank holding company itself, indicating for each shareholder or beneficial owner the name and address; the country of citizenship or incorporation; and the number of shares and percentage of each class of voting securities owned, controlled, or held with power to vote.

Directors and officers. Listing of each principal shareholder, director, trustee, executive officer, or person exercising similar functions, regardless of title or compensation, of the bank holding company, showing the following:

1. Name and address (city and state and country)
2. Title or position with the bank holding company and all subsidiaries of the bank holding company
3. Title or position with any other business company in which the person is a director, trustee, partner, or principal officer
4. Principal occupation, if other than with the bank holding company organization
5. Number of shares and percentage of each class of voting securities owned, controlled, or held with power to vote in the bank holding company subsidiaries of the bank holding company; and any other business company, if more than 25 percent of its outstanding voting securities are held.

Insider loans. (The term ''insider'' means any executive officer, or any person exercising similar functions, of the bank holding company organization, regardless of title or compensation, or any shareholder who holds more than a 10 percent ownership interest in the bank holding company. An ''interest'' of any insider is any corporation, partnership, business trust, or similar organization in which the insider has more than a 25 percent ownership interest.) Listing of each loan made by the bank holding company organization to an insider and his or her interests if the aggregate of such loans to any one insider and his or her interests is more than 10 percent of the equity capital accounts of the bank holding company.

For each such loan, the following information must be provided:

1. Name of borrower; title, position, or other designation that makes the borrower an insider
2. Name of lending institution
3. Date originated; original amount of the loan and current balance; original current interest rate; and the lending institution's interest rate on comparable loans to borrowers other than insiders, in effect on the origination date and on the most recent renewal date
4. Description and value of the collateral

Commentary. The Y-6 Annual Report of Domestic Bank Holding Companies does indeed contain organizational data, detail on subsidiaries, intracompany transactional summary data, and information on ownership, related interests, and loans to insiders that would be relevant to investors and analysts in understanding a bank holding company, if made available despite any claim of confidentiality, besides being of regulatory value.

Y-9 Bank Holding Company Financial Supplement
This filing is required for bank holding companies with consolidated assets of $50 million or more. Bank holding companies with consolidated assets of $50 million to $100 million need file parent company only balance sheets and income statements at year-end. And bank holding companies that have consolidated assets of $100 million to $300 million file consolidated and parent only balance sheets and income statements at year-end; while those with $300 million or more in consolidated assets file consolidated and parent company only balance sheets and income statements at end of the first six months of their fiscal year as well as at year-end.

Y-7 Annual Report of Foreign Banking Organizations
This report is required by section 225.5(b) of Regulation Y of the Board of Governors of the Federal Reserve System, as authorized by section 5(c)

of the Bank Holding Company Act (12 U.S.C. 1844(c), and sections 8 and 13(a) of the International Banking Act of 1978 (12 U.S.C. 3106 and 3108(a)).

The Y-7 Annual Report is required to be filed by companies that are organized under the laws of a foreign country *and* that are engaged in the business of banking in the U.S.A. through subsidiary banks, subsidiary commercial lending companies, or their own branches or agencies.

In Section I of the report, such foreign banking organizations are required to submit financial information to assess their ability to be a continuous source of strength and support to their U.S.A. banking operations.

In Section II of the report, foreign banking organizations that are also directly engaged in nonbanking activities in the U.S.A., or indirectly through an investment in a related company, are also required to provide information on nonbanking activities in the U.S.A., so that compliance with applicable statutes and regulations can be assured.

A foreign government or an agency of a foreign government is exempt from the filing requirement. Otherwise, the filing requirement applies to each foreign banking organization, as defined by section 211.23(a)(a) of Regulation K of the Board of Governors of the Federal Reserve System, including the following:

1. A bank holding company, as defined by section 2(a) of the Bank Holding Company Act of 1956, that is organized under the laws of a foreign country and is principally engaged in the banking business outside the United States.

2. A foreign bank, as defined by section 1(b)(7) of the International Banking Act of 1978, that maintains a branch or agency in a state of the United States or the District of Columbia, and/or owns, controls, or holds with power to vote 25 percent or more of the outstanding voting securities of a commercial lending company organized under the laws of any state of the United States (an ''Article 12 New York Investment Company''), but a bank organized under the laws of Puerto Rico and defined as a ''foreign bank'' by section 1(b)(7) of the International Banking Act of 1978 is not required to file.

Note: The term "Article 12 New York Investment Company" really should be written "Article XII", referring to that article in the New York State Banking Law (sections 507–519); and "Investment Company" really refers to banking organizations organized as subsidiaries having the power to receive money for transmission and to transmit money between the U.S. and any foreign country and otherwise to engage in foreign banking and investing. They may be "Agreement Corporations," such as state-chartered, Edge Act type of banking subsidiaries.

GAO EVALUATION OF FEDERAL RESERVE'S BANK HOLDING COMPANY DATA BASE

The General Accounting Office, in its *Report to the Chairman, Federal Financial Institutions Examination Council* dated June 1, 1982 and entitled "Information About Depository Institutions' Ancillary Activities Is Not Adequate for Policy Purposes", evaluates the Federal Reserve's Bank Holding Company Data Base as follows:

> Information on bank holding companies is reported to the Federal Reserve Board by means of a number of different reports and compiled on the bank holding company data base for research, statistical, and supervisory purposes. However, financial information is available for only a minor portion of the bank holding companies. For 1981, only about 775 of the approximately 3,640 holding companies will have their financial information compiled on this data base. The remaining holding companies are not required to file financial statements in a form which lends itself to computerization. In response to our recent report which addressed this subject, the Federal Reserve Board told us that it plans to computerize the financial data.
>
> Not only is the information compiled on the bank holding company data base limited, it is often difficult to use for analysis purposes. Problems we noted include the following:
> 1. The financial and structural information on the companies is frequently duplicated because of the tiered ownership of some holding companies.

2. The type of business conducted by many subsidiaries is not shown.
3. Often the information needed to distinguish whether a subsidiary is operated by a bank or directly by the holding company is not indicated.
4. Financial information on all the ancillary activities of banks and many nonbanking activities is not available.

The review, "Financial Developments of Bank Holding Companies in 1982" by Anthony G. Cornyn of the Federal Reserve Board's Division of Banking Supervision and Regulation, which appeared in the July 1983 issue of the *Federal Reserve Bulletin*, is based on data from a sample of 394 bank holding companies that had more than $100 million in consolidated assets as of year-end 1982 (as of December 31, 1982. 4,557 registered bank holding companies were in existence). These 394 holding companies controlled aggregate assets of $1,596.1 billion, or about 70 percent of the assets controlled by U.S. commercial banking institutions. The data used in the review were drawn from the Federal Reserve's Bank Holding Company Financial Supplement (Form FR Y-9).

This review discusses trends in earnings and profitability, balance sheet composition, asset quality, and capital. A summary follows.

Earnings and Profitability

Growth in net operating income (before securities transactions and extraordinary items) slowed in 1981–82 to 5.8 percent, compared with 8.6 percent in 1980–81, 9.5 percent in 1979–80, and 20.2 percent in 1978–79. Bank holding companies in the largest size category ($5 billion or more in consolidated assets) gained 4.5 percent in N.O.I for 1981–82, compared to 8.9 percent for 1980–81, 9.3 percent for 1979–80, and 19.4 percent for 1978–79. It is pointed out that corporate profits in general were down about 22 percent for 1981–82. The growth in earnings reflected strong gains in both net interest income and noninterest revenue that more than offset relatively sharp increases in loan-loss provisions and noninterest expenses.

The slow pace of growth in earnings was reflected both in lower return on average assets and in return on average equity. N.O.I. divided by average assets for the 394 bank holding companies was flat at 0.63 percent for 1982, compared to 0.65 percent for 1981, 0.66 percent for 1980, and 0.68 percent for 1979. This compared with the N.O.I. on average assets, for the largest size bank holding companies of 0.57 percent for 1982, 0.60 percent for 1981, 0.60 percent for 1980, and 0.62 percent for 1979. The return on average equity (N.O.I. divided by average equity) for the 394 bank holding companies was 13.2 percent for 1982, 14.0 percent for 1981, 14.5 percent for 1980, and 14.7 percent for 1979. The largest bank holding companies did no better than the 13.2 percent for 1982, compared with 14.2 percent for 1981, 14.7 percent for 1980, and 15.1 percent for 1979.

A feature of the Cornyn study is its computation of the contribution of nonbank subsidiaries of the 394 bank holding companies to their consolidated earnings (Net Income), indicating that this rose to 9.3 percent for 1982, compared to 4.9 percent in 1981, 3.6 percent in 1980, 4.6 percent in 1979, and 4.3 percent in 1978.

Balance Sheet Changes

Over the 1976–80 period, assets of the 394 bank holding companies expanded at the compounded annual rate of about 12.8 percent. In recent years, however, the asset growth of bank holding companies slowed considerably—in 1982, total assets increased 9.9 percent, compared to 9.7 percent in 1981.

Composition of assets in the 1978–82 period changed significantly over the 1978–82 period. Holdings of non-interest-bearing cash balances and investment securities were reduced relative to total assets, while loans and lease-financing receivables and holdings of money market instruments were increased. Dependence on deposit sources of funds continued to decline in 1982 in relative terms, while the role of short- and long-term borrowings in meeting their funding needs continued to expand.

Asset Quality

Data on nonperforming assets were not readily available for all of the bank holding companies included in the survey, but data on the 25 largest bank holding companies show that nonperforming assets rose about 77 percent in 1982. This raised that group's ratio of nonperforming assets to total loans to 3.1 percent at year-end 1982, compared with 1.9 percent at year-end 1981, but still well below the year-end peak of 4.4 percent in 1976.

Capital

The bank holding companies raised in excess of $2.2 billion of common and preferred equity and another $1.3 billion in equity-related offerings during 1982, a record year for such external capital financing. A large portion of the total was raised through the use of three recent financing innovations: adjustable-rate preferred stock, equity-for-debt exchanges, and mandatory convertible securities. The adjustable-rate preferred stocks were the largest in dollar volume of the financing, and most were also designed to be perpetual, so that they qualify as *primary capital* under the capital adequacy guidelines of the Federal Reserve and the Comptroller of the Currency.

However, the equity to assets ratios of the 394 bank holding companies were still relatively low, at 4.92 percent for year-end 1982, compared with 4.76 percent at end of 1981 and 4.67 percent at year-end 1980. The largest bank holding companies, those with total assets of $5 billion or more, showed equity to assets ratio of 4.49 percent at year-end 1982, compared with 4.30 percent at year-end 1981, and 4.14 percent at end of 1980.

Based on the more meaningful ratio of equity to risk assets (risk assets figured as total assets less cash and due from depositories, U.S. Treasury securities, and obligations of U.S. Government agencies and corporations), the 394 bank holding companies showed such equity cushion as 6.33 percent at close of 1982, compared with 6.21 percent at year-end 1981 and 6.35 percent at year-end 1980. The largest bank holding companies (those with total assets of $5 billion or over) had equity to risk assets ratios of 5.67 percent at year-end 1982, compared with 5.53 percent at close of 1981, and 5.69 percent at year-end 1980.

Mr. Cornyn concluded that the extraordinarily large volume of external primary capital financing in 1982 was the result not only of the recent financing innovations and the more receptive market but also of other factors, including:

1. The slowdown in the rate of internal capital generation experienced by the industry over the last several years
2. The desire of some banking organizations to build capital in anticipation of some relaxation of interstate banking restrictions (in essence positioning themselves to capitalize on any investment opportunities that may arise)
3. The concern of management, investors, and rating agencies over the adequacy of capital stirred by perceptions of increased risk in the economic and financial environment
4. The regulatory pressures placed on banking institutions to address the long-term decline in capital ratios.

Commentary: The factors summarized by Mr. Cornyn also largely apply to those that have prevailed during 1983 and into 1984.

Whether or not the Federal Financial Institutions Examination Council develops a *Uniform Bank Holding Company Report* (*infra*), it is to be hoped that the Board of Governors of the Federal Reserve System will continue such studies as the Cornyn study of the suitable bank holding company groupings, as appropriate utilization of the FR Y-9 data filed and as general guides to bank holding companies' performance.

Chapter 3

Bank Holding Company Powers and Policies

Bank holding companies may be classified as follows:

One-bank or multibank. In a decreasing number of states, the multibank holding company is not permitted except for those having "grandfather rights" by virtue of their existence at the time of enactment of the prohibitory legislation.

> *Interstate* multibank holding companies are rarer. The Bank Holding Company Act of 1956, however, granted "grandfather rights" to then existing interstate multibank holding companies, exempting them from the Act's prohibition of interstate acquisitions of banks unless specifically authorized by the states in which the target banks were located.

Organizationally, single bank holding company, or tiered holding companies. A tiered holding company occurs when a bank holding company indirectly controls a subsidiary through another holding company which owns, controls, or holds with power to vote 25 percent or more of any class of voting securities, or otherwise controls the subsidiary.

> Tiered bank holding company structures have the extra leverage imparted by the additional tiers of holding companies, each with its own

capital structure leverage, superimposed upon the operating subsidiaries, each with their own leverage. It will be recalled that the Public Utility Holding Company Act of 1935 required the elimination in public utility holding company structures of holding companies beyond the "second degree" (two tiers), because of the excessive leverage otherwise created.

Diversified bank holding companies or non-diversified into bank-related financial services besides basic banking. Such diversification may be found engaged in by subsidiary banks themselves, to the extent deemed to be organizationally feasible, or by separate nonbank subsidiaries, controlled by the parent holding company directly or through separate subsidiary holding companies, depending upon the nature of the specialization and volume, and extent of the specialized personnel required.

The banking industry has become increasingly concerned with the entry in recent years by nonbanks—free themselves from banking type regulation and restraints—into types of financial services which with regulation banks are permitted to provide, and additional types of financial services which banks and their holding companies despite "deregulation" (broader range of permissible financial services) are not yet permitted to provide, but would like to do so. Additional legislation and/or regulatory continued liberalization of the concept of "bank-related" permissible services appeared to be likely as of early 1984. Comprehensive legislation was planned in the Senate for the Second Session of the 98th Congress, and in the meantime, the "regulatory moratorium" on granting of charters to nonbank banks (sic) declared by the Comptroller of the Currency on April 6, 1983 was extended to March 31, 1984.

Bank-Related Activities

The Banking Act of 1956 (Bank Holding Company Act of 1956, 12 USC 1841 *et seq.* (May 9, 1956)) specifically permitted bank holding companies to engage in the following activities:[9]

- Ownership and management of holding company property
- Provision of permitted services to subsidiary banks

- Operation of safe deposit company

- Liquidation of property acquired by subsidiary banks

In addition, other nonbanking activities would be permitted to bank holding companies if found by the Board of Governors of the Federal Reserve System to be "so closely related to the business of banking or managing or controlling banks as to be a proper incident thereto."

The Bank Holding Company Act Amendments of 1970, P.L. 91-607 (December 31, 1970) extended regulation by the Board of Governors of the Federal Reserve System to one-bank holding companies as well, and similarly subjected nonbanking activities to the bank-related test. In addition, acquisitions by both one-bank and multibank holding companies were subjected to the test that any activity engaged in must "reasonably be expected to produce benefits to the public, such as greater convenience, increased competition, or gains in efficiency, that outweigh possible adverse effects, such as undue concentration of resources, decreased or unfair competition, conflicts of interest, or unsound banking practices." The 1970 Amendments also expanded the board's authority to determine that a company controls a bank; revised the rules and expanded the authority of the board with respect to foreign activities of domestic-based holding companies and domestic activities of foreign-based holding companies; and prohibited any bank to extend services to customers on tie-in arrangements.

Over time since, the Board of Governors expanded the list of bank-related activities, so that by July 1983, when the board effected a further expansion of permissible nonbanking activities for its Regulation Y (Bank Holding Companies and Change in Bank Control, 12 CFR 225), the list of permissible activities deemed bank-related as listed in Regulation Y had grown to include the following:[10]

Making or acquiring, for its own account or for the account of others, loans and other extensions of credit (including issuing letters of credit and accepting drafts), such as would be made by a mortgage, finance, credit card, or factoring company.

Operating as an industrial bank, Morris Plan bank, or industrial loan company, in the manner authorized by state law so long as the institution does not both accept demand deposits and make commercial loans.

Servicing loans and other extensions of credit for any person.

Performing or carrying on any one or more of the functions or activities that may be performed or carried on by a trust company (including activities of a fiduciary, agency, or custodian nature), in the manner authorized by federal or state law, so long as the institution does not make loans or investments or accept deposits other than those generated by these types of activities.

Acting as investment or financial adviser to the extent of (1) serving as the advisory company for a mortgage or a real estate investment trust; (2) serving as investment adviser, as defined in the Investment Company Act of 1940, to an investment company registered under that Act; (3) providing portfolio investment advice to any other person, observing in such activity the standards of care and conduct applicable to fiduciaries; (4) furnishing general economic information and advice, general economic statistical forecasting services and industry studies (but not "management consulting"); and (5) providing financial advice to state and local governments, such as with respect to the issuance of their securities.

Leasing personal property or acting as agent, broker or adviser in leasing such property provided:

1. The lease is to serve as the functional equivalent of an extension of credit to the lessee of the property
2. The property to be leased is acquired specifically for the leasing transaction under consideration or was acquired specifically for an earlier leasing transaction
3. The lease is on a nonoperating basis
4. At the inception of the initial lease the effect of the transaction (and, with respect to governmental entities only, reasonably anticipated future transactions) will yield a return that will compensate the lessor for not less than the lessor's full investment in the property plus the

estimated total cost of financing the property over the term of the lease, from:

(a) Rentals

(b) Estimated tax benefits (investment tax credit, net economic gain from tax deferral from accelerated depreciation, and other tax benefits with a substantially similar effect)

(c) The estimated residual value of the property at the expiration of the initial term of the lease, which in no case shall exceed 20 percent of the acquisition cost of the property to the lessor

(d) In the case of a lease of not more than seven years in duration, such additional amount, which shall not exceed 60 percent of the acquisition cost of the property, as may be provided by an unconditional guarantee by a lessee, independent third party or manufacturer, which has been determined by the lessor to have the financial resources to meet such obligation, that will assure the lessor of recovery of its investment and cost of financing

5. The maximum lease term during which the lessor must recover the lessor's full investment in the property plus the estimated total cost of financing the property shall be 40 years

6. At the expiration of the lease (including any renewals or extensions with the same lessee), all interest in the property shall be either liquidated or re-leased on a nonoperating basis as soon as practicable but in no event later than two years from the expiration of the lease. However, in no case shall the lessor retain any interest in the property beyond 50 years after its acquisition of the property.

All of the above enumerated provisos are applicable to the leasing of personal property, except (4)(d) which is not applicable.

Leasing real property or acting as agent, broker, or adviser in leasing such property provided:

Making equity and debt investments in corporations or projects designed primarily to promote community welfare, such as the economic rehabilitation and development of low-income areas.

Providing data processing and data transmission services, data bases or facilities (including data processing and data transmission hardware, software, documentation, and operating personnel) for the internal operations of the holding company or its subsidiaries.

Providing to others data processing and transmission services, facilities, data bases or access to such services, facilities, or data bases by any technologically feasible means, were:

1. Data to be processed or furnished are financial, banking, or economic, and the services are provided pursuant to a written agreement so describing and limiting the services
2. The facilities are designed, marketed, and operated for the processing and transmission of financial, banking, or economic data
3. Hardware in connection therewith is offered only in conjunction with software designed and marketed for the processing and transmission of financial, banking, or economic data, and where the general purpose hardware does not constitute more than 30 percent of the cost of any packaged offering.

Acting as insurance agent or broker in offices at which the holding company or its subsidiaries are otherwise engaged in business (or in an office adjacent thereto) with respect to the following types of insurance:

1. Any insurance that (a) is directly related to an extension of credit by a bank or bank-related firm of the kind described in this regulation (Regulation Y), or (b) is directly related to the provision of other financial services by a bank or such a bank-related firm.
2. Any insurance sold by a bank holding company or a nonbanking subsidiary in a community that has a population not exceeding 5,000 (as shown by the last preceding decennial census), provided the principal place of banking business of the bank holding company is located in a community having a population not exceeding 5,000.

Acting as underwriter for credit life insurance and credit accident and health insurance which is directly related to extensions of credit by the bank holding company system. (To assure that engaging in the underwriting of credit life and credit accident and health insurance can reasonably be expected to be in the public interest, the Board of Governors will only approve applications in which an applicant demonstrates that approval will benefit the consumer or result in other public benefits. Normally such a showing would be made by a projected reduction in rates or increase in policy benefits due to bank holding company performance of this service.)

Providing courier services (1) for the normal operations of the holding company and its subsidiaries; (2) for checks, commercial papers, documents, and written instruments (excluding currency or bearer-type negotiable instruments) as are exchanged among banks and banking institutions; (3) for audit and accounting media of a banking or financial nature and other business records and documents used in processing such media.

Providing management consulting advice (not on a daily or continuing basis, except as shall be necessary to instruct the client institution on how to perform such services for itself; see also the board's interpretation of bank management consulting advice (12 CFR 225.131)) to nonaffiliated bank and nonbank depository institutions, including commercial banks, savings and loan associations, mutual savings banks, credit unions, industrial banks, Morris Plan banks, cooperative banks, and industrial loan companies, provided that:

1. Neither the bank holding company nor any of its subsidiaries own or control, directly or indirectly, any equity securities in the client institution
2. No management official, as defined in 12 CFR 212.2(h) of the bank holding company or any of its subsidiaries serves as a management official of the client institution except where such interlocking relationships are permitted pursuant to an exemption granted under 12 CFR 212.4(b)
3. The advice is rendered on an explicit fee basis without regard to correspondent balances maintained by the client institution at any depository institution subsidiary of the bank holding company
4. Disclosure is made to each potential client institution of (a) the names of all depository institutions which are affiliates of the consulting com-

pany, and (b) the names of all existing client institutions located in the same county(ies) or SMSA(s) as the client institution.

Performing appraisals of real estate.

Providing securities brokerage services, related securities credit activities pursuant to the Board's Regulation T (12 CFR 220), and incidental activities such as offering custodial services, individual retirement accounts, and cash management services, *provided* that the securities brokerage services are restricted to buying and selling securities solely as agent for the account of customers and do not include securities underwriting or dealing or investment advice or research services.

> In connection with the above enumerated nonbanking activities, the Fed points out in Regulation Y that any bank holding company may engage, or retain or acquire an interest in a company that engages solely in one or more of the enumerated nonbanking activities, including such incidental activities as are necessary to carry on the activities so specified. As to whether *banks* can offer brokerage services to the general public directly or by contracting out the execution and clearing functions to independent broker dealers; or conduct these securities activities in operating subsidiaries which have been registered with the Securities and Exchange Commission (SEC) as broker dealers or investment advisors, the Office of the Comptroller of the Currency on October 26, 1983 announced a review which would include determining whether all national banks should conduct these activities in operating subsidiaries. The SEC, for its part, proposed new rules that would subject banks engaging in discount or other brokerage activities under SEC supervision, including a redefinition of the term ''broker'' under the Securities Exchange Act of 1934 so that it would include a bank. The OCC and the SEC agreed to consult on the issue. In a subsequent letter to the SEC in December 1983, the Justice Department stated that ''the SEC's legal basis for asserting authority to regulate banks that engage in the specified securities activities is unclear.''

In addition to the above listed nonbanking activities specified by the Fed's Regulation Y, the Fed on a case-by-case basis has authorized the acquisition by bank holding companies, and operation, of savings and loan associations (e.g., Citicorp, 68 *Federal Reserve Bulletin* 656, 1982; Interstate Financial Corp., 68 *Federal Reserve Bulletin* 316, 1982; D. H.

Baldwin & Co., 63 *Federal Reserve Bulletin* 280, 1977; American Fletcher Corp., 60 *Federal Reserve Bulletin* 868, 1974; see also, Staff of the Federal Reserve Board, *Bank Holding Company Acquisitions of Thrift Institutions,* September 1981).

Further important banking legislation, introduced as S. 2181 late in the First Session of the 98th Congress for consideration in the Second Session of the 98th Congress in 1984, by Senator Garn of Utah, comprehensively includes in its proposals a number of provisions "to develop comprehensive financial services legislation to address significant issues facing our financial system and to focus Congressional attention on them." S. 2181 includes provisions to permit depository institutions, through holding companies, to offer new nonbanking services, including:

- Underwriting and dealing in mortgage-backed securities

- Mutual funds

- Underwriting state and municipal revenue bonds

- Real estate brokerage investment and development

- Insurance brokerage and underwriting.

On the other hand, S. 2181 would:

- Limit acquisitions among the nation's largest bank holding companies, savings and loan holding companies, and securities and insurance companies

- Prohibit real estate construction activities

- Strengthen the ban on bank insurance sales tie-ins

- Apply the Douglas Amendment (contained in the Bank Holding Company Act of 1956, requiring consent of states in which targeted bank acquisitions are located) to cross-industry acquisitions by holding companies

- Apply the restrictions contained in the McFadden Act (imposing geographic restrictions on establishment of national bank branches to states permitting same; the Act was originally enacted February 25, 1927 and is still referred to as the McFadden Act although amended since) to future banking branching of any thrift institution acquired by a bank holding company

- Preempt state laws that authorize banks to engage in insurance activities outside that state that are different from those authorized for state-chartered banks within that state

- Permit bank holding companies and others to acquire "consumer banks" making consumer loans, residential mortgage loans and similar investments without limitations, as well as lend as much as 5 percent of assets in small business loans or leases, inventory or floor planning, and similar loans. These limited commercial volumes would therefore specifically exclude "consumer banks" as being commercial banks for the purposes of the Bank Holding Company Act.

Commentary: It is apparent that the wide range of proposed additional nonbanking activities for bank holding companies and their banks is aimed to provide the "level playing field" in competing with nonbanks which have proliferated in recent years in the financial services field, subject however to mollifying restraints.

Bank Holding Company Policies

Not all bank holding companies, even among the giants, maximize diversification into nonbank financial services. Emphases on banking and the mix of financial services in operations will vary with the market opportunities visualized and the personnel resources available, with competition an increasing factor, and the state of the economy in areas served.

One notable exception to maximization in financial services among the giant bank holding companies is the First Bank System, headquartered in Minneapolis-St. Paul. This is a multibank system, interstate in holdings ("grandfathered" because it was in existence when the Bank Holding

Company Act of 1956 was enacted), consisting of 88 commercial banks and 5 trust companies with some 154 banking offices located in Minnesota, Wisconsin, North Dakota, South Dakota and Montana, and 2 trust companies located in Florida and Arizona; and a current bank-related services volume that generated growing and profitable operations in mortgage banking, leasing, commercial finance, and insurance brokerage, besides a joint venture with another bank holding company for automated teller machines and electronic point-of-sale payment system for retail purchases. First Bank System's policy:

> "In the next few years, as the financial services industry adapts to changes caused by deregulation, First Bank System will focus on developing and strengthening its banking business, diversifying only gradually into new banking-related activities."

Part II

Analysis of Unconsolidated and Consolidated
Statements of Bank Holding Companies

Chapter 4

Unconsolidated Statements

Unconsolidated statements of a parent bank holding company indicate its own financial condition and sources of financial flows, which may be compared with its own fixed charges, maturities, and requirements for its own operating expenses and dividends to stockholders. In addition, the holding company's unconsolidated statements will indicate its loans to and investments in subsidiaries, and the nature and extent of the holding company's external financing in supplying funds both for its own needs and for such "downstream" financing for its subsidiaries. One of the economies of scale for a parent holding company would be its ability to obtain external financing more readily and less expensively than its individual subsidiaries and to be in position to pass along the savings to subsidiaries.

Conversely, the unconsolidated statements of a parent holding company would indicate the extent of "upstream" loans to the holding company from subsidiaries and investments in the parent holding company's securities by subsidiaries. Unless supported by schedules with the necessary detail, or unless accompanied by unconsolidated statements in turn of subsidiaries, the parent holding company's unconsolidated statements would not identify specific subsidiaries and details involved in "downstream", "upstream", or "cross stream" loans and investments.

The Garn-St. Germain Depository Institutions Act of 1982 (P.L. 97-320, October 15, 1982) in its Title IV completely revised the Federal Reserve Act's section 23A, which governs loans to affiliates of member banks and other FDIC-insured institutions, to provide among other things, for the following changes, as summarized by the Board of Governors of the Federal Reserve System[10]:

1. Limited the aggregate amount of "covered transactions" between a bank and any one affiliate to 10 percent of the bank's capital and surplus (20 percent in the case of all affiliates).

     The term "affiliate" continued to be defined to include any company which controls the bank and any other company that is controlled by the company that controls the bank, and a bank subsidiary of the member bank; but the Act also defined as an "affiliate" any company interlocked with either a bank or its parent holding company.
2. Required that covered transactions between a bank and its affiliates be on terms and conditions consistent with safe and sound banking practices. (The Act authorized the Board of Governors of the Federal Reserve System to define as an "affiliate" any company of which a bank owns 25 percent or more when transactions with that company could have adverse effects on the bank.)
3. Eliminated restrictions on transactions among bank subsidiaries at least 80 percent owned of a holding company, except for the restriction on the purchase of low quality assets.
4. Expanded the definition of "affiliate" to include among others any organization sponsored and advised on a contractual basis by a bank or its affiliate, and any investment company advised by a bank or its affiliates.
5. Expanded the types of collateral permitted on bank loans and extensions of credit to affiliates, while requiring that these new types of collateral have a high value relative to the loan.

Commentary. These liberalized provisions governing intra-organizational transactions are welcomed by holding company managements for maximized efficiencies for the holding company organization as a whole. However, effective supervision and examinations by the regulatory banking agencies of holding company intra-organizational transactions would increase in importance in order to minimize problem situations. In the words of a study by the General Accounting Office (Comptroller General):

> "Sometimes a holding company's attempt to maximize its operations as a whole works to the detriment of specific subsidiaries. In extreme cases, holding companies have used subsidiary banks' funds to cover problems in the operations of other subsidiaries in the same companies. For example, in one instance often cited by bank regulators, the management of Hamilton Bancshares, Inc., a large holding company, required a subsidiary bank to purchase poor loans made by a mortgage company subsidiary. Ultimately, the bad loans placed such a drain on the bank's funds that the bank failed."[12]

Unconsolidated statements of bank holding companies admittedly have limitations for complete analysis of the entire holding company structure. Nevertheless, such unconsolidated data for the parent holding company alone would provide indications of: (1) holding company liquidity; (2) holding company loans to and investments in subsidiaries, as well as external loans and investments, if any; (3) the holding company's sources and uses of funds for its own requirements; and (4) the holding company's own financing and capital structure.

HOLDING COMPANY LIQUIDITY

"Liability management" has gained such acceptance in management of holding company liquidity that a giant bank holding company among others defines liquidity as the ability of a financial institution to access (sic) a wide variety of funding sources, including short-term negotiable Certificates of Deposit, commerical paper, and other market-based liabilities, in meeting requirements for maturities of other borrowings, deposit withdrawals, and customers' borrowing needs (as well as shortfalls in sources of operating funds).

To be sure, bank holding companies with established funding sources can under normal general financial conditions readily borrow funds required for liquidity. However, it is well to remember the words of caution given by a governor of the Board of Governors of the Federal Reserve System in 1974:[13]

> "To finance their rapid asset expansion, many larger banks, in particular, have turned to *heavy reliance on liability management* involving the issuance of market-type deposit certificates and other liabilities to raise whatever added funds are wanted. Such instruments have proved not only highly interest-sensitive but also highly confidence-sensitive in time of stress. Undue banker confidence in their abilities as liability managers has sometimes contributed to the making of *excessive loan commitments*. Such promises to lend are a practical part of everyday banking, but those promises have not always been prudently limited to amounts that banks could effectively handle in times of strong credit pressures."

In general, "primary" liquidity (cash assets) and "secondary reserves" (marketable securities and other assets readily marketable or convertible into cash avails, with minimum risk of loss) may be compared to total assets; and to indicated current liabilities, as indicators of holding company liquidity.

> Under provisions of the Banking Act of 1933, the since-eliminated statutory specifications for liquidity of bank holding companies were that cash and readily marketable assets, by five years from date of enactment of that Act (June 16, 1933), were to equal a minimum of 12 percent of the par value of the bank stocks held by the holding company. Such minimum ratio was to be increased by 2 percent per year until such assets should amount to 25 percent of the aggregate par value of the bank stocks held by the holding company. The Act specified that the holding company shall reinvest in readily marketable assets, other than bank stock, all net earnings over and above 6 percent per annum on the book value of its own shares outstanding, until such assets shall amount to the 25 percent of the aggregate par value of all bank stocks controlled by it.
>
> Such statutory provisions were considered rigid in prescribing fixed liquidity percentages for such bank holding affiliates of member banks. Thus the Bank Holding Company Act of 1956 and subsequent amendments thereto contain no such requirements, and the above parts of Section 5144 Revised Statutes (12 U.S.C.61) were subsequently eliminated.

Nor has the Board of Governors of the Federal Reserve System provided for any specific liquidity requirements, either by its own regulation (Regulation Y) or by delegation (12 C.F.R. 265, Rules Regarding Delegation of Authority, specifically 12 C.F.R. 265.2, which includes defined delegation to district Federal Reserve Banks of powers to act on bank holding company applications). It might be argued, however, that under Section 5(b) of the Bank Holding Company Act as amended (''The Board is authorized to issue such regulations and orders as may be necessary to enable it to administer and carry out the purposes of this Act and prevent evasions thereof''), the Board of Governors has the implied power to prescribe liquidity requirements in view of its statutory power (Section 3(c)of the Act): ''in every case, the Board shall take into consideration the financial and managerial resources and future prospects of the company or companies and the banks concerned and the convenience and needs of the community to be served.''[14]

In the absence of prescribed minimum liquidity requirements, the ratios of cash and marketable securities to indicated current liabilities, as well as to total assets, of leading bank holding companies vary widely. This wide variation reflects differences in financial policies, including: (1) trade-off between profitability and risk by maintaining a low level of liquidity in hand, and instead maximizing by employment of funds for investments in and loans to subsidiaries, both existing units and new acquisitions; and (2) liability management by willingness to depend upon the holding company's share of the market for such short-term (money market) funds as commercial paper, time certificates of deposit, Eurodollar borrowing, and repurchase agreement transactions. Ready access to the capital markets, for funding such short-term borrowings as commercial paper and as a source of new long-term debt financing would also influence the maintenance of low levels of liquidity in hand.

A parent bank holding company's requirements for liquidity may arise in connection with: (1) advances to needy subsidiaries, either directly or through repurchase agreements; (2) shortfalls in income from subsidiaries needed to cover the parent holding company's own fixed charges, maturities, and legal expenses; and (3) maintenance of the holding company's own cash dividends to stockholders. Timing problems in connection with short- and/or long-term financing might also require liquidity-in-hand pending the financing's consummation. In general, a parent bank holding company reasonably supplied with its own liquidity or liquidity sources is not under pressure to overreach in charges to subsidiaries for advances, investments, and fees for services, or on the other hand, for "upstream" loans from subsidiaries, within the permissible limits.

Besides the limitations (supra) on extensions of credit to the parent bank holding company by subsidiary banks, or to other affiliates (with certain exceptions), and on the investments in or collateral loans on the securities of same: (1) Section 106 of the 1970 amendments to the Bank Holding Company Act (as well as regulations of the Board of Governors of the Federal Reserve System) prohibit a bank holding company and certain of its subsidiaries from entering into certain tie-in arrangements involving extension of credit or provisions of property or services; and (2) in the case of national bank subsidiaries of a holding company, the approval of the Comptroller of the Currency is required if total dividends declared by the national bank in any calendar year exceed the bank's net profits as defined for that year, combined with its retained net profits for the preceding two years. It might also be held to constitute "an unsafe or unsound practice," which the Comptroller of the Currency can prohibit under the Financial Insurance Supervisory Act, for a national bank to pay dividends which the Comptroller might find in his opinion to be an unsafe or unsound practice in view of the financial condition of the bank.

As noted supra, final revision of Article 9 of Regulation S-X does not require bank holding companies to report "current assets" and "current liabilities" classifications in their balance sheets as required for commercial and industrial companies under Article 5 of Regulation S-X of the SEC. This provision of Article 9 in turn reflects similar provision for Regulation F of the Board of Governors of the Federal Reserve System. Nevertheless, ratios of cash and marketable securities to total assets and indicated current liabilities are of analytical interest for the reasons discussed above.

Liquidity ratios of cash and marketable securities reported in hand at given times should not be taken to indicate the full extent of available liquidity, since cash inflows from loans to and investments in subsidiaries, money market availabilities, and other borrowings, might be relied upon for gross funds to cover particular short-term liabilities.

Summary. Bearing in mind the above caveats as to jumping to hasty conclusions regarding liquidity ratios, low ratios of cash and marketable securities, relative to total assets and current liabilities of parent bank holding companies, may be fairly indicative of dependence upon invested assets (loans and investments) for liquidity needs, and/or dependence upon external sources. As noted supra, one of the basic economies of scale of a holding company should be its ability to provide funds for its subsidiaries for their current needs and expansion, and this implies reasonable liquidity position of the parent bank holding company for its own needs, a question of fact in each case.

LOANS AND INVESTMENTS

A parent bank holding company's invested position, beyond any portfolio in marketable securities for liquidity purposes, would be indicated by its total position in loans and investments.

Such loans to and investments in subsidiaries constitute the bulk of assets of most parent bank holding companies, reflecting their basic function as sources of such support, for both bank and nonbank subsidiaries. In various cases, nonbank subsidiaries have been the recipients of most of the advances extended to subsidiaries by the parent holding company. An additional aspect of parent holding company support for nonbank subsidiaries may be the extension of such advances in whole or in part on a non-interest basis.

Citicorp's (parent company only) condensed balance sheet (Appendix C) reports as of December 31, 1983 an invested position largely ($11,359 million or 47 percent of total assets) in investments in and advances to subsidiaries other than banks, compared to investments in and advances to Citibank, N.A. and other subsidiary banks of $6,862 million (28 percent of total assets). Citicorp's support for subsidiaries other than banks is further indicated by no dividends paid by such nonbank subsidiaries to Citicorp in 1982 and 1983, compared to dividends received of.$252 million in 1982 and $272 million in 1983 from bank subsidiaries, both covering Citicorp's own dividends to stockholders of $252 million in 1982 and $272 million in 1983.

Such support of nonbank subsidiaries, and the ploughing back into equity of such subsidiaries of any of their earnings, reflects Citicorp's continuing expansion geographically and in range of financial services and new markets. Domestically, Citicorp's subsidiaries now have deposit-taking capabilities of various kinds in some 17 states and some form of operations in 41 states and the District of Columbia. Internationally, in addition to established activity in institutional banking, business loans, and capital markets, expansion in host countries has in 1983 included acquisitions of a 70-branch bank in Spain; a 9-branch bank in Belgium; a small bank in Austria; and expansion in Diners Club franchises in a number of countries throughout the world.

The bottom line to such expansion in individual banking is that already in 1983, such banking by Citicorp generated net income of $202 million, compared to $66 million in 1982; and a contribution of return on equity of 17.7 percent, compared to 7.4 percent for 1982. According to John S. Reed, vice chairman of Citicorp who oversees the individual banking core business, "performance of the individual bank reflects both current business endeavors and significant expansion activities intended to provide for future earnings."

Citicorp's successful strategy of emphasizing consumer banking, which began some ten years ago, included in 1982 acquisition of the Fidelity Savings and Loan Association of California, now known as Citicorp Savings and reported to be profitable and showing "solid growth"; and in 1983 acquisition of two additional savings and loan associations, the First Federal of Chicago, with $4 billion in assets and 60 branches in Illinois (a "unit banking" state, without state-wide branch banking for commercial banks); and the Biscayne Savings and Loan of Miami, with $1.8 billion in assets and 34 branches in Florida.

STATEMENT OF CHANGES IN FINANCIAL POSITION

The Statement of Changes in Financial Position (Exhibit C) indicates the main categories of sources and uses of funds of a parent bank holding company, unconsolidated, for its own indicated requirements as well as those of subsidiaries: (1) funds derived from operations (net income, minus equity in undistributed net income of subsidiaries); (2) other sources of funds, including internal sources (such as decreases in cash balances with subsidiary banks, and reductions in advances and loans, as well as investments; and external sources of financing); (3) uses of funds, including the parent company's own cash dividends, increases in advances and loans, as well as in investments, repayment of indebtedness, and increases in cash balances with subsidiary banks.

As indicated in Exhibit C, Citicorp (parent company only basis) financed externally in 1983 by the substantial amount of $2,314 million in debt, convertible notes, and redeemable preferred stock; $540 million in preferred stock; and $655 million in purchased funds and other short-term borrowing. The last-named types of borrowing are associated with *liability management*. Major reasons for the long-term financing no doubt included the Federal regulatory requirements for maintenance of minimum ratios of primary capital and total capital relative to total assets (*infra*); and expansion plans. However, as of the close of 1983 most of the long-term funds raised in 1983 were deposited in Citicorp's subsidiary banks ($3,354 million), and not yet applied to expansion. Thus Citicorp's (parent company only) balance sheet as of December 31, 1983 showing $5,521 million in deposits with subsidiary banks (principally interest-bearing), compared with $1,687 million as of December 31, 1982, is a temporary condition of excessive liquidity which will in future translate into increased investments in subsidiary banks and nonbanks as opportunities for further expansion develop (Citicorp, the parent company itself, keeps a relatively light portfolio of investment securities on hand ($331 million December 31, 1982, which it reduced to $232 million December 31, 1983).

Summary. The analyst will find that the Statement of Changes in Financial Position is of particular interest for analysis of a bank holding company's flows of funds and its patterns of sources and use of funds. These flows will reflect the holding company's function of providing funds for subsidiaries with economies of scale.

Besides being comprehensive as to sources and uses beyond merely the income statement, the Statement of Changes in Financial Position is on a funds basis, so that net income is adjusted to a cash flow basis by deduction of the equity in undistributed income of subsidiaries and undistributed securities gains or losses of subsidiaries, to reflect funds derived from operations.

CONSOLIDATED STATEMENTS

Holding Company Financing and Capital Structure
The financing of bank holding company requirements indicated for a given statement period will give clues as to policies and possible constraints in the financing of needs. In addition, more bank holding companies are providing explanation and discussion of financing policies in annual reports to stockholders.

Citicorp's debt policies. In "Managing the Liability Side of the Balance Sheet" (a presentation by Citicorp's treasury division to security analysts on March 6, 1979), the following debt policies of Citicorp were explained by Mr. Edward L. Palmer, Chairman of the Executive Committee:

1. To lengthen the maturities of liabilities. Lengthening the maturities of liabilities increases day-to-day liquidity. The more liabilities that are long-term, the less money has to be taken out of the markets on any given day . . . and hence the greater the liquidity.

> But "lengthening the maturities of liabilities also reduces flexibility which could pose a problem especially if interest rates do not behave as projected." Explaining the greater liquidity, if there are $100 million in liabilities with a 10-day maturity, then "we have to find an average of $10 million a day; with a 20-day maturity, $5 million a day; and with a one-year maturity, less than $300 thousand a day to maintain the same level of funding. No matter how you look at it, from a liquidity point of view, 30-year debt is better than 30-day debt.

2. To develop as many new and different sources of funding as possible. "We seek as many sources in as many countries, in as many currencies, and through as many different types of instruments as we can around the world," including all the money markets in the world and in more than 90 different currencies, and new sources of funding.

> New sources of funding have included floating rate notes; debt denominated in Australian dollars; zero coupon bonds; and auctioning of

TABLE 3 Citicorp and Subsidiaries Year-End Debt and Equity (millions)

	Commercial Paper (less than 1 year)	Purchased Funds and Other Borrowings (less than 1 year)	(by original maturities) Intermediate Debt (1–15 years)	Long-Term Debt (15 years and over)	Preferred and Common Stockholders' Equity
1978	$2,963	$8,676	$1,726	$1,170	$3,186
1979	3,889	14,549	2,233	1,911	3,598
1980	4,935	17,594	3,351	2,216	3,891
1981	5,349	17,017	5,586	2,486	4,281
1982	5,352	17,505	7,709	2,467	4,815
1983	4,087	18,212	9,372	2,460	5,771

Source: Citicorp Annual Reports.

91-day commercial paper which has been a new way of funding the holding company as well as extending the maturity of the holding company's commercial paper.

Table 3 compares the volume of commercial paper, purchased funds and other borrowings, and by original maturities at issuance, intermediate debt (Citicorp regards 1 to 15 years as suitable maturity classification for intermediate debt of banks) and long-term debt, for the year-ends from 1978 through 1983, for Citicorp and its subsidiaries. The major expansion in debt has been in short-term (maturities less than one year) and in intermediate debt (one to fifteen years in maturity).

More specifically, the maturity distribution on intermediate and long-term debt outstanding at year-ends also shows the major expansion in the shorter maturity ranges. Thus since year-end 1980, when money market rates reached record levels, Citicorp's combined intermediate and long-term debt has shown the following maturity distribution:

	1980	1982	1983
Due within 1 year	15%	24%	17%
Due 1-5 years	31	49	51
Due 6-10 years	21	7	16
Due 11-15 years	15	13	10
Due 15 years and over	18	8	6
Total	100%	100%	100%

Thus it may be concluded that although longer-term debt is preferable to short-term debt for funding purposes, all things being equal, market conditions and circumstances including the prevailing outlook for money rates will determine the choice and mix of financing.

Capital structure. The above-referenced presentation to security analysts by Citicorp treasury division executives also ''plainly stated'' that the debt-to-equity ratio, as such, has ''little significance'' to Citicorp.

From the standpoint of general financing fundamentals, debt is more advantageous than equity because (1) it is lower cost capital—interest thereon is tax deductible to the issuer—than preferred and common stock—dividends on which are not tax deductible to the issuer; and (2) debt provides more effective earnings leverage for the common stock than preferred stock—if the overall earnings on total capital structure are in excess of the net cost of the debt.

Banks are particularly highly leveraged, and thus on a consolidated basis so are their holding companies, because their capital structure leverage is in addition to their volume of deposits and the leverage they provide relative to equity. A customary method of compiling total deposits leverage as well as capital structure leverage is as follows:

Citicorp and Subsidiaries Total Capitalization as of December 31, 1983 (amounts in millions)

		Capital Structure	Capital Base
Deposits	$79,794		59.3%
Purchased Funds, Other Borrowings, and Other Liabilities	36,869		27.4
Total	$116,663		86.7%
Capital:			
Intermediate and Long-Term Debt	$12,181	67.7%	9.0
Preferred Stock	580	3.2	0.4
Common Equity	5,231	29.1	3.9
Total	$17,992	100.0%	13.3%
Total Assets	$134,655		100.0%

Source: Citicorp 1983 Annual Report.

Viewed objectively these leverage ratios, which are typical among the giant bank holding companies, are indeed high, considering that banking is a highly cyclical type of operation with domestic and international vulnerability to fluctuation in volume of deposits and earning assets, as well as in interest rates, and in provision for credit losses.

Yet giant bank holding companies such as Citicorp successfully operate with such highly charged leverage ratios, and one might well wonder whether there are limits to such leveraging. Two limits have emerged in recent years:

1. Minimum capital guidelines promulgated by the federal regulatory banking agencies
2. Coverage of fixed charges by earnings available therefore (*times fixed charges earned*).

Minimum capital guidelines. In June 1983, the Board of Governors of the Federal Reserve System and the Comptroller of the Currency announced minimum capital guidelines for the seventeen banking organizations designated as *multinationals,* including Citicorp. The 17 are the following:

BankAmerica Corporation
Bank of Boston Corporation
Bankers Trust New York Corporation
Chase Manhattan Corporation
Chemical New York Corporation
Citicorp
Continental Illinois Corporation
Crocker National Corporation
First Chicago Corporation

First Interstate Bancorp
Irving Bank Corporation
Manufacturers Hanover
Corporation
Marine Midland Banks, Inc.
Mellon National Corporation
Morgan, J.P. & Co., Inc.
Security Pacific Corporation
Wells Fargo & Company

Institutions affected by the guidelines are categorized officially as either *multinational* organizations (as designated by their respective supervisory agency); *regional* organizations (all other institutions with assets in excess of $1 billion, which may include some institutions located in money centers); or *community* organizations (less than $1 billion in total assets).

The minimum capital guidelines are used in the examination and supervisory process, and among their objectives is the introduction of greater uniformity, objectivity, and consistency into the supervisory approach for assessing *capital adequacy* as a framework "for assessing the capital of well-managed national banks, state member banks, and bank holding companies."

Two principal ratio measurements of capital are used: (1) *primary capital* to total assets and (2) *total capital* to total assets.

Primary capital is defined by the federal banking agencies as consisting of common stock; perpetual preferred stock; capital surplus; undivided profits; reserves for contingencies and other capital reserves; mandatory convertible instruments; the allowance for possible loan and lease losses; and any minority interest in the equity accounts of consolidated subsidiaries.

Total capital includes the *primary capital* components as shown plus limited-life preferred stock; and qualifying notes and debentures.

Minimum capital guidelines ratios: A minimum level of *primary capital to total assets* is established at 5 percent for *multinational* and *regional* organizations; and 6 percent for *community* organizations. Generally, however, banking organizations are expected to operate *above* the minimum *primary capital ratios.* Also, those banking organizations that have a higher-than average percentage of their assets exposed to risk, or have a higher than average amount of off-balance sheet risk, "may be expected to hold additional *primary capital* to compensate for this risk."

The *total capital to total assets* guidelines consist of three broad zones:

	Multinational and Regional	Community
Zone 1	Above 6.5%	Above 7.0%
Zone 2	5.5% to 6.5%	6.0% to 7.0%
Zone 3	Below 5.5%	Below 6.0%

Generally, the nature and intensity of supervisory action will be determined by the zone in which an institution falls. While an institution's position in the quantitative capital zones will normally trigger the following supervisory responses, qualitative analysis will continue to be used in determining minimum levels of capital for banking organizations:

For banking institutions operating in zone 1, the federal supervisory agencies will: presume that capital is adequate if the *primary capital ratio* is acceptable to the regulator and is above the minimum level; and intensify analysis and action when unwarranted declines in capital ratios occur.

For banking organizations operating in zone 2, the federal supervisory agencies will: presume that the institution may be undercapitalized, particularly if the *primary* and *total capital* ratios are at or near the minimum guidelines; engage in extensive contact and discussion with the management and require the submission of comprehensive capital plans acceptable to the regulator; and closely monitor the capital position over time. The agencies' approach to institutions operating in zone 3 will include: a very strong presumption that the bank is undercapitalized; frequent contact with management and a requirement to submit a comprehensive capital plan, including a capital-augmentation program that is acceptable to the regulator; and continuous analysis, monitoring, and supervision.

Commentary. The Minimum Capital Guidelines were issued jointly by the Board of Governors of the Federal Reserve System and the Office of the Comptroller of the Currency on December 17, 1981 and revised June 13, 1983. The full details are found in *Federal Reserve Regulatory Service* (Board of Governors of the Federal Reserve System), 3--1506, Transmittal 30, August 1983.

The impact of the Minimum Capital Guidelines is illustrated by Citicorp's substantial increases in 1983 in its *primary capital* to $6.6 billion, up $1.0 billion or 19 percent compared with year-end 1982; and in its *total capital,* to $9.6 billion as of December 31, 1983, an increase of $1.8 billion over year-end 1982. As a result, the improvement in the capital ratios of Citicorp and Subsidiaries through 1983 compared as follows:

**Citicorp and Subsidiaries Capital
as Percent of Total Assets
(percent of Fourth Quarter
Average Assets)**

Year-End	Primary Capital	Total Capital
1979	4.0%	6.0%
1980	4.0	6.1
1981	4.2	6.1
1982	4.3	6.1
1983	5.1	7.4

Source: Citicorp 1983 Annual Report.

Citicorp reports that the substantial increase in its capital ratios during 1983 reflects both the increase in capital from internal and external sources, and a management decision "to grow assets selectively." Internal sources included increases in retained earnings and in loan loss allowances; and external financing included two issues of perpetual preferred stock totaling $540 million and twelve separate issues of debt totaling $2,515 million.

In early 1984, Citicorp further increased *primary capital* and *total capital* by $350 million in guaranteed subordinated Capital Notes due in 1996 and by $100 million of perpetual preferred stock. This $450 million increase in *primary capital* substantially exceeded the amount ($350 million) from external sources by which Citicorp committed itself to increase by March 31, 1984 as a condition specified by the Federal Reserve Board for approving Citicorp's acquisition of two savings and loan associations in January 1984.

In addition, the commitment to the Federal Reserve Board in January 1984 also included the meeting of a *primary capital*-to-average total assets ratio of not less than 5.25 percent for the fourth quarter of 1984, "subject to reasonable economic and market conditions."

Citicorp's 1983 annual report states that it can meet that 5.25 percent commitment for *primary capital*-to-average total assets ratio for the fourth quarter of 1984 principally through: (1) earnings retained during 1984;

(2) increasing the commercial and consumer loan loss allowances during 1984; (3) restricting the 1984 asset growth rate to less than the growth rate of retained earnings and the loan loss allowances; and (4) raising additional primary capital from external sources.

Compliance with these *capital adequacy* requirements will thus serve to constrain the aggressive expansion which Citicorp and other leading bank holding companies have achieved in recent years. But with allowable minimum ratios relative to total assets of 5% in *primary capital* and 6.5% in *total capital,* the indicated leverage is still quite high, especially compared to conventional thinking not so many years ago that 10% was a conservative minimum for equity as a percentage of risk assets.

Debt-to-equity ratios have become more important under the official minimum capital guidelines, because primary capital ratios are given first emphasis compared with total capital ratios, and as noted above, the components of primary capital are equity in nature.

However, it might be argued that the ratios of both primary capital and total capital to total assets in effect understate the capital adequacy in its meaningful sense, relative to risk assets. If cash and due from banks, deposits at interest with banks, and U.S. Treasury and Federal Agency securities, as of December 31, 1983 are subtracted from the reported total assets of Citicorp and Subsidiaries (consolidated), the indicated net assets at presumed risk of $116.4 billion would be covered by 5.7 percent in *primary capital* and 8.2 percent in *total capital*.

Ratio of Earnings to Fixed Charges
A basic test of the ability of a bank holding company and its subsidiaries to carry its total debt for funding and total long-term capital requirements is the earnings coverage of interest and other fixed charges.

This ratio should be reported in annual reports to stockholders and in Form 10-K annual reports submitted to the Securities and Exchange Commission. It is specially computed in accordance with specifications of the Securities and Exchange Commission and cannot be calculated from the data included in such annual reports, because of the ''interest factor'' in rents, and amortization.

The ratio of earnings available for fixed charges, and/or the ratio of earnings available for fixed charges and preferred stock dividends (called the "ratio" by the SEC) is specified in Regulation S-K of the SEC for inclusion in Registration Statements filed under the Securities Act of 1933 for public offerings and for inclusion in the Prospectus that is a part of the Registration Statement. Since this "ratio" is thus required for the information of investors, it should also be required for the continued information of holders of debt securities and stockholders.

For purposes of computing the consolidated ratio (as called for) of income to fixed charges, income represents net income plus income taxes and fixed charges. Fixed charges, excluding interest on deposits, represent interest expense (excluding interest paid on deposits), and the interest factor in rents.[15] In the past five years, Citicorp's consolidated ratio has compared as follows:

Citicorp and Subsidiaries (consolidated)

Ratio of Income to Fixed Charges

1979	1.42
1980	1.26
1981	1.18
1982	1.30
1983	1.37

Source: Prospectus dated January 17, 1984 for
Citicorp Person-to-Person, Inc. (a wholly owned
subsidiary of Citicorp).

Citicorp's consolidated ratios of income to combined fixed charges and preferred stock dividends, but excluding interest on deposits, were the same ratios as indicated above for the ratios of income to fixed charges only, because of the relatively small amounts of preferred stock outstanding.

Including interest on deposits in total interest charges, Citicorp's consolidated ratios of income to combined fixed charges and to combined fixed charges and preferred stock dividends, were as follows:

Citicorp and Subsidiaries (consolidated)

**Ratio of Income to Fixed Charges
(including interest on deposits) and
Preferred Stock Dividends**

1979	1.11
1980	1.08
1981	1.06
1982	1.10
1983	1.14

Source: Prospectus dated January 17, 1984 for
Citicorp Person-to-Person, Inc. (a wholly owned
subsidiary of Citicorp).

Summary. As indicated by the appended Table 4, the largest bank holding
companies as of December 31, 1983 carry substantial multiples to total assets relative to total capital (intermediate and long-term debt, preferred
stock, and common equity). In turn, total capital structures vary widely in
their proportions of long-term debt (including intermediate debt with
maturities at issuance of one year and longer). The official minimum capital guidelines, by requiring minimum ratios of primary capital to total assets, will require strengthening of such capital ratios but the required
minimum would still provide high leverage.

OTHER CONSOLIDATED BANK HOLDING COMPANY RATIOS

In addition to the capital adequacy ratios, exemplified by the official minimum capital ratios, and the earnings times fixed charges and preferred
stock dividends ratios, a number of additional ratios of bank holding company statements on a consolidated basis may be computed to focus on aspects of financial condition and operating performance.

Asset Ratios
Asset Leverage: Customarily computed by dividing total assets by common
stockholders equity, to indicate the leverage provided for the common

TABLE 4 Largest Bank Holding Companies

Total Capital Ratios (Consolidated Basis) as of December 31, 1983

	Total Assets (millions)	*Total Capital (millions)	Percent of Total Capital Long-Term Debt	Equity
Citicorp	$134,655	$17,992	67.7%	32.3%
BankAmerica	121,176	7,565	32.1	67.9
Chase Manhattan	81,921	5,916	39.6	60.4
Mfrs. Hanover	64,332	5,218	48.8	51.2
J.P. Morgan	58,023	4,112	19.3	80.7
Chemical New York	51,165	3,012	23.5	76.5
First Interstate	44,423	3,535	40.8	59.2
Continental Illinois	42,097	3,078	40.8	59.2
Security Pacific	40,382	3,454	47.4	52.6
Bankers Trust N.Y.	40,003	2,212	19.1	80.9
First Chicago	36,323	2,346	25.7	74.3
Wells Fargo	27,018	2,880	53.2	46.8
Mellon National	26,433	2,042	28.5	71.5
Crocker National	23,393	1,435	14.3	85.7
Marine Midland	22,872	1,586	34.1	65.9
InterFirst	21,736	1,549	30.0	70.0
First Bank System	20,871	1,544	27.9	72.1
Norwest	19,854	2,580	55.6	44.4
Bank of Boston	19,538	1,447	30.4	69.6
Texas Commerce	19,499	1,132	10.0	90.0
Republic of Texas	19,082	1,327	26.4	73.6
Irving Bank Corp.	18,586	1,174	29.0	71.0
First City Bancorp	17,263	1,007	12.0	88.0
NBD Bancorp	13,245	914	12.7	87.3
NCNB (NC)	12,808	874	30.3	69.7

Source: Annual Reports.
*Intermediate and long-term debt. Preferred stock, if any, and common equity.

stock by senior capital (preferred stock, short-term and long-term debt, and intermediate debt) and the deposits.

As of December 31, 1983 Citicorp's asset leverage was a high 15.73 times, which served to magnify the 0.611 percent rate of the common stock's applicable net income, to total assets, to a 15.73 percent rate of the common stock's applicable net income for 1983 (net income of $860 million minus dividends on preferred stocks of $37 million, or $823 million).

Earnings Assets Leverage: Measures the number of times the earnings assets (deposits at interest, holdings in investment securities and in trading account, and total loans) were 21.90 times the common stockholders equity of Citicorp as of December 31, 1983, and averaged 20.63 times during 1983 (average earnings assets divided by average equity). Besides the earnings assets, substantial fees, commissions, and miscellaneous revenue are derived from operations amounting to over 12 percent of total revenue during 1983, against 9.8 percent in 1982.

Loans Ratios: Because total loans are the largest of the earnings assets and are both highest earning and highest risk assets, a number of ratios may be computed to highlight their features.

1. Volume: At year-end 1983, total loans (exclusive of unearned discount only) totaled $91,054 million, or 67 percent of total assets; up 4 percent for 1983 over year-end 1982; and alone over 15 times the year-end 1983 stockholders equity. The year-end 1983 total loans of $91,054 million (exclusive of unearned discount only) were over 114 percent of total deposits, the same ratio as at year-end 1982 and indicating the absence of any self-imposed limit on the relative carrying volume of loans.

2. Allowance for possible losses on loans: The year-end 1983 balances in this evaluation reserve, their percentage to total loans (before deduction of the allowances but exclusive of unearned discount) and the comparative provision for possible losses in the Income Statement and net charge-offs (net after recoveries), compare in recent years as follows, for Citicorp:

TABLE 5-A Citicorp (consolidated)

Year	*Commercial Loans (millions)	Allowance for Possible Losses (millions)	% Allowance Re Loans (percent)	Provision for Losses (millions)	Net Charge-offs (millions)
1979	$49,517	$328	0.66%	$83	$60
1980	54,610	359	0.66	86	49
1981	59,114	400	0.68	102	60
1982	62,518	490	0.78	282	192
1983	60,242	540	0.90	293	241

*Gross of allowance for possible losses.

Source: Citicorp Annual Reports.

TABLE 5-B Citicorp (consolidated)

Year	*Consumer Loans (millions)	Allowance for Possible Losses (millions)	% Allowance Re Loans (percent)	Provision for Losses (millions)	Net Charge-offs (millions)
1979	$13,477	$129	0.94%	$151	$125
1980	15,811	147	0.92	212	195
1981	18,528	173	0.93	222	196
1982	23,205	190	0.82	201	184
1983	28,995	226	0.78	232	196

*Gross of allowance for possible losses.

Source: Citicorp Annual Reports.

TABLE 5-C Citicorp (consolidated)

Year	*Total Loans (millions)	Allowance for Possible Losses (millions)	% Allowance Re Loans (percent)	Provision for Losses (millions)	Net Charge-offs (millions)
1979	$62,994	$457	0.73%	$234	$185
1980	70,421	506	0.72	298	244
1981	77,642	573	0.74	324	256
1982	85,723	680	0.79	483	376
1983	89,237	766	0.86	525	437

*Gross of allowance for possible losses.

Source: Citicorp Annual Reports.

Commentary: Citicorp points out in its 1983 annual report to stockholders that "after absorbing all known loan losses in current earnings, the total allowance for future losses has been increased by $309 million over the last five years" (checked per the above tabulation), with the increase in the allowance outpacing the growth in loans.

However, the 1983 increase in net write-offs is "primarily related to debt servicing considerations on certain government and financial institution lending" (classifications by Citicorp of its commercial loans in its 1983 annual report include $2,341 million in loans to financial institutions in its domestic offices, which includes loans to governments and official institutions of $475 million; and in overseas offices, $5,914 million in loans to financial institutions and $4,074 million in loans to governments and official institutions.)

> The Securities and Exchange Commission, as indicated in Citicorp's 1983 annual report, requires that an allowance for loan losses applicable to loans related to foreign activities be disclosed in a note to the financial statements. Citicorp makes no such allocation and no portion of the allowance for possible losses on commercial loans or allowance for consumer credit losses is restricted to any individual loans or groups of loans.
>
> However, "for the purpose of meeting the requirement under generally accepted accounting principles to calculate earnings and assets attributable to foreign operations, $301 million at December 31, 1983, $251 million at December 31, 1982, and $194 million at December 31, 1981 of such allowances is allocated to foreign operations."

3. Foreign operations: Based on the classifications given in Citicorp's 1983 annual report (consolidated), the following relative proportions of operatons in the U.S. and in foreign countries may be calculated.

Cross-border and foreign currency outstandings. Financing activities of Citicorp outside the U.S. may cross country borders and involve a currency other than the borrower's local currency. "Country risk" arises because although the borrower may be creditworthy in terms of the local currency, the country's foreign exchange reserves may be at least temporarily insufficient for the borrower to obtain the foreign currency required to repay the foreign currency loan.

TABLE 6-A Citicorp (consolidated)

Average Total Assets (millions)

	1983	1982	1981
U.S.A.	$52,370 (41.0%)	$44,456 (36.6%)	$39.744 (34.3%)
Total Foreign	75,553 (59.0%)	77,634 (63.4%)	76.151 (65.7%)
Total	$127,923 (100.0%)	$121,482 (100.0%)	$115,895 (100.0%)
Other North America	$2,651 (2.1%)	$2,467 (2.0%)	$2,119 (1.8%)
Brazil	6,058 (4.7%)	5,591 (4.6%)	4,858 (4.2%)
Other Caribbean, Central and South America	12,458 (9.7%)	13,091 (10.8%)	12,962 (11.2%)
Europe, Middle East and Africa	30,461 (23.8%)	30,813 (25.4%)	32,539 (28.1%)
Asia/Pacific	22,438 (17.6%)	20,404 (16.8%)	16,517 (14.3%)
Other Foreign	1,487 (1.1%)	4,660 (3.8%)	7,156 (6.1%)
Total Foreign	$75,553 (59.0%)	$77,634 (63.4%)	$76,151 (65.7%)

Source: Citicorp 1983 Annual Report.

As prescribed by the Securities and Exchange Commission and federal banking regulators, *supra,* Citicorp in its 1983 Annual Report indicates that such outstandings include all loans, deposits at interest with banks, acceptances, other interest-bearing investments and other monetary assets, both cross-border and also intra-country when denominated in foreign currency. Adjustments are made to include the excess of local currency outstandings over local currency liabilities, if any, for each country and to allow for external guarantees and collateral. The data summarize the year-end 1983 outstandings by major groups of countries and for individual countries in excess of 1 percent of total assets "profiled" as to commercial banks (including both private and government-owned commercial banks), public sector customers (including governments, central banks, development banks and other official institutions, and enterprises that are majority-owned by the government), and other private sector customers for each country group. Countries with outstandings between .75 percent and 1 percent of total assets are also reported in the aggregate with similar profile.

Citicorp reports that it manages such "country risk" exposure through a system of country-by-country limits on total cross-border and foreign currency outstandings.

In general, the characteristics of an institution's country exposure will be considered a factor in the application of the *capital adequacy* guidelines used by the federal banking agencies (supra).

As indicated in table 6, reproduced from Citicorp's 1983 Annual Report, Citicorp's total adjusted world-wide cross-border and foreign currency outstandings were $50.1 billion on December 31, 1983, compared with $50.7 billion on December 31, 1982.

Of the year-end 1983 amount, $24 billion, or about one-half, was to borrowers in "industrial countries", a category which includes all members of the Organization for Economic Cooperation and Development (OECD) in Western Europe except Portugal, Yugoslavia, Greece, and Turkey. Approximately $20 billion or 15 percent of Citicorp's total assets was to borrowers in the non-oil developing countries. The remaining $6 billion of outstandings was mainly to the oil exporting countries and to the offshore banking centers. Outstandings to Eastern Europe totaled approximately $200 million, equivalent to about 0.2 percent of total assets. Outstandings at the end of 1983 in eleven foreign countries exceeded 1 percent of Citicorp's total assets, as shown in table 6; and in three additional countries, outstandings were between .75 percent and 1 percent of total assets.

Commentary. It is apparent from the preceding tables on foreign operations that Citicorp and its subsidiaries still do business largely in foreign countries, although both the percentages of assets and revenues attributed to foreign operations have declined relative to U.S. operations in the past years, and conversely the assets and revenues from operations in the U.S. have risen relative to foreign operations and the indicated rate of net income on average total assets of U.S. operations topped that on foreign operations in 1983.

A feature of foreign operations is the continued relative superiority of rates of net income on average total assets of operations in Brazil and other Caribbean, Central American, and South American areas (the bunching of countries is Citicorp's own). Consequently, if Citicorp and its subsidi-

TABLE 6 Cross-Border and Foreign Currency Outstandings[1] at Year End Adjusted for Net Local Currency Outstandings, External Guarantees and Collateral

IN BILLIONS OF DOLLARS	Cross-Border and Foreign Currency Outstandings				Adjust-Ments[5]	1983 Total Adjusted Outstandings	1982 Total Adjusted Outstandings
	Banks	Public Sector	Private Sector	Total			
Outstandings by Country of Obligor Primarily Based On Official International Monetary Fund Categories[2]							
Industrial Countries	$9.9	$ 1.3	$ 8.6	$19.8	$4.5	$24.3	$25.4
Centrally Planned Economies of Eastern Europe	.2	—	—	.2	—	.2	.3
Oil Exporting Developing Countries[3]	.8	1.1	1.9	3.8	(.4)	3.4	3.3
Non-Oil Developing Countries							
Net Oil Exporters[4]	.7	2.2	1.3	4.2	(.1)	4.1	4.2
Major Exporters of Manufactures	2.8	3.3	4.6	10.7	.2	10.9	10.6
Other Net Oil Importers	.8	1.8	1.3	3.9	.2	4.1	3.8
Low Income	.3	.2	.1	.6	—	.6	.7
Offshore Banking Centers	.9	.1	1.4	2.4	.1	2.5	2.4
Total	$16.4	$10.0	$19.2	$45.6	$4.5	$50.1	$50.7

Outstandings for Selected Countries

Outstandings Exceeding 1% of Total Assets:

Australia	$.1	$—	$1.3	$1.4	$.2	$1.6	$1.4
Brazil	.9	2.3	1.4	4.5	.1	4.7	4.4
Canada	.6	.1	.6	1.3	.8	2.1	2.3
Federal Republic of Germany	.3	—	1.1	1.4	.9	2.3	3.3
France	1.5	.1	.1	1.7	—	1.7	1.6
Japan	3.9	—	1.6	5.5	1.3	6.8	6.8
Korea	.6	.1	.9	1.6	.2	1.8	2.0
Mexico	.5	1.5	1.0	3.0	(.1)	2.9	2.9
Phillippines	.2	.4	—	1.5	.1	1.4	1.4
United Kingdom	1.2	.2	1.4	2.8	1.0	3.8	4.0
Venezuela	.3	.5	.7	1.5	—	1.5	1.4
Countries With Outstandings between ¾% and $% of Total Assets[6]	.9	.4	2.3	3.6	(.1)	3.5	3.3

(1) Outstandings include all loans, deposits at interest with banks, acceptances, other interest-bearing investments and other monetary assets.

(2) Centrally planned economies of Eastern Europe and offshore banking centers are identified based on Bank for International Settlements classifications.

(3) Principally OPEC countries.

(4) Predominantly Ecuador, Malaysia, Mexico and Peru.

(5) Amounts primarily represent excess of local currency outstandings over local currency liabilities, if any, for each country included in category. Additionally, adjustments are made to assign externally guaranteed outstandings and outstandings for which tangible, liquid collateral is held outside of the obligor's country to the country of the guarantor and the country in which the collateral is held respectively.

(6) Countries included are Argentina, Greece and Hong Kong.

Legally binding cross-border and foreign currency commitments, including irrevocable letters of credit and commitments to extend credit, after adjustment to assign externally guaranteed commitments to the country of guarantor, amounted to $.7 billion in Australia, $.6 billion in Canada, $.7 billion in the Federal Republic of Germany, $.7 billion in France, $.7 billion in Japan, $.5 billion in Korea and $2.4 billion in the United Kingdom at December 31, 1983. Commitments were not material in relation to adjusted outstandings in any other country with outstandings exceeding 1% of total assets.

Source:—Citicorp 1983 Annual Report.

TABLE 6-B Citicorp (consolidated)

Geographic Total Revenue Sources (millions)

	1983		1982		1981	
U.S.A. Operations	$2,915	(49.5%)	$2,339	(45.7%)	$1,935	(47.7%)
Total Foreign	2,968	(50.5%)	2,782	(54.3%)	2,118	(52.3%)
Total	$5,883	(100.0%)	$5,121	(100.0%)	$4,053	(100.0%)
Other North America	$77	(2.6%)	$47	(1.7%)	$18	(0.9%)
Brazil	401	(13.5%)	452	(16.3%)	344	(16.2%)
Other Caribbean, Central and South America	617	(20.8%)	565	(20.3%)	491	(23.2%)
Europe, Middle East and Africa	1,182	(39.8%)	1,253	(45.0%)	915	(43.2%)
Asia/Pacific	718	(24.2%)	649	(23.3%)	595	(28.1%)
Other Foreign	−27	(−0.9%)	−184	(−6.6%)	−245	(−11.6%)
Total Foreign	$2,968	(100.0%)	$2,782	(100.0%)	$2,118	(100.0%)

Source: Citicorp 1983 Annual Report.

TABLE 6-C Citicorp (consolidated)

Geographic Net Income Sources (millions)

	1983		1982		1981	
U.S.A.	$392	(45.6%)	$215	(29.7%)	$185	(34.8%)
Total Foreign	468	(54.4%)	508	(70.3%)	346	(65.2%)
Total	$860	(100.0%)	$723	(100.0%)	$531	(100.0%)
Other North America	$19	(4.1%)	3	(0.6%)	−2	(−0.6%)
Brazil	168	(35.9%)	174	(34.3%)	124	(35.8%)
Other Caribbean, Central and South America	114	(24.3%)	94	(18.5%)	92	(26.6%)
Europe, Middle East and Africa	204	(43.6%)	270	(53.1%)	184	(53.2%)
Asia/Pacific	191	(40.8%)	180	(35.4%)	162	(46.8%)
Other Foreign	−228	(−48.7%)	−213	(−41.9%)	−214	(−61.8%)
Total Foreign	$468	(100.0%)	$508	(100.0%)	$346	(100.0%)

Source: Citicorp 1983 Annual Report.

TABLE 6-D Citicorp (consolidated)

Percentage Net Income on Average Total Assets

	1983	1982	1981
U.S.A. Average Assets (millions)	$52,370	$44,456	$39,744
U.S.A. Net Income (millions)	$392	$215	$185
Percentage Net Income on Average Total Assets	0.75%	0.48%	0.47%
Foreign Average Assets (millions)	$75,553	$77,026	$76,151
Foreign Net Income (millions)	$468	$508	$346
Percentage Net Income on Average Total Assets	0.62%	0.66%	0.45%
Area Percentage Net Income on Average Total Assets:			
Other North America	0.72%	0.12%	−0.09%
Brazil	2.77%	3.11%	2.55%
Other Caribbean, Central and South America	0.92%	0.72%	0.71%
Europe, Middle East and Africa	0.67%	0.88%	0.57%
Asia/Pacific	0.85%	0.88%	0.98%
Other Foreign	−15.33%	−4.57%	−2.99%

Source: Citicorp 1983 Annual Report.

aries can avoid additional voluntary or compulsory provision for credit losses, and net additions to the allowances for possible loan losses, which depend upon international developments, the superiority of net income rates in Latin American areas would continue to justify Citicorp's operations in these areas.

If the referenced allocations by Citicorp of the allowances for possible loss to foreign operations were applied to assets reported for the Latin American area, the percentage of such provision would appear as follows:

Total Average Assets (millions)	1983	1982	1981
Brazil	$6,058	$5,591	$4,858
Other Caribbean, Central and South America	12,458	13,091	12,962
Total for Latin America	$18,516	$18,682	$17,820
Total Allowances for Possible Losses on Foreign Operations	$301	$251	$194
Percentage	1.62%	1.34%	1.04%

Nonaccrual and Renegotiated Loans: Nonaccrual commercial loans are those in which, as a result of doubt as to collection, income is recognized only to the extent cash is received.

Renegotiated commercial loans are those on which the rate of interest has been reduced as a result of the borrower's inability to meet the original terms.

Citicorp's procedures for classifying nonaccrual commercial loans are as follows:

1. The loan is placed on a nonaccrual basis when evaluation procedures have determined that the payment of interest or principal is doubtful of collection.
2. In any case where interest or principal is past due for 90 days or more, the loan is automatically placed on nonaccrual basis unless an affirmative determination is made by senior credit management that the condition is not indicative of doubt as to the collectibility of principal or interest.
3. Any interest accrued on a loan placed on a nonaccrual basis is reversed and charged against current earnings. Interest on nonaccrual loans is thereafter included in earnings only to the extent actually received in cash.

Citicorp reports that its experience, as well as the experience of others, generally has shown that a substantial percentage of nonaccrual and renegotiated loans do not have to be written off: and that actual interest collections averaged 11.63 percent in 1983 and 10.29 percent in 1982.

Citicorp's commercial loan policy with regard to the provision for possible losses on loans in the Income Statement, is to consider the level of net loan losses for the year as a significant factor in determining the appropriate level for such provision. Based on management's judgment as to the appropriate level of the allowance for possible losses (the valuation account which is deducted from gross commercial loans, along with unearned discount), the amount actually provided may be greater or less than the net loan losses for the year. Determination of the amount by which the provision should exceed or be less than the net loan losses (net of recoveries) is based on management's current evaluation of the anticipated impact of domestic and international economic conditions; changes in the character and size of the portfolio; past and expected future loss experience; and other pertinent indicators.

Citicorp's consumer loans are written off upon reaching a predetermined number of days past due on a contractual basis. The number of days is set at an appropriate level by loan product and by country, to result in the recognition of losses on a basis which makes the likelihood of subsequent recovery of those losses fall between 20 percent and 30 percent. Consumer credit

TABLE 7-A Citicorp (consolidated)

Nonaccrual and Renegotiated Loans as Percentage of Total Loans

Year-End	Total Nonaccrual and Renegotiated Loans (millions)	*Total Loans (millions)	Percentage of Total Loans (percent)
1979	$1,095	$62,537	1.75%
1980	799	69,915	1.14
1981	1,036	77,139	1.34
1982	1,662	85,043	1.95
1983	2,110	88,471	2.38

*Net, after allowance for possible losses, and after unearned discount.

Source: Citicorp Annual Reports.

TABLE 7-B Citicorp (consolidated)

International Nonaccrual and Renegotiated Loans as Percentage of Total Loans

Year-End	Total International Nonaccrual and Renegotiated Loans (millions)	*Total Loans (millions)	Percentage of Total Loans (percent)
1979	$536	$62,537	0.86%
1980	343	69,915	0.49%
1981	575	77,139	0.75
1982	1,111	85,043	1.31
1983	1,638	88,471	1.99

*Net, after allowance for possible losses, and after unearned discount.

Source: Citicorp Annual Reports.

loss expense is charged to earnings in an amount that results in an allowance "sufficient to cover anticipated losses based on the mix of the portfolio, past and expected future loss experience, and economic conditions and trends."

Three possible measurements of the relative size of total nonaccrual and renegotiated loans may be computed: (1) as percentage of total loans; (2) as percentage of total assets; and (3) as percentage of stockholders' equity (including the allowance for possible loan losses).

Commentary. It will be noted that most of the nonaccrual and renegotiated loans at year-end 1983 were international loans ($1,638 million international nonaccrual and renegotiated loans, or 78 percent, compared to total nonaccrual and renegotiated loans of $2,110 million).

The increase for 1983 over 1982 of $527 million in international nonaccrual and renegotiated loans compared with a *decline* of $79 million for the same years in domestic nonaccrual and renegotiated loans. Of the year-end 1983 total of $2,110 million in international nonaccrual and renegotiated loans, approximately one-half was to borrowers in Central and South America, principally to the following indentified countries:

Citicorp (consolidated) Year-End 1983

Nonaccrual and Renegotiated Loans (millions)

Argentina	$192
*Brazil	144
Mexico	106
Venezuela	398

*The $144 million at year-end 1983 in nonaccrual and renegotiated loans for Brazil compared with Citicorp's 1983 average total assets of $6,058 million in that country, or 2.38%.

TABLE 8-A Citicorp (consolidated)

Nonaccrual and Renegotiated Loans as Percentage of Total Assets

Year-End	Total Nonaccrual and Renegotiated Loans (millions)	Total Assets (millions)	Percentage of Total Assets (percent)
1979	$1,095	$106,371	1.03%
1980	799	114,920	0.70%
1981	1,036	119,232	0.87%
1982	1,662	129,997	1.28%
1983	2,110	134,655	1.57%

Source: Citicorp Annual Reports.

TABLE 8-B Citicorp (consolidated)

International Nonaccrual and Renegotiated Loans as Percentage of Total Assets

Year-End	International Nonaccrual and Renegotiated Loans (millions)	Total Assets (millions)	Percentage of Total Assets (percent)
1979	$536	$106,371	0.50%
1980	343	114,920	0.30%
1981	575	119,232	0.48%
1982	1,111	129,997	0.85%
1983	1,638	134,655	1.22%

Source: Citicorp Annual Reports.

Commentary. Although often used as the base for percentage calculation of the relative amount of nonaccrual and renegotiated loans, total assets are the largest of the possible bases for such computation and least relevant, in our judgment, in relationship. We prefer either the first method of measurement—percentage of total loans—or the third method of measurement—percentage of total stockholders' equity.

TABLE 9-A Citicorp (consolidated)

Year-End	*Total Stockholders' Equity (millions)	Total Nonaccrual and Renegotiated Loans (millions)	Percentage of Stockholders' Equity (percent)
1979	$4,055	$1,095	27.0%
1980	4,397	799	18.2%
1981	4,854	1,036	21.3%
1982	5,602	1,662	29.7%
1983	6,542	2,110	32.3%

*Includes Total Allowance for Possible Loan Losses.

Source: Citicorp Annual Reports.

TABLE 9-B Citicorp (consolidated)

Year-End	*Total Stockholders' Equity (millions)	International Nonaccrual and Renegotiated Loans (millions)	Percentage of Stockholders' Equity (percent)
1979	$4,055	$536	13.2%
1980	4,397	343	7.8%
1981	4,854	575	11.8%
1982	5,602	1,111	19.8%
1983	6,542	1,638	25.0%

*Includes total allowance for possible loan losses.

Source: Citicorp Annual Reports.

Commentary. In computing the preceding tables of nonaccrual and renegotiated loans to stockholders' equity including the total allowance for possible loan losses, the latter as the base for the calculation is most relevant as a measurement of *exposure* of equity to possible charge-offs. It should be understood, however, that in addition to the existing total stockholders' equity including the existing total allowance for possible loan losses, Citicorp's large ''plow back'' of net income over the cash dividends paid on the equity are substantial sources of additional equity to serve as cushions for coverage of marginal assets. In addition, equity financing in future as additions to primary capital would further strengthen the equity cushions.

Retained Earnings (total and ratios of Net Income): In the past five years, Citicorp has plowed back $2,129 million in net income over total cash dividends paid, a retained earnings ratio of 68 percent. As Table 9C indicates, this is a substantial internal growth factor.

TABLE 9C Citicorp (consolidated)

Year	Net Income (millions)	Total Cash Dividends (millions)	Retained Earnings and Ratio (millions and percent)
1979	$541	$160	$381 (70%)
1980	499	174	325 (66%)
1981	531	198	333 (63%)
1982	723	222	501 (69%)
1983	860	271	589 (68%)

Source: Citicorp Annual Reports.

Net Income: Paradoxically, although the earnings factors for Citicorp have been favorable in recent years, the market times earnings ratios have been quite modest, seemingly traceable to the imposed minimum primary capital ratio and to disquiet over the publicity given to the general international loans situation. Table 10 compares market times earnings ratios and dividend yields on Citicorp common stock in recent years.

TABLE 10 Citicorp (consolidated)

Common Stock Market Multiples

Net Income per share:	1983	1982	1981	1980	1979
On Common and Common Equivalents	$6.48	$5.60	$4.20	$4.02	$4.34
Fully Diluted basis	$6.15	$5.30	$4.01	$3.78	$4.10
Market Times Fully Diluted					
Net Income per share:					
Market high	7.56	7.55	7.57	6.54	5.80
Market low	4.96	4.06	5.21	4.50	4.94
Market close	6.04	6.13	6.29	6.40	5.79
Annual Dividend Yields					
on Market Price:					
Market high	4.0%	4.3%	5.1%	5.7%	4.9%
Market low	6.2%	8.0%	7.5%	8.4%	6.4%
Market close	5.1%	5.3%	6.2%	5.8%	5.5%

Source: Citicorp annual reports.

"Net Net" Income. This is not an officially recognized net income concept, but we suggest it as an analytical concept for the reasons outlined below. It is derived by deducting, from the net income, the net loan losses (loan losses, less recoveries), or adding thereto the net recoveries (recoveries less loan losses).

The idea of deducting further the net loan losses from or adding the net recoveries to, the reported net income is suggested for the following reasons: (1) it is consistent with the comprehensive view of the statement of income, i.e., that all types of gains and losses should be noted, appropriately identified as to their nature (operating, nonoperating, recurring, nonrecurring, extraordinary, etc.); (2) it is consistent with the "matching" principle that such complete gains or losses as occur in the given accounting period should be noted; and (3) it would afford a more completely net concept of net income, given effect not only to securities gains (or losses) after tax effect, but also charge-offs and recoveries on loans, the normally largest earning asset.

Of course, the net net income and net net available for fixed charges, based on the "net net" concept, would fluctuate more widely than income before securities gains (or losses) from year to year, and more widely than the net income (as reported) concept. Each concept, however, would have its place in analysis of the fluctuation, and the overall "net net" concept would be the most inclusive and indicative of change in position for a given accounting period. High income before securities gains (or losses) and loan charge-offs or recoveries might characterize banks making higher-yielding but higher-risk investments and loans; but these might create high securities losses and loan charge-offs which should be noted for complete analysis of (1) operating performance; and (2) asset quality. The same situation might exist for overaggressive nonbank subsidiaries of a bank holding company.

Net net income of Citicorp (consolidated) in recent years and its market price multiples on a per share fully diluted common stock basis has compared as follows:

	1983	1982	1981	1980	1979
Net Income as reported, applicable to the Common Stock (millions)	$833.8	$729.9	$537.9	$505.6	$552.0
Less: Net Loan Losses (charge-offs on loans less recoveries) (millions)	437.0	376.0	256.0	244.0	185.0
Net Net Income (millions)	$396.8	$353.9	$281.9	$261.6	$367.0
Net Net Income per share Common (fully diluted basis)	$2.92	$2.57	$2.11	$1.96	$2.73
Market Times Fully Diluted Net Net Income per share:					
Market high	15.92	15.56	14.39	12.63	9.66
Market low	10.45	8.37	9.89	8.06	7.42
Market close	12.71	11.13	8.65	8.30	8.13

Source: Citicorp annual reports.

Net Assets per $1,000 of Funded Debt; Underlying Equity Coverage of Funded Debt: These two ratios indicate two aspects of the asset coverage of funded debt regardless of whether or not the funded debt issues are secured by pledge of specific assets. In bank holding company and subsidiary banks' finance, funded debt issues are unsecured, but asset and equity coverages are nevertheless of analytical interest because such strong and conservative coverages really reflect limits on levels of funded debt and the fixed charges involved. Indenture provisions of this type are often found in funded debt issues, prescribing minimal equity coverage of funded debt to avoid prohibition of payment of dividends and pledge of assets as security for borrowings.

Net Assets per $1,000 of Funded Debt. Citicorp's consolidated balance sheet as of December 31, 1983 (Appendix C) showed the following coverage of intermediate and long-term debt by net total assets (at market values for investment securities), compared to December 31, 1982.

TABLE 11 Citicorp and Subsidiaries (millions)

	Dec. 31, 1983	Dec. 31, 1982
Total assets (at market values for Investment securities)	$134,626	$130,018
Less: Deposits and all other liabilities except intermediate and long-term debt	116,663	114,616
Net assets	17,963	$15,402
Intermediate and long-term debt	12,181	10,526
Coverage	1.48 times	1.46 times
Coverage in net assets per $1,000 of intermediate and long-term debt	$1,475	$1,463

Source: Citicorp 1983 Annual Report.

It might well be argued that such net assets coverage should not be a criterion in analysis of funded debt of bank holding companies, because such issues are not secured by pledge of assets; and that instead, the multiples of earnings times fixed charges are more relevant. Yet even in the case of unsecured funded debt, in general funded debt analysis the net asset coverage is indicative of debt leverage.

Underlying Equity Times Funded Debt. Another conventional ratio in general analysis of funded debt is in turn its coverage by the underlying total shareholders' equity, to indicate the equity cushion junior to the debt.

Citicorp's ratios of underlying equity times intermediate and long-term debt also reflect its high debt leverage. Back at the close of 1974, for instance, the total intermediate and long-term debt of $1,022,482,000 (in thousands) was covered by Shareholders' Equity, reflecting market values for Investment Securities, of $1,834,828,000, or 1.80 times. In recent years, the ratio has compared as follows:

TABLE 12 Citicorp and Subsidiaries

	Intermediate and Long-term Debt (millions)	*Shareholders' Equity (millions)	Equity Times Debt
Dec. 31, 1979	$4,501	$3,451	0.77
Dec. 31, 1980	5,922	3,590	0.60
Dec. 31, 1981	8,422	3,871	0.46
Dec. 31, 1982	10,526	4,855	0.46
Dec. 31, 1983	12,181	5,811	0.47

*Reflects market values for Investment Securities.

Book Value Per Share of Common Stock; Market Times Book Value: Net equity applicable to the common stock may be expressed on a per share basis, so that comparison may be made with market prices for the stock and the market times book value ratio calculated.

The indicated book value (equity) for the common stock of any bank holding company, consolidated, as reported in Annual Reports to Stockholders and in Form 10-K Annual Reports to the SEC, not including minority interest in subsidiaries and after full asset preference of preferred stock, if any, is the sum of common capital, surplus and retained earnings, minus common stock in treasury at cost.

The Common Equity should be adjusted analytically to reflect current market values for the portfolio of securities; if possible, for understatement of net carrying values of fixed assets (bank premises, other real estate owned, furniture and fixtures, and leasehold improvements); and for any serious likelihood of liability on litigation, etc.

In addition, an arbitrary formula sometimes used for adjusted computation of book value calls for the sum of common capital, surplus, and retained earnings, minus the cost of treasury stock if any, and half of the total allowance for possible losses on loans. Such a formula obviously can be improved upon, at least in part, on the basis of at least generally available data, and commentary by bank management. Whether the current additions to the allowance for possible losses on loans, made by provision for possible losses on loans found in the statement of income as a charge to operating expenses, and the ratio of the total allowance for possible losses on loans to the total loans, are over-provided might be checked by noting the total of recognized charge-offs on loans and the subsequent recoveries from such charge-offs credited to the allowance for possible losses on loans. This, however, is a quantitative approach which may result in given years in misleading implications for conservative and realistic management who actually adequately provide for additions to the allowance for possible loans on loans from the income statement, and for charge-offs.

Citicorp's provision for loan loss expense in recent years has been realistic with a margin to spare over loan losses, thanks to recoveries, as table 13 indicates. In view, however, of continued credit uncertainties internationally, particularly in Latin America where Citicorp and its subsidiaries had $18,516 million in average total assets in 1983, it would be appropriate to follow the referenced formula, and add one-half of the total allowances for possible losses on loans to the reported book value (even though such allowances are regulatorily included in *Primary Capital* in full).

On such a basis, market prices for Citicorp common stock have accorded its Book Values low valuations in recent years, as table 14 indicates.

When all is said and done, however, it might be argued that, as a general rule, book value should be secondary in importance for valuation purposes to current earnings and dividends, and to prospective earnings and dividends (discounted to present value).

Some hold that book values are meaningful for bank holding company and bank stocks, and for other common stocks in the financial group of companies, because they reflect largely liquid assets; and calculation of book values per share of common stock is conventional for such stocks. Granted such liquidity in assets instead of large proportionate amounts of fixed assets, the volume leverage and earnings rates on invested assets and the net income margin relative to total revenues might all be low, so that the rate of net income on book value and earnings as well as dividends per share would be low. These factors in turn would lead to low price-earnings ratios (market times earnings) and market prices for the common stock that would represent discounts of book value. On the other hand, if these earnings factors are favorable, the price-earnings ratios would generally be high, leading to high market multiples of book value. In either event, the primary determinant generally would be earning power and its corollary, dividends.

TABLE 13 Citicorp and Subsidiaries

Loan Loss Experience (millions of dollars)

	1983	1982	1981	1980	1979
Provision for Loan Loss Expense:					
Commercial Loans	$293	$284	$102	$86	$ 83
Consumer Loans	227	189	203	212	151
Total	520	473	305	298	234
Loan Losses:					
Commercial Loans	292	245	127	109	119
Consumer Loans	283	266	270	262	205
Total	575	511	397	371	324
Less: Recoveries:					
Commerical Loans	51	53	67	60	59
Consumer Loans	87	82	74	67	80
Total Recoveries	138	135	141	127	139
*Net Loan Losses (after Recoveries):					
Commercial Loans	241	192	60	49	60
Consumer Loans	196	184	196	195	125
Total	437	376	256	244	185

Source: Citicorp Annual Reports.

*Year-end combined Allowances for Possible Losses on Loans compare as follows: (millions)

	1983	1982	1981	1980	1979
Year-End Allowances:					
On Commercial Loans	$540	$490	$400	$359	$328
On Consumer Loans	226	190	173	147	129
Total Allowances	766	680	573	506	457
Net Loan Losses in Year	437	376	256	244	185
Excess	329	304	317	262	272

TABLE 14 Citicorp (consolidated)

Book Values and Market Prices for Common Stock

	1983	1982	1981	1980	1979
Book value per share:					
*As reported	$41.75	$38.02	$30.24	$29.56	$27.85
**Adjusted	$44.85	$40.56	$32.53	$31.02	$29.70
Market prices per share (N.Y. Stock Exchange):					
High	46 ½	40	30 ⅜	24 ¾	26 ⅝
Low	30 ½	21 ½	20 ⅞	17	20 ¼
Close	37 ⅛	32 ½	25 ¼	24 ¼	23 ¾
Market times adjusted book value:					
High	1.04	0.99	0.93	0.80	0.90
Low	0.68	0.53	0.64	0.55	0.68
Close	0.83	0.80	0.78	0.78	0.80
Year-end shares	1983	1982	1981	1980	1979
outstanding (millions)	124.6	127.3	125.3	122.6	123.9

*Giving effect to market values for holdings of investment securities.

**Adjusted to include one-half of total year-end allowances for possible losses on loans.

Source: Citicorp Annual Reports.

Average Assets and Earnings Leverage: For bank holding companies of the diversified type, with nonbank as well as bank subsidiaries, analysis of the single consolidated statement of income would be only an overall composite resulting from total operations. More meaningful for judgments as to the success of diversification would be separate statements of income for the major services and products provided.

Citicorp presented for the first time in its 1983 Annual Report classifications of its Core Businesses (International Banking, Individual Banking, and Capital Markets), each with its total revenue, income before taxes and net income, average assets, and the rate of return (net income) both on average assets and on equity, for 1983 compared with 1982. These data are welcomed for additional insights, although strictly speaking, the classifications are organizational groupings rather than by separate lines of activity.

An alternative form of disclosure as to nonbank subsidiaries was last presented by Citicorp (the parent company itself) in the 1980 Annual Report—for subsidiaries other than banks, combined balance sheet, statement of income, statement of changes in stockholders' equity, and statement of changes in financial position (but no such separate breakout of subsidiaries of Citibank, N.A. was given). In 1980, net income of Citicorp's subsidiaries other than banks was $15 million on revenue of $1,580 million, compared with 1979 totals of $59 million in net income and $1,052 million revenue, and 1978 totals of $49 million in net income and $596 million in revenue. No dividends have been received by Citicorp from its nonbank subsidiaries since the $66 million in 1981 and $39 million in 1979; but interest received from nonbank subsidiaries totaled $652 million in 1980, $380 million in 1979, and $148 million in 1978 (not separately reported from nonbank subsidiaries in 1981, 1982, and 1983).

Table 15 on Citicorp's Core Business Results adds to the data provided in the 1983 Annual Report: the net income margin (percent of total revenue) and the key role of the leverage ratio (average assets times equity) in linking the return (net income) on average assets with the return (net income) on equity, for example as follows:

Institutional Banking:

Return on Average Assets	times	Leverage Ratio (Average Assets times Equity)	=	Return on Equity
0.87%	×	25.6 times	=	22.3%

The Core Business Results are impressive as to both volume and profit margins, particularly for the Individual Banking Core's results in 1983: (1) each of its three overseas divisions (Latin America, the Pacific, and Europe) as well as its United States operations reported "solid" earnings; (2) total revenue rose 26 percent in 1983 over 1982, best rise of the three Cores; (3)

net income more than tripled from 1982 to 1983 (*note:* the net income is after provision for possible loan losses, noted in tables *supra* on loan loss experience), as net income margin on total revenue rose from 3.4 percent in 1982 to 8.3 percent in 1983; and (4) return (net income) on equity rose to 17.7 percent in 1983, compared to 7.4 percent in 1982. The Individual Banking Core thus became the second largest contributor to net income among the Cores in 1983.

Net Interest Rate Spread; Sensitivity to Changes in Interest Rates: Net Interest Rate Spread (the difference between rate of interest revenue and rate of interest expense) on a taxable equivalent basis, is a basic indicator of the principal source of profitability (the earning assets, loans and investments) that should be noted in analysis.

Expressed as percentages of average interest-earning assets, and separately stated for domestic and international net interest spreads, Citicorp's consolidated net interest spreads have risen in recent years, featured by the superiority of domestic spreads as compared with international spreads:

Citicorp (consolidated)

Net Interest Rate Spreads (Taxable Equivalent Basis)

	1983	1982	1981
Domestic	4.29%	4.12%	3.89%
International	3.53%	3.54%	2.67%
Total	3.74%	3.49%	2.60%

Source: Citicorp 1983 Annual Report.

Sensitivity to changes in interest rates on loans, the largest of the earning assets, is an indicator of interest rate risk—the longer the maturities at predetermined interest rates, the greater the vulnerability to narrowing of the net interest rate spreads on loans. Should interest rates rise in the future, the higher market rates would not be reflected in the predetermined rates on existing loans, but the interest cost of funds would rise.

TABLE 15 Citicorp
Core Business Results

	1983	1982
Institutional Banking		
Total Revenues (millions)	$2,896	$2,857
Income before taxes (millions)	1,319	1,335
Net Income (millions)	758	751
Net Income Margin (percent of Total Revenues)	26.2%	26.3%
Average Assets (billions)	87	85
Net Income on Average Assets (percent)	.87%	.88%
Leverage Ratio (Average Assets times Equity)	25.6	25.7
Net Income on Equity (percent)	22.3%	22.6%
Individual Banking		
Total Revenues (millions)	$2,427	$1,921
Income before taxes (millions)	345	109
Net Income (millions)	202	66
Net Income Margin (percent of Total Revenues)	8.3%	3.4%
Average Assets (billions)	29	23
Net Income on Average Assets (percent)	.69%	.29%
Leverage Ratio (Average Assets times Equity)	25.7	25.5
Net Income on Equity (percent)	17.7%	7.4%
Capital Markets		
Total Revenues (millions)	$587	$527
Income before taxes (millions)	204	183
Net Income (millions)	128	119
Net Income Margin (percent of Total Revenues)	21.8%	22.6%
Average Assets (billions)	10	8
Net Income on Average Assets (percent)	1.26%	1.38%
Leverage Ratio (Average Assets times Equity)	25.6	25.7
Net Income on Equity (percent)	32.2%	35.4%
Other Items:		
Total Revenues (millions)	(27)	(184)
Income before taxes (millions)	(262)	(377)
Net Income (millions)	(228)	(213)
Average Assets (billions)	2	5
Citicorp Consolidated:		
Total Revenue (millions)	$5,883	$5,121
Income before taxes (millions)	1,606	1,250
Net Income (millions)	860	723
Net Income Margin (percent of Total Revenues)	14.6%	14.1%

TABLE 15 (Continued)

Core Business Results

	1983	1982
Average Assets (billions)	128	121
Net Income on Average Assets (percent)	.67%	.59%
Leverage Ratio (Average Assets times Equity)	24.6	26.8
Net Income on Equity (percent)	16.5%	15.8%

Note: The above classifications of Core Business Results include the following categories of operations:

Institutional Banking: Corporate, banking, and government markets (loans and financial services); electronic banking for commercial applications; foreign exchange trading; trade finance.

Individual Banking: Financial services for consumers, domestic and international (including transactional services: checking accounts, money orders, travelers checks, and credit cards); savings (products ranging from passbooks to certificates of deposit); loans (types ranging from overdraft loans to mortgage loans); private banking and investment division to service the "affluent market"; global travel and entertainment services, etc.

Capital Markets: This classification includes investment and merchant banking; international private banking; investment management; venture capital investment; securities processing; and economic information services. The Capital Markets Group "integrates Citicorp's advisory and fund-raising expertise within the broad array of services offered to our customers," according to Citicorp's annual report.

Other Items: The components of Citicorp's activities that are not identified with the three Core Businesses are presented in the aggregate within this category. These items primarily include (1) general corporate expenses, such as corporate-level staff costs (other than those charged to the Core Businesses), costs associated with corporate-level assets and other expenses not charged to Core Businesses; (2) the earnings and funding costs related to the investment portfolio (with a volume of approximately $1 billion) that is managed at the corporate level; and (3) tax expenses retained at the corporate level after charging the Core Businesses the statutory federal tax rate, with appropriate adjustments for certain items that are not subject to tax or are taxed at different rates.

Source: Citicorp 1983 Annual Report.

TABLE 16 Citicorp (consolidated)

Gross Commercial Loans (millions)

Dec. 31, 1983:	Due Within One Year	Due in Over One Year but Within 5 Years	Due Over 5 Years	Total
In Domestic Offices:				
Commercial and Industrial	$10,354	$2,651	$1,905	$14,910
Mortgage and Real Estate	1,899	895	1,181	3,975
All Other Loans	1,582	450	309	2,341
Total Domestic Offices	13,835	3,996	3,395	21,226
In International Offices	24,143	10,264	4,995	39,402
Combined Totals	$37,978	$14,260	$8,390	$60,628
Loans Due After One Year:				
At predetermined interest rates		$5,178	$3,890	
At floating or adjustable interest rates		$9,082	$4,500	
Totals		$14,260	$8,390	
Dec. 31, 1982				
In Domestic Offices:				
Commercial and Industrial	$10,828	$3,453	$2,134	$16,415
Construction and Land Development Loans Secured Primarily by Real Estate	1,461	907	547	2,915
All Other Loans	4,058	524	253	4,835
Total Domestic Offices	16,347	4,884	2,934	24,165
In International Offices	22,143	11,994	5,500	39,637
Combined Totals	$38,490	$16,878	$8,434	$63,802
Loans Due After One Year:				
At predetermined interest rates		$6,039	$2,934	
At floating or adjustable interest rates		$10,839	$5,491	
Totals		$16,878	$8,434	

Source: Citicorp Annual Reports.

Citicorp's consolidated gross commercial loans at year-end 1983 were largely short-term (due within one year), and carried mostly floating or adjustable interest rates on loans maturing in over one year. This was true of both domestic and international loan volume, as table 16 indicates.

SUMMARY

The preceding ratios and analytical approaches are among the techniques of analysis that would be meaningful for analysis of consolidated bank holding company reports, illustrated by reference to Citicorp's annual reports. Additional ratios and analysis of specific topics would suggest themselves to the analyst.

Project to develop Uniform Bank Holding Company Performance Reports (UBHCPR): The Comptroller General of the U.S., in his *Report to the Congress* entitled "Federal Financial Institutions Examination Council Has Made Limited Progress Toward Accomplishing Its Mission," dated February 3, 1984, has this to say about the possibility of development of a UBHCPR, presumably similar to the Uniform Bank Performance Report (UBPR). (Such UBHCPR would make supervisory instead of merely statistical use of bank holding company reports possible, based on a number of ratios calculated computer-wise from the data in the reports, for each specific bank holding company compared with its peer group, similar to the techniques used in the UPBR.)

> The UBHCR project (of the Task Force on Surveillance Systems organized by the Federal Financial Institutions Council) was begun in July 1979 with the intended goal of establishing a uniform bank holding company performance report...
> ...The Federal Deposit Insurance Corporation, the Office of the Comptroller of the Currency, and the Federal Reserve System each had their own interest for establishing a UBHCPR. Basically, the FDIC's interest was in improving financial data on small (under $50 million total

assets) bank holding companies...the OCC believes it needs data timeliness and quality of bank holding company reports of the FRS, particularly regarding those BHCs with consolidated assets in excess of $100 million. The FRS agrees that a new and improved BHC performance report (over its in-house model) is needed...but the postponement it requested on the project while the FRS staff worked on a new BHC report has continued and, at the completion of the Comptroller General's Report referred to, no UBHCPR has been established.

As in the case of the UBPR, the value of a UBHCPR would lie in the additional detail submitted in improved and uniform reports and in the variety of ratios possible to compute therefrom by computer by the federal banking agencies that would be available in UBHCPR reports on individual bank holding companies, compared to peer group, available to holding company managements and to the public.

Chapter 5

Uniform Bank Call Report

The Federal Financial Institutions Council approved for use by the three federal banking agencies (the Board of Governors of the Federal Reserve System, the Federal Deposit Insurance Corporation, and the Office of the Comptroller of the Currency) a revision to the Reports of Condition and Income (Call Reports) filed quarterly by all insured commercial banks. This revision was implemented as of the March 31, 1984 report date.

Four sets of report forms were developed. The specific reporting requirements applicable to each bank depend upon the size of the bank and whether it has any foreign offices (including an International Banking Facility (IBF)).

> The Comptroller General in his report referenced *supra* reports that most FFIC principals and top agency officials consider the revisions to the Report of Condition and Income (Call Report) as particularly significant. Two of the foremost reasons are given as the changing financial services industry and the development and expanding use by bank regulators of the Council's UBPR as a supervisory tool, to identify and predict the impact of new risks on the safety and soundness of banks on a more timely basis.

Of course more detail and supporting schedules are required for such objectives, as follows:

Report of Condition

Schedule RC	Balance sheet
Schedule RC-A	Cash and balances due from depository institutions
Schedule RC-B	Securities
Schedule RC-C	Loans and lease financing receivables
Schedule RC-D	Assets held in trading accounts in domestic offices only (to be completed only by banks with $1 billion or more in total assets)
Schedule RC-E	Deposit liabilities
Schedule RC-F	Other assets
Schedule RC-G	Other liabilities
Schedule RC-H	Selected balance sheet items for domestic offices
Schedule RC-I	Selected assets and liabilities of IBFs
Schedule RC-J	Repricing opportunities for selected balance sheet categories
Schedule RC-K	Quarterly averages
Schedule RC-L	Commitments and contingencies
Schedule RC-M	Memoranda
Schedule RC-N	Past due, nonaccrual and renegotiated loans and lease financing receivables
Schedule RC-O	Other data for deposit insurance assessments

Report of Income

Schedule RI	Income Statement
Schedule RI-A	Equity capital
Schedule RI-B	Charge-offs and recoveries and changes in allowance for loan and lease losses
Schedule RI-C	Applicable income taxes by taxing authority
Schedule RI-D	Income from international operations
Schedule RI-E	Explanations (of various items in Schedules RI, RI-A and RI-B)

WHO MUST REPORT ON WHAT FORMS

Every national bank, state member bank, and insured state nonmember bank is required to file consolidated Reports of Condition and Income normally as of the last business day of each calendar quarter, i.e., the report date. The specific reporting requirements depend upon the size of the bank and whether it has any foreign offices. Banks must file the appropriate forms as described below:

1. Banks with foreign offices: Banks of *any* size that have any "foreign" offices (as defined below) must file quarterly the *Consolidated Reports of Condition and Income for a Bank with Domestic and Foreign Offices* (FFIEC 031). For purposes of these reports, all of the following constitute "foreign" offices:
   (a) an International Banking Facility (IBF);
   (b) a branch or consolidated subsidiary in a foreign country, Puerto Rico, or a U.S. territory or possession; or
   (c) a majority-owned Edge or Agreement subsidiary.
   However, for purposes of these reports, a branch at a U.S. military facility located in a foreign country is a "domestic" office.
2. Banks without foreign offices and with assets of $300 million or more: Such banks that have only domestic offices must file quarterly the *Consolidated Reports of Condition and Income for a Bank with Domestic Offices Only and Total Assets of $300 Million or More* (FFIEC 032).
3. Banks without foreign offices and with assets of $100 million or more but less than $300 million: Such banks that have only domestic offices must file quarterly the *Consolidated Reports of Condition and Income for a Bank with Domestic Offices Only and Total Assets of $100 Million or More but Less than $300 Million* (FFIEC 033).
4. Banks without foreign offices and with assets of less than $100 million: Such banks that have only domestic offices must file quarterly the *Consolidated Reports of Condition and Income for a Bank with Domestic Offices Only and Total Assets of Less than $100 Million* (FFIEC 034).

Frequency of Reporting

The reports are required to be submitted quarterly by all banks. However, some schedules are required on a less frequent basis for some banks.

1. For all banks, Schedule RI-C, Applicable Income Taxes by Taxing Authority, is to be filed *only* at year-end.
2. In addition, for banks with domestic offices only and total assets of less than $100 million (those banks filing the FFIEC 034), Schedule RI-A, Changes in Equity Capital, and Schedule RI-B, part II, Changes in Allowance for Loan and Lease Losses, are to be filed only at year-end. All other banks must report these schedules quarterly.

Differences in Detail of Reports

The amount of detail required to be reported varies among the four versions of the report, with the report for banks with less than $100 million in assets and with only domestic offices (FFIEC 034) having the least amount of detail and the report for banks with foreign offices (FFIEC 031) having the most. Also, within FFIEC 031 and FFIEC 032, banks with assets of $1 billion or more must provide detail on assets held in trading accounts (in Schedule RC-D) and U.S. and non-U.S. addressee information on customers' liability on acceptances outstanding (Schedule RC-M, item 5) that smaller banks filing these reports do not. Similarly, within FFIEC 034, banks with less than $25 million in assets have somewhat less detailed requirements in Schedule RC-K, Quarterly Averages, and Schedule RI, Income Statement, than do larger banks filing FFIEC 034.

In addition, the required basis of reporting the loan detail in Schedules RC-K (Quarterly Averages), RC-N (Past Due, Nonaccrual, and Renegotiated Loans and Lease Financing Receivables), RI (Income Statement), and RI-B, part 1 (Charge-Offs and Recoveries on Loans and Leases), but *not* in Schedule RC-C (Loans and Lease Financing Receivables), is different for banks over and under $300 million in assets with no foreign offices. For a more detailed discussion, refer to ''Reporting of Loan Detail by Banks with Assets of Less Than $300 Million and No Foreign Offices'' below in these General Instructions.

Shifts in Reporting Status

All shifts in reporting status (except as noted below for banks establishing a foreign office) are to begin with the March Reports of Condition and Income. Such a shift will take place only if the reporting bank's total assets as reflected in the Report of Condition for June of the previous year equal or exceed the total asset criteria specified below.

Shifts requiring a change in report form:

1. *Upon establishment of a foreign office*—A bank, regardless of size, with only domestic offices that establishes or acquires any "foreign" office as described above, including an IBF, must begin filing the FFIEC 031 (Consolidated Reports of Condition and Income for a Bank with Domestic and Foreign Offices) for the first quarterly call report date following the commencement of operations by the "foreign" office. However, a bank with "foreign" offices that divests itself of *all* its "foreign" offices must continue filing the FFIEC 031 through the end of the calendar year in which the cessation of all operations of its "foreign" offices was completed.
2. *At $100 million or more in total assets for banks with domestic offices only*—A bank will begin filing the FFIEC 033 instead of the FFIEC 034.
3. *At $300 million or more in total assets for banks with domestic offices only*—A bank will begin filing the FFIEC 032 rather than the FFIEC 033.

Shifts requiring the reporting of additional information without a change in report form:

1. *At $25 million or more in total assets for banks with domestic offices only*—A bank must report additional loan information on Schedule RC-K, Quarterly Averages, and on Schedule RI, Income Statement.
2. *At $1 billion or more in total assets*—A bank, with or without foreign offices, must begin reporting detailed information on assets held in trading accounts (Schedule RC-D) and U.S. and non-U.S. addressee in-

formation on customers' liability on acceptances outstanding (Schedule RC-M, item 5).

Once a bank begins to file the report form applicable to a bank with a larger amount of total assets (except as noted for banks with foreign offices), it *must* continue to file that form unless it establishes a foreign office or its assets increase to an even larger total asset category.

PREPARATION OF THE REPORTS

Banks are required to prepare and file the Reports of Condition and Income in accordance with these instructions. All reports shall be prepared in a consistent manner.

The bank's financial records shall be maintained in such a manner and scope so as to ensure that the Reports of Condition and Income can be prepared and filed in accordance with these instructions and reflect a fair presentation of the bank's financial condition and results of operations.

Questions and requests for interpretations of matters appearing in any part of these instructions should be addressed to the appropriate federal bank supervisory authority (i.e., the Federal Reserve Banks, the Comptroller of the Currency, or the Federal Deposit Insurance Corporation). Such inquiries will be referred for resolution to the Reports Task Force of the Federal Financial Institutions Examination Council.

SIGNATURES

Officer Declaration
The Reports of Condition and Income filed with the appropriate supervisory agency shall be signed at the places and in the manner indicated on the forms by a duly authorized officer of the bank.

Director Attestation

National and state member banks. The correctness of the Report of Condition shall be attested to by at least three directors of the reporting bank, other than the officer signing the report, as indicated on the form.

State nonmember banks. The correctness of the Report of Condition shall be attested to by at least two directors of the reporting bank, other than the officer signing the report, as indicated on the form.

SUBMISSION OF THE REPORTS

The reports are to be submitted on the report forms provided by the supervisory agencies for each report date. No caption on the report forms shall be changed in any way. No item is to be left blank. An entry must be made for each item, i.e., an amount, a zero, the word "none," an "X," or an "N/A."

All reports shall be made out clearly and legibly by typewriter or in ink. Reports completed in pencil will not be accepted.

State member banks may submit computer printouts in a format identical to that of the report form, including all item and column captions and other identifying numbers.

Where to Submit the Reports

The completed and manually signed original reports shall be submitted as follows:

National banks and state nonmember banks—to the Federal Deposit Insurance Corporation.

State member banks—to the appropriate Federal Reserve Bank.

In addition, *national banks* must provide one copy of the Reports of Condition and Income to the appropriate Federal Reserve Bank and one copy to the appropriate district Deputy Comptroller.

State banks should refer to their appropriate state bank supervisory authorities for information concerning state requirements for providing copies of the Reports of Condition and Income submitted to federal bank supervisory authorities.

Legible photocopies are preferred. However, when carbons are used to prepare copies, the copies must be legible and prepared carefully to ensure that the figures and other information appear in the correct position on all copies.

All copies shall bear the same signatures as on the originals, but these signatures may be facsimiles or photocopies.

Submission Date

The completed Reports of Condition and Income shall be submitted no more than 30 calendar days after the report date. Earlier submission would aid the regulatory agencies in reviewing and processing the reports and is encouraged.

15-day extension. Any bank with more than one foreign office, other than a "shell" branch or an IBF, may take an additional 15 days to submit its reports. Such banks are urged to use the additional time only if absolutely necessary and to make every effort to report as soon as possible, preferably within the 30-day period.

Amended Reports

A bank's primary federal bank supervisory authority may require filing amended Reports of Condition or Income if reports as previously submitted contain significant errors as determined by the supervisory authority.

SCOPE OF THE "CONSOLIDATED BANK" REQUIRED TO BE REPORTED IN THE SUBMITTED REPORTS

In their Reports of Condition and Income submitted to the federal bank supervisory agencies, banks shall include the following on a consolidated basis in both the Report of Condition and the Report of Income:

1. the bank's head office
2. all branches of the bank, domestic and foreign
3. any International Banking Facility (IBF) established by the bank
4. all majority-owned Edge and Agreement subsidiaries, including their IBFs, their foreign and domestic branches, and their significant subsidiaries
5. all majority-owned foreign banks held directly by the reporting bank pursuant to Section 25 of the Federal Reserve Act
6. all majority-owned bank premises subsidiaries
7. all other majority-owned subsidiaries that are "significant," EXCEPT *domestic* subsidiaries that are commercial banks, savings banks, or savings and loan associations that must file separate Reports of Condition and Income (or separate reports of a comparable nature) with any state or federal financial institutions supervisory authority (see the Glossary entry for "subsidiaries" for the definition of "significant subsidiary")
8. all "significant" majority-owned subsidiaries of "significant" majority-owned subsidiaries of the bank
9. all nonsignificant majority-owned subsidiaries that the bank has elected to consolidate on a consistent basis in both the Report of Condition and the Report of Income.

Each bank shall account for any investments in unconsolidated subsidiaries, associated companies, and those corporate joint ventures over which the bank exercises significant influence according to the equity method of accounting. The equity method of accounting is described in Schedule RC, item 8. (Refer to the Glossary entry for "subsidiaries" for the definitions of the terms subsidiary, associated company, and corporate joint venture.)

Exclusions from the Coverage of the Consolidated Report
Subsidiaries held on a temporary basis. If control of a subsidiary by the parent bank is likely to be temporary, the subsidiary is not to be consolidated for purposes of the report. Thus, the bank's investments in such subsidiaries are not eliminated in consolidation but will be reflected in the reports in the balance sheet item for "Investments in unconsolidated subsidiaries

and associated companies'' (Schedule RC, item 8) and other transactions of the bank with such subsidiaries will be reflected in the appropriate items of the reports in the same manner as transactions with unrelated outside parties.

Trust accounts. For purposes of the Reports of Condition and Income, the reporting bank's trust department is *not* to be consolidated into the reporting bank's balance sheet or income statement. Thus, assets held in or administered by the bank's trust department and the income earned on such assets are excluded from the consolidated reports except when trust funds are deposited by the trust department of the reporting bank in the commercial or some other department of the reporting bank.

When such trust funds are deposited in the bank, they are to be reported as deposit liabilities in Schedule RC-E in the deposit category appropriate to the beneficiary. Interest paid by the bank on such deposits is to be reported as part of the reporting bank's interest expense.

However, there are two exceptions:

1. *uninvested trust funds (cash)* held in the bank's trust department, which are *not* included on the balance sheet of the reporting bank, *must* be reported in Schedule RC-O, Other Data for Deposit Insurance Assessments; and
2. the *fees* earned by the trust department for its fiduciary activities and the *operating expenses* of the trust department are to be reported in the bank's income statement (Schedule RI) on a gross basis as if part of the consolidated bank.

Custody accounts. All custody and safekeeping activities (i.e., the holding of securities, jewelry, coin collections, and other valuables in custody or in safekeeping for customers) are *not* to be reflected on any basis in the balance sheet of the Report of Condition unless cash funds held by the bank in safekeeping for customers are commingled with the general assets of the reporting bank. In such cases, the commingled funds would be reported in the Report of Condition as deposit liabilities of the bank.

RULES OF CONSOLIDATION

For purposes of these reports, all offices (i.e., branches, subsidiaries, and IBFs) that are within the scope of the consolidated bank as defined above are to be reported on a consolidated basis. Unless the report form captions or the line item instructions specifically state otherwise, this consolidation shall be on a line-by-line basis, according to the caption shown. As part of the consolidation process, the results of all transactions and all outstanding asset/debt relationships between offices *included* in the scope of the consolidated bank are to be *eliminated* in the consolidation and must be *excluded* from the consolidated Reports of Condition and Income. (For example, eliminate in the consolidation (1) loans made by the bank to a consolidated subsidiary and the corresponding liability of the subsidiary to the bank, (2) a consolidated subsidiary's deposits in the bank and the corresponding cash or interest-bearing asset balance of the subsidiary, and (3) the intercompany interest income and expense related to such loans and deposits of the bank and its consolidated subsidiary.) On the other hand, the results of all transactions and all outstanding asset/debt relationships between an office that is consolidated and an office *excluded* from the scope of the consolidated reports are *not* eliminated but are *entered* in the appropriate line items of the reports.

Subsidiaries of subsidiaries. For a subsidiary of a bank which is in turn the parent of one or more subsidiaries:

1. Each subsidiary shall consolidate its majority-owned subsidiaries in accordance with the consolidation requirements set forth above.
2. Each subsidiary or consolidated subsidiary shall be carried upward to the next succeeding "parent" level to determine whether consolidation, based on tests of significance, is required.
3. Each subsidiary shall account for any investments in unconsolidated subsidiaries, corporate joint ventures over which the bank exercises significant influence, and associated companies according to the equity method of accounting.

Minority interests. A minority interest arises when the reporting bank owns less than 100 percent of the stock of a consolidated subsidiary. The minority interest consists of the shares of stock not owned by the reporting bank. Report minority interests in the reporting bank's consolidated subsidiaries in Schedule RC, item 20, "Other liabilities," and identify these interests in Schedule RC-G of the Report of Condition. Report income (or loss) associated with such minority interests in "Other noninterest expense" in Schedule RI of the Report of Income.

Intrabank transactions. (For banks with foreign offices.) While all intrabank transactions are to be excluded from the consolidated Reports of Condition and Income, a few intrabank items that are eliminated in consolidation are required to be identified and reported. For example,

1. Schedule RC-H of the Report of Condition requires reporting of
    (a) the net amount of "due from" or "due to" balances between domestic offices and foreign offices of the consolidated bank, and
    (b) the net amount of "due from" or "due to" balances between domestic offices of the reporting bank and the IBF of the domestic offices of the reporting bank.
2. Schedule RI-D of the Report of Income requires the reporting of intrabank interest charges between types of offices of the bank.

FDIC insurance assessments. For domestic offices of the reporting bank, all deposits of subsidiaries that are consolidated and, therefore, eliminated from reported deposits in domestic offices (Schedule RC, items 13(a), 13(a)(1), and 13(a)(2)) must be reported in Schedule RC-O, item 4(a) or 4(b), as appropriate.

Cutoff dates for consolidation. All *branches* must be consolidated as of the report date. For purposes of consolidation, the date of financial statements of a *subsidiary* should, to the extent practicable, match the report date of the parent bank, but in no case differ by more than 93 days from the report date.

REPORTING BY TYPE OF OFFICE (For banks with foreign offices.)

Some information in the Reports of Condition and Income is to be reported by type of office (e.g., for domestic offices, for foreign offices, or for IBFs) as well as for the consolidated bank. Where information is called for by type of office, the information reported shall be the office component of the consolidated item unless otherwise specified in the line item instructions (e.g., as in the case of certain items in Schedule RI-D of the Report of Income). That is, as a general rule, the office information shall be reported at the same level of consolidation as the fully consolidated statement, shall reflect only transactions with parties outside the scope of the consolidated bank, and shall exclude all transactions between offices of the consolidated bank as defined above.

In addition to the type-of-office components of the corresponding consolidated bank items, some supporting schedules also require the reporting of the net amount of certain intrabank transactions that are eliminated from the Report of Condition.

**PUBLICATION REQUIREMENTS FOR THE REPORT
OF CONDITION**

State Nonmember Banks
There is no federal publication requirement for state nonmember banks. Such banks should refer to their appropriate state banking authorities for state publication requirements.

State Member Banks
Section 9 of the Federal Reserve Act, as amended, requires that the Reports of Condition submitted by state member banks to Federal Reserve Banks as required by the Board of Governors of the Federal Reserve System ''shall be published by the reporting banks in such manner and in accordance with

such regulations as the said Board may prescribe.'' (There is no requirement that the Report of Income be published.) Pursuant to this provision of law, the Board of Governors of the Federal Reserve System has prescribed the following regulations for publication of the Report of Condition.

The face page of each Report of Condition that is submitted by a state member bank to the Federal Reserve Bank of its district, pursuant to the requirements set by the Board of Governors of the Federal Reserve System, shall be published by the member bank within 10 calendar days of the required date of submission of the report. Upon application, and for good cause shown, the Reserve Bank may permit an extension of this period. Such extensions are not ordinarily granted for more than 10 days.

Such publication of the report shall be in a newspaper published in the place where the bank is located or, if there is no newspaper published in the place where the bank is located, in a newspaper that is published in the same or adjoining county and is in general circulation in the place where the bank is located. For the purpose of this regulation, the term ''newspaper'' means a publication with a general circulation published not less frequently than once a week, one of the primary functions of which is the dissemination of news of general interest.

Except as otherwise provided in the instructions below, the published information shall agree in every respect with that shown on the face of the Report of Condition submitted to the Federal Reserve Bank.

A copy of the published report from the newspaper where published shall be attached to the Certificate of Publication (either form FR 2109pf or form FR 2109ps) that accompanies the reporting forms and shall be submitted to the Federal Reserve Bank.

The report shall be published either (1) in the format of the face page of the Report of Condition (Schedule RC), with certain exceptions discussed below, or (2) in a format that meets the publication requirements both of the Federal Reserve and of the relevant state banking authority. These two publication formats are described below.

(1) *Use of the FFIEC forms for publication:*
    If the face of the Report of Condition (Schedule RC) is used for publication, form FR 2109pf shall be used for the Certificate of Publication.

The published information shall agree in every respect with that shown on Schedule RC submitted to the Federal Reserve Bank, with the following exceptions:

a. The heading that appears on the reverse side of form FR 2109pf shall be used as the heading of the published version of Schedule RC.

b. All item numbers may be omitted, and any item for which no amount is shown on the bank's submitted copy of Schedule RC may be stricken from the publisher's copy.

c. Any part of the printed caption appearing in parentheses may be omitted on the publisher's copy if not applicable to the reporting bank.

d. Item references included in the line titles may be stricken from the publisher's copy.

e. Where applicable, the publisher's copy shall show information pertaining to the interest rate, maturity, and the amount outstanding of each note and debenture issued, even though this information is not required to be shown on the Report of Condition submitted to the Reserve Bank. Issues that mature serially may be identified briefly as such. For example, the publishers copy might refer to $10,000,000 of 8.5 percent notes maturing annually in amounts of $1,000,000 from December 1984 through December 1993. Variations in interest rates and amounts maturing annually must be specifically identified. This supplementary information may be published as a footnote to the publisher's copy or underlined in the appropriate place.

f. The declaration and attestation section that appears on the reverse side of form FR 2109pf shall be shown at the end of the publication copy. All signatures shall be the same in the published statement as in the original report submitted to the Federal Reserve Bank. On the report for publication, the signatures may be typewritten, otherwise copied, or manually signed.

(2) *Joint publication meeting requirements of both the Federal Reserve and the state banking authority:*

Under the following conditions, the Federal Reserve will accept for purposes of the publication requirement a single, joint publication of a state member bank's Report of Condition submitted to the state banking department and to the Federal Reserve Bank, pursuant to the requirements of state law and of the Federal Reserve Act, respectively. For a joint publication, form FR 2109ps shall be used for the Certificate of Publication.

Condition A: The heading that appears on the reverse side of form FR 2109ps shall be used as the heading of the published version of Schedule RC.

Condition B: The declaration and attestation section that appears on the reverse side of form FR 2109ps shall be shown at the end of the publication copy. If desired, or if required under state procedures, the phrase ''and the state banking authority'' may be changed as appropriate in the declaration and attestation statements.

All signatures shall be the same in the published statement as in the original report submitted to the Federal Reserve Bank. If required by the state, the published statement may show the signatures of more than one officer (in addition to the attestation of three or more directors), provided that one of the signatures is that of the officer who signed the bank's Report of Condition submitted to the Reserve Bank.

On the report for publication, the signatures may be typewritten, otherwise copied, or manually signed.

An affidavit may also be included if required by the state.

Condition C: With the exceptions noted under paragraphs (1)(b), (1)(c), (1)(d), and (1)(e) of this section on publication, the published copy must be in such a form that the information submitted to the Federal Reserve on the Schedule RC can be derived from the published copy. Depending on the details of the published copy, such derivation can be accomplished in a number of ways.

For example, where the state requires publication of additional detail not called for by the Report of Condition, publication of the additional detail will satisfy Federal Reserve requirements provided that (1) the Federal Reserve version can be derived from the state version by the simple addition of components and (2) the accounting, consolidation, and other requirements of the Federal Reserve version are followed.

Similarly, where the state requires less detail to be shown in published reports than does the Federal Reserve, and the state authority agrees to accept publication of the more detailed information required on the bank's Report of Condition, Schedule RC, the Federal Reserve permits joint publication provided that the accounting, consolidation, and other requirements of Schedule RC are followed.

Where the state requires additional items that are neither components nor aggregates of items appearing on the Report of Condition (e.g., memoranda items), such additional items may be shown on the published copy wherever appropriate.

National Banks

National banks are required by 12 USC 161 to publish the "statement of resources and liabilities," Schedule RC of the consolidated Report of Condition submitted to the Comptroller of the Currency, in a local newspaper of general circulation. There is no requirement that the Report of Income be published.

Banks conducting international operations must publish a fully consolidated statement including both foreign and domestic activities. Proof of publication shall be retained by the bank. The condition statement must be published within 20 days following the Comptroller's call that these reports be filed.

A printer's copy of Schedule RC of the Report of Condition will be provided to each national bank for publication purposes. Any item of Schedule RC for which no amount is shown by the bank may be stricken from the published statement. The published statements of banks with foreign offices must be identified as being on a fully consolidated basis. Banks without any consolidated subsidiaries should delete references to subsidiaries from the title of the published statement. The caption "published in response to call made by Comptroller of the Currency, under Title 12, United States Code, Section 161," which appears on the printer's copy together with the attestation of the officer responsible for signing the report and directors' signatures, must also be published.

The bank must ensure that the published statement is printed in large enough type to be clearly readable.

Banks may elect to publish the Report of Condition in dollars and cents instead of in the rounded amounts required on the report submitted to the Comptroller.

RELEASE OF INDIVIDUAL BANK REPORTS

All schedules of the Reports of Condition and Income submitted by each reporting bank, including the optional narrative statement in Schedule RC-N, past due, nonaccrual, and renegotiated loans and lease financing receivables, will be made available to the public upon request by the federal bank supervisory authorities with the exception of column A, ''Past due 30 through 89 days and still accruing,'' of Schedule RC-N.

APPLICABILITY OF GENERALLY ACCEPTED ACCOUNTING PRINCIPLES TO REGULATORY REPORTING REQUIREMENTS

It should be noted that while it is the agencies' intention to follow generally accepted accounting principles (GAAP) wherever these are appropriate, the Reports of Condition and Income are supervisory and regulatory documents, not primarily accounting documents. Because of the special supervisory, regulatory, and economic policy needs served by these reports, these instructions do not in all cases follow GAAP or the opinions and statements of the Accounting Principles Board (APB) or the Financial Accounting Standards Board (FASB). In reporting transactions not covered in principle by these instructions, banks may follow GAAP. However, in all such circumstances, a specific ruling shall be sought promptly from the appropriate federal bank supervisory agency.

There may be areas in which a bank wishes more technical detail on the application of accounting standards and procedures to the requirements of these instructions. Such information may often be found in the appropriate entries in the Glossary section of these instructions or, in more detail, in APB Opinions and FASB Statements. Selected opinions and statements of these accounting organizations are referenced in the instructions where appropriate. The accounting entries in the Glossary are intended only to serve as an aid in specific reporting situations; they do not, and are not intended to constitute a comprehensive statement on bank accounting.

ACCRUAL BASIS REPORTING

Banks with total assets of $10 million or more as of December 31, 1981, shall prepare all schedules of the Reports of Condition and Income on an accrual basis. Banks with total assets of less than $10 million as of December 31, 1981, may, at their option, report on a cash basis (with the four exceptions listed below) until January 1, 1985. All reports for periods beginning on or after that date must be prepared on an accrual basis.

The federal bank supervisory agencies encourage banks below $10 million in assets to begin to report on an accrual basis as soon as possible.

All banks, whether reporting on an accrual or cash basis, *must* report the following on an accrual basis:

1. income from installment loans;
2. amortization of premiums paid on investment securities
3. income taxes
4. depreciation on premises and fixed assets.

Banks reporting on an accrual basis may report particular accounts on a cash basis, except for the four listed above, if the results would not differ significantly from those obtained using an accrual basis. Trust department income may be reported on a cash basis.

All banks reporting on an accrual basis shall establish and maintain an allowance for loan and lease losses. Banks with assets of less than $10 million which report on the cash basis may elect to either:

1. establish and maintain at an adequate level an allowance for loan and lease losses, or
2. account for loan and lease losses on an actual net charge-off basis.

Such banks are strongly encouraged to adopt the first option.

For banks on an accrual basis of reporting, no interest or discount shall be accrued on any asset which must be carried in nonaccrual status.

REPORTING OF LOAN DETAIL BY BANKS WITH ASSETS OF LESS THAN $300 MILLION AND NO FOREIGN OFFICES

All banks regardless of size are required to report their loans oustanding as of the report date in Schedule RC-C, Loans and Lease Financing Receivables, in the standardized loan categories specifically defined in the instructions for that schedule.

There are four other schedules that require the reporting of certain data by loan category:

Schedule RC-K	Quarterly Averages
Schedule RC-N	Past Due, Nonaccrual, and Renegotiated Loans and Lease Financing Receivables
Schedule RI	Income Statement
Schedule RI-B, part 1	Charge-Offs and Recoveries on Loans and Leases

In these four schedules also, all banks with $300 million or more in assets or with any foreign offices (as defined for these reports)(i.e., those banks that are required to report on FFIEC 031 or 032) are required to report detailed loan data in terms of the standardized loan categories defined in these instructions. However, for these four schedules, but *not* for Schedule RC-C, banks with less than $300 million in assets *and* with no foreign offices (i.e., those banks that are required to report on FFIEC 033 or 034) are permitted to report the detailed loan data requested in these schedules in terms of general loan categories that are based upon *each bank's own* internal loan categorization system. (Banks with assets of less than $25 million are exempt from reporting any loan detail on Schedules RC-K and RI.)

There are four general loan categories that are used in these schedules for all banks with assets of less than $300 million and no foreign offices:

1. real estate loans
2. installment loans
3. credit cards and related plans
4. commercial (time and demand) and all other loans

In addition, for some of these schedules and for some of the banks with less than $300 million in assets, data for the following loan categories will be reported in memoranda items:

5. agricultural loans (to be reported on all four of the above schedules by banks with agricultural loans, as reported in Schedule RC-C, item 3, exceeding five percent of total loans)
6. obligations (other than securities) of states and political subdivisions in the U.S. (to be reported on Schedules RC-K and RI by banks with assets of $100 million or more but less than $300 million)
7. loans to foreign governments and official institutions (to be reported on Schedule RI-B, part 1, by banks with assets of $100 million or more but less than $300 million)

For banks with assets of less than $300 million and no foreign offices and *only* for purposes of Schedules RC-K, RC-N, RI, and RI-B, part 1 (but *not* for purposes of Schedule RC-C), the first five of these seven general loan categories are flexibly defined as follows in accordance with the manner in which each bank characterizes such loans in its own recordkeeping systems or for its own internal purposes:

Real estate loans As each reporting bank determines for itself, such loans may be those loans made or booked in the bank's real estate department, or the coverage may be determined by other criteria. Depending on each bank's internal practices, such loans may or may not include loans secured by junior liens on real estate; loans secured by commercial properties; loans secured by farm properties; etc. Thus, at the reporting bank's option, the coverage of real estate loans in these four schedules for a bank with less than $300 million in assets and with no foreign offices is not necessarily the same as the coverage of the "Loans secured by real estate" category that the bank is required to report in Schedule RC-C, item 1.

Installment loans As each reporting bank determines for itself, such loans may be those loans made or booked in the bank's installment loan department or those made on an installment basis, or the coverage may be determined by other criteria. Depending on each bank's internal practices, such loans may or may not include business installment loans; installment loans for farmers; some loans secured by junior liens on real estate; some single payment loans; some loans with irrregular payment schedules or with balloon payments; some loans arising out of prearranged overdraft plans; etc. Thus, at the reporting bank's option, the coverage of "installment loans" in these four schedules for a bank with less than $300 million in assets and with no foreign offices is not necessarily the same as the coverage of the "Other loans to individuals for household, family, and other personal expenditures" category that the bank is required to report in Schedule RC-C, item 6(b).

Credit cards and related plans As each reporting bank determines for itself, depending on its internal practices, such loans may or may not include business as well as consumer use of such cards; may or may not cover prearranged overdraft plans as well as credit cards. Thus, at the reporting bank's option, the coverage of "credit cards and related plans" for these four schedules for a bank with less than $300 million in assets and with no foreign offices is not necessarily the same as the coverage of the "Credit cards and related plans" category that the bank is required to report in Schedule RC-C, item 6(a).

Commercial (time and demand) and all other loans This category is a residual category and, for each bank, its contents will depend on the contents of the three preceding categories as reported in these four schedules. This residual category will consist mainly of loans for commercial and agricultural purposes and loans to financial institutions but, depending on each reporting bank's internal practices and choices for reporting in these four schedules, it may or may not include, for example, commercial real estate loans, business installment loans, business credit card loans, consumer single payment loans, junior lien loans, etc. Thus, the coverage of commercial (time and demand) and all other loans for these four schedules for a bank with less than $300 million in assets and with no foreign offices is unlikely to be the same as the coverage of the "Commercial and industrial loans" category that the bank is required to report in Schedule RC-C, item 4.

Agricultural loans As each reporting bank determines for itself, such loans may be those loans made or booked in an agricultural loan department, or the coverage may be determined by other criteria. Depending on each bank's internal practices, such loans may or may not include loans secured by farmland or other farm real estate; loans to farmers secured by nonfarm property; consumer installment loans made to farmers; etc. Thus, at each reporting bank's option, the coverage of agricultural loans in these four schedules for a bank with less than $300 million in assets and with no foreign offices is not necessarily the same as the coverage of the "Loans to finance agricultural production and other loans to farmers" category that the bank is required to report in Schedule RC-C, item 3.

While, for purposes of reporting in Schedules RC-K, RC-N, RI, and RI-B, part 1, by banks with less than $300 million in assets and with no foreign offices, the definitions of the above five categories are left to the choice of each reporting bank, each bank *must* use consistent definitions and coverages of these categories in each of the four schedules.

For the two additional loan category memoranda items that appear in some of these four schedules for banks with assets of $100 million or more but less than $300 million (i.e., for those banks filing the FFIEC 033), "Obligations (other than securities) of states and political subdivisions in the U.S." in Schedules RC-K and RI and "Loans to foreign governments and official institutions" in Schedule RI-B, part 1, the definitions and coverages of these two categories when used in these schedules *must* be exactly the same as the definitions and coverages of the two corresponding loan categories in Schedule RC-C, items 8 and 7, respectively.

MISCELLANEOUS GENERAL INSTRUCTIONS

Rounding

For banks with total assets of less than $10 billion, all dollar amounts must be reported in thousands, with the figures rounded to the nearest thousand. Items less than $500 will be reported as zero.

For banks with total assets of $10 billion or more, all dollar amounts may be reported in thousands, but each bank, at its option, may round the figures reported to the nearest million, with zeros reported in the thousands column. For banks exercising this option, amounts less than $500,000 will be reported as zero.

Rounding may result in details not adding to their stated totals. The only permissible differences between totals and the sums of their components are those attributable to the mechanics of rounding.

On the Report of Condition, "Total assets" (Schedule RC, item 12) and "Total liabilities, limited-life preferred stock, and equity capital" (Schedule RC, item 29), which must be equal, must be derived from unrounded numbers and then rounded in order to ensure that these two items are equal as reported.

Negative Entries
Except for the items listed below, negative entries are not appropriate on the Report of Condition and shall not be reported. Hence, assets with credit balances must be reported in liability items and liabilities with debit balances must be reported in asset items, as appropriate, and in accordance with these instructions. The four items for which negative entries may be made, if appropriate, are:

1. Schedule RC, item 8, "Investments in unconsolidated subsidiaries and associated companies,"
2. Schedule RC, item 26, "Undivided profits and capital reserves,"
3. Schedule RC, item 27, "Cumulative foreign currency translation adjustments," (for banks with foreign offices), and
4. Schedule RC-C, item 10, "Lease financing receivables (net of unearned income)" (item 9 in FFIEC 034).

When negative entries do occur in one or more of these four items, they shall be recorded in parentheses rather than with a minus ($-$) sign.

On the Report of Income, negative entries may appear as appropriate. Income items with a debit balance and expense items with a credit balance must be reported in parentheses.

Verification
All addition and subtraction should be doubled-checked before reports are

submitted. Totals and subtotals in supporting materials should be cross-checked to corresponding items elsewhere in the reports.

Before a report is submitted, all amounts should be compared with the corresponding amounts in the previous report. If there are any unusual changes from the previous report, a brief explanation of the changes should be attached to the submitted reports.

Banks should retain workpapers and other records used in the preparation of these reports.

SEPARATE BRANCH REPORTS

Each U.S. bank shall submit for each of its branches located in a foreign country, Puerto Rico, or a U.S. territory or possession (including trust territories) a *Foreign Branch Report of Condition* (FFIEC 024) once a year as of the end of December, unless the appropriate federal bank supervisory authority specifically requires some other frequency of reporting.

SUMMARY ON THE MARCH 31, 1984 UNIFORM BANK CALL REPORT

According to release dated November 3, 1983 by the Federal Financial Institutions Examination Council (FFIEC) the Office of Management and Budget (OMB) approved the 1984 call report revisions that had been announced by the FFIEC on June 29, 1983. The revisions became effective for the Reports of Condition and Income filed by all insured commercial banks as of the March 31, 1984 report date.

These revisions are the last of a series of amendments to the Call Reports that began in March 1983.

The Appendix reproduces sample forms in full for the revised uniform Bank Call Report that became effective as of the March 31, 1984 report date.

The FFIEC summarizes the changes in the finally revised uniform Bank Call Report as follows:

1. The revised Call Reports are different in several ways from those issued for public comment originally in June 1982. The majority of the changes were made to reduce the reporting burden of the original proposals. The most significant change allows banks with total assets of less than $300 million and no foreign offices to report the loan detail required on several of the schedules according to the bank's own internal loan categories rather than the standardized categories used in the Report of Condition Schedule of loan balances outstanding. Banks with assets of less than $25 million are not required to report any income or quarterly average balance data for specific types of loans.

2. The number of loan categories that must be aggregated and reported by the nation's largest banks in the Report of Condition have been reduced by 25 percent from the previously required report.

3. Deposit data called for in the Report of Condition emphasizes the distinction between transaction and non-transaction balances as well as between interest-bearing and non-interest bearing balances.

4. The Income Statement section of the Report of Income is presented on a single tier net income basis in the net interest margin format.

5. In response to objection by many bankers to the previous Call Report requirement that loans to states, counties, and political subsidivisions be reported in the same item as securities issued by these instrumentalities, the 1984 Call Report provides separate categories under loans and securities to report these different types of obligations. Bonds issued by industrial development authorities will, as a general rule, be reported as securities if rated by a national rating service, and as loans if they are not rated.

The newly revised Call Report forms, including the Schedules, provide the data base for the numerous ratios, percentages and dollar amounts calculated and compiled by computer for the Uniform Bank Performance Report (UBPR).

Chapter 6

The Uniform Bank Performance Report

The Federal Financial Institutions Examination Council (FFIEC) developed the Uniform Bank Performance Report (UBPR) as an analytical tool for bank supervisory, examination and management purposes. According to the FFIEC:

> It shows, in a convenient format, the impact of management decisions and economic conditions on a bank's performance and balance sheet composition. The performance and composition data contained in the report may be used as an aid in making decisions concerning the adequacy of earnings, liquidity, capital, asset and liability management, and growth management. Bankers and examiners alike may use the report to further their understanding of the bank's financial condition and through such understanding become more effective in the performance of their duties.

A UBPR is produced for each commercial bank in the United States which is supervised by the Board of Governors of the Federal Reserve System, Federal Deposit Insurance Corporation, or the Office of the Comptroller of the Currency. The report is computer-generated from a data base derived from public and non-public sources. It contains several years of data which are updated quarterly. These data are presented in the form of ratios, percentages, and dollar amounts computed mainly from Reports of Condition and Income submitted by the bank. Each UBPR also contains corresponding average data for the bank's peer group and percentile rankings for most ratios. The UBPR therefore permits evaluation of a bank's current condition, trends in its financial performance, and comparisons with the performance of its peer group.

A User's Guide for the Uniform Bank Performance Report is also available containing the basic guidelines necessary for using the UBPR, including a suggested method of analyzing the report, technical information, and also ratio definitions.

Contents of a UBPR

The Table of Contents of a UBPR includes the following:

Sections
    Summary Ratios
    Income Information
        Income Statement—Revenues and Expenses
        Relative Income Statement and Margin Analysis
        Non-Interest Income and Expense Ratios
    Balance Sheet Information
        Balance Sheet—Assets Section
        Balance Sheet—Liabilities and Capital
        Balance Sheet—Percentage Composition of Assets and Liabilities
        Analysis of Loan Loss Reserve and Loan Mix
        Analysis of Past Due, Nonaccrual and Renegotiated Loans
        Optional Narrative Statement (concerning the figures submitted on the past due, nonaccrual and renegotiated loans and lease financing receivables report)
        Sources and Uses of Funds
        Analysis of Repricing Opportunities
        Liquidity and Investment Portfolio
        Capital Analysis

Other Information
   Summary Information for Bank in State
   Foreign Office Trends
   Peer Group Information
Bank and Bank Holding Company Information (Bank's number
   and its Certificate and Charter Numbers; name of its Holding
   Company, if any, and the Holding Company's number and
   address)

Sample Copy of Summary Ratios, BPR

Appended herewith is the page of Summary Ratios of the BPR for
Citibank, N.A., principal bank subsidiary of Citicorp. The *User's Guide*
explains:

"TE" means tax equivalent.

"X" means number of times (multiple).

"Volatile liability dependence" means total volatile liabilities less temporary investments divided by the sum of net loans, lease financing receivables and investment securities with remaining maturities of more
   than one year ("volatile liabilities") are the sum of all time deposits of
   over $100 thousand, Federal Funds purchased, and securities sold
   under agreements to repurchase, interest-bearing demand notes (note
   balances) issued to the U.S. Treasury, and other liabilities for
   borrowed money).

"Peer group" data show how a group of banks with similar characteristics have performed during a particular period. This concept provides
   a frame of reference for evaluating the bank's financial condition.
There are three general UBPR peer group formations. The primary formation (consisting of 25 peer groups) is used based on a combination
   of factors: asset size, branch system versus non-branch system, and
   metropolitan versus non-metropolitan location. All banks within the
   same peer group are of similar size, type, and location. Second and
   third peer group formations refer to state averages: the second is the

TABLE 17

Cert #7213 DSB #02364990
Charter #1461

Citibank, N. A. New York City, New York

Summary Ratios

Earnings and Profitability	1983			1982			1981			1980		1979	
Average Assets ($000)	108256500**			106497000**			103226061			96400022**		88305962	
Net Income ($000)	756000			883000			673776			649378		561621	
# Banks in Peer Group	22			22			21			18		17	
	Bank	Peer 01	PCT	Bank	Peer 01	PCT	Bank	Peer 01	PCT	Bank	Peer 01	Bank	Peer 01
Percent of Average Assets:													
Net Interest Income (TE)	3.05	2.80	69	3.11	2.86	65	2.57	2.82	40	2.60	2.74	2.71	2.81
+ Non-Interest Income (TE)	1.12	.95	82	1.10	.87	78	1.11	.80	90	.98	.76	.66	.66
− Overhead Expense	2.53	2.35	60	2.41	2.36	52	2.19	2.25	54	2.12	2.13	2.05	2.07
− Provision for Loan Losses	.30	.40	34	.28	.33	34	.17	.25	27	.12	.25	.12	.25
= Pretax Net Oper Inc (TE)	1.34	1.00	78	1.52	1.02	82	1.33	1.13	77	1.34	1.12	1.20	1.15
Net Operating Income	.70	.54	73	.84	.56	86	.67	.60	72	.68	.57	.65	.59
Adj. Net Oper Income	.75	.62	73	.91	.63	86	.73	.68	63	.70	.63	.68	.70
Adj. Net Income	.69	.52	78	.78	.51	86	.60	.54	68	.61	.53	.59	.57
Net Income	.70	.54	73	.83	.53	86	.65	.56	72	.67	.56	.64	.58
Percent of Avg Earning Assets:													
Interest Income (TE)	13.71	11.29	91	15.99	14.04	91	17.33	15.85	90	14.92	13.45	12.62	11.63
Interest Expense	10.07	7.88	91	12.20	10.78	91	14.22	12.65	90	11.71	10.24	9.37	8.31
Net Int Income (TE)	3.65	3.33	69	3.78	3.41	69	3.11	3.44	31	3.21	3.41	3.26	3.50

Loan Losses, Reserves and Non-Performing Loans and Leases

Net Loan Loss to Avg Total LNS	.38	.52	34	.35	.41	30	.19	.30	23	.18	.34	.15	.27
Earn Cover of Net LN Losses (×)	6.54	4.44	86	8.13	4.86	86	12.38	7.73	80	13.53	7.19	14.75	7.78
Loss Resv to Net LN Losses (×)	2.14	2.77	34	2.22	2.90	30	3.64	4.22	42	3.75	4.02	4.80	3.87
Loss Reserve to Total Loans	.81	1.16	04	.73	1.07	04	.66	1.00	09	.61	.97	.65	1.00
% Non-Performing Loans & Lease	3.05	4.17		NA	NA		NA	NA		NA	NA	NA	NA

Liquidity and Rate Sensitivity

Volatile Liability Dependence	73.06	60.11	60	80.62	64.98	82	80.56	65.26	86	81.91	66.72	83.64	64.27
Net Loans to Total Assets	61.06	59.30	65	61.49	59.89	65	62.26	58.79	63	59.10	55.88	56.79	55.42
Net Assets Repricable in 1 Yr or Less to Assets	-1.32	-.26	47	NA	NA	NA	NA	NA	NA	NA	NA	NA	NA

Capitalization

Prim Capital to Total Assets	5.72	5.15	86	5.39	4.91	86	5.06	4.74	86	4.71	4.52	4.52	4.55
Cash Dividends to Net Income	35.98	46.37	23	28.54	44.02	09	33.84	43.27	22	32.65	43.15	34.19	39.92
Ret Earns to Avg Total Equity	8.47	6.48	78	12.21	7.30	91	9.61	7.84	68	10.37	8.14	9.75	8.40

Growth Rates

Assets	2.13	2.26	52	6.03	6.61	30	2.58	9.29	22	5.79	11.78	18.14	15.88
Primary Capital	8.33	9.05	56	12.89	9.95	73	10.26	11.01	45	10.24	10.92	11.14	10.96
Total Loans	1.49	3.03	47	4.78	8.90	26	8.12	15.58	22	10.06	13.91	15.39	15.09
Volatile Liabilities	-3.27	-5.53	60	2.31	5.65	26	2.38	14.40	09	1.19	18.29	22.45	17.02

**One or More Mergers, Consolidations, or Purchases Have Occurred during the Period.

state average for all commercial banks within the state; and the third is derived with the state of averages based on specific asset sizes.

For any given time period presented in the UBPR, the bank is included in a peer group most closely aligned with its own characteristics at that particular time.

In the appended sample copy of Summary Ratios, "01" refers to the first peer group.

"Pct" refers to the percentile ranking of the bank's ratio (how high or low the bank's ratio is in relation to its peer group).

To calculate the percentile ranking for a particular ratio, the corresponding ratios for each bank in the peer group are arranged in order, from the highest to the lowest value. All banks with the same ratio value are assigned the same rank within the peer group. Once the bank's rank is determined, the percentile ranking is calculated by the familiar statistical method: the rank is multiplied by 100 and the result is divided by the number of banks in the peer group plus one. The numerical value of the percentile ranking will range from 99 to 0.

A high or low percentile ranking does not automatically imply a good or bad or satisfactory or unsatisfactory rating. However, when analyzed in context with other data, an opinion can be rendered as to the relevance of a high or low ranking to an individual bank's performance.

Commentary. It will be noted that Citibank, N.A. showed generally favorable comparisons with its peer group. In general, however, we have reservations about the comparison with any peer group because the peer group does not necessarily indicate a desirable norm. But the comparison may serve as a starting point for further judgment and evaluation.

Availability

The Uniform Bank Performance Report (UBPR) may be ordered for individual banks. There is also a state average report and a peer group report. Each report may be ordered as indicated below. All requests must be in writing and must include full payment with the order. The following is the current fee schedule for requested reports:

Type of Order	Price per Copy
Number of printed copy UBPRs:	
1–49	$25.00
50–99	$22.50
100 +	$21.25
Magnetic Tape Print Images (for photocopy machine processing):	
1–24 (reports)	Not available
25–99	$21.25
100 +	$20.00
Bank requesting additional copy of its UBPR	$ 6.00
State Average Report (covers all states)	$25.00
Peer Group Report (covers all UBPR peer groups)	$25.00
UBPR User's Guide	$ 2.50

All requests must be sent to:
> UBPR
> Department 4320
> Chicago, Illinois 60673

Make check payable to:
> Federal Financial Institutions Examination Council

SUMMARY

The UBPR with its various reports and its comprehensive content of ratios and comparisons is a must for analysis of bank statements.

There is nothing, of course, to prevent the analyst from working out other ratios and analytical constructions bearing on topics of interest regarding a particular bank or specialized groups of banks.

It should be noted that:

1. The UBPRs and its various reports refer only to individual banks, not to bank holding companies, unconsolidated or consolidated.
2. The UBPR was not designed to replace on-site examinations or investigations but to supplement present management and examination procedures.

Notes

Chapter One

[1]Securities Act Release 6384, March 3, 1982 (47 FR 11476).

[2]Release Nos. 33-6458 and 34-19570 (17 CFR Parts 210, 231, 240 and 241).

[3]The SEC solicited public comments on the proposed revision of Article 9 and Guide 3 in Release 33-6417, July 9, 1982, found in 47 FR 32158 (July 26, 1982).

[4]FASB Exposure Draft, Proposed Statement of Financial Accounting Concepts, "Reporting Income, Cash Flows and Financial Position of Business Enterprises," November 16, 1981 (delayed in adoption).

[5]American Institute of Certified Public Accountants, Inc., *Audits of Banks* (Prepared by the Banking Committee), 1983.

[6]*Ibid.*

[7]This is consistent with the SEC's Regulation S-K, whose Item 404 was revised in Securities Act Release 6441, December 13, 1982 (47 FR 5566).

[8]Robert V. Roosa (partner, Brown Brothers Harriman & Co.), "International Financial Crisis?" *Remarks* at Institute on International Banking and Finance, Southern Methodist University, Dallas, Texas, November 10, 1982.

Chapter Three

[9]Staff of Board of Governors of the Federal Reserve System, *The Bank Holding Company Movement to 1978: A Compendium*, September 1978, p. 46.

[10]Board of Governors of the Federal Reserve System, *Federal Reserve Regulatory Service*, Regulation Y, Sec. 225.5.

Chapter Four

[11]Rose, J. T. and Talley, S. H., "The Banking Affiliates Act of 1982: Amendments to Section 23A," *Federal Reserve Bulletin,* November 1982.

[12]Comptroller General of the United States, "Federal Supervision of Bank Holding Companies Needs Better, More Formalized Coordination," *Report* to the Congress, February 12, 1980, pp. 5, 6.

[13]Holland, Robert C., Member of the Board of Governors of the Federal Reserve System, *Statement* before the Subcommittee on Bank Supervision and Insurance of the Committee on Banking and Currency, U.S. House of Representatives, December 12, 1974.

[14]Heller, Pauline B., *Handbook of Federal Bank Holding Company Law,* 1976, p. 350.

[15]In computing the ratio of earnings to fixed charges or the ratio of combined fixed charges and preferred stock dividends, Regulation S-K (17 CFR 229.503) of the SEC specifies that "Fixed Charges" shall mean the following:

(a) Interest, whether expensed or capitalized;

(b) Amortization of debt expense and discount or premium relating to any indebtedness, whether expensed or capitalized;

(c) Such portion of rental expense as can be demonstrated to be representative of the interest factor in the particular case; and

(d) Preferred stock dividend requirements, which shall be increased to an amount representing the pre-tax earnings which would be required to cover such dividend requirements, by the income tax factor as follows:

Preferred Stock Dividend Requirements

100% minus Income Tax Rate

Bibliography

Bank Holding Companies

Brown, D. M., "The Effect of State Banking Laws on Holding Company Banks," Federal Reserve Bank of St. Louis *Review,* August/September 1983.

Conover, C. T. (Comptroller of the Currency), "What Should a Bank Holding Company Be?" *Remarks* before the Association of Bank Holding Companies, November 19, 1982.

Curry, T. J. and Rose, J. T. (Staff of the Board of Governors of the Federal Reserve System), *Multibank Holding Companies: Recent Evidence on Competition and Performance in Banking Markets,* January 1982.

Elliott, D. F. and Biggs, D. C., "The Pros and Cons of a One-Bank Holding Company," *Hoosier Banker,* July 1982.

Frieder, L. A. and Apilado, V. P., "Bank Holding Company Expansion: A Refocus on Its Financial Rationale," *Journal of Financial Research,* Spring 1983.

Jeffries, M. H. Jr., "Holding Company Advantages," *Southern Banker,* March 1983.

Karna, A. S. and Graddy, D. B., "Bank Holding Company Leverage and the Return on Stockholders Equity," *Journal of Bank Research,* Spring 1982.

Kendrick, J. J., "New Tax Law Benefits Bank Holding Company Formations," *Independent Banker,* October 1982.

Pozen, R. C., "The 1982 Tax Act and Bank Holding Companies," *Bank Administration,* February 1983.

Rose, J. T., "Bank Holding Company Affiliations and Market Share Performance," *Quarterly Journal of Monetary Economics,* January 1982.

Rose, J. T. and Talley, S. H. (Staff of Board of Governors of the Federal Reserve System), *Financial Transactions Within Holding Companies,* May 1983.

Stover, R. D., "A Reexamination of Bank Holding Company Acquisitions," *Journal of Bank Research,* Summer 1982.

Banking and Related Lines

Committee on Insurance and Committee on Developments in Investment Securities, of the Corporation, Banking and Business Law Section of the American Bar Association, "The Changing Environment for Financial Services and Products," *Business Lawyer,* February 1983.

Earley, J. S. and Evans, G. R., "The Problem Is Bank Liability Management," *Challenge,* January/February 1982.

Gardner, E. P. M., "Capital Adequacy and Banking Supervision—Towards a Practical System," *Journal of Bank Research,* Summer 1982.

Gorinson, S. M., "Depository Institutions Deregulatory Refrom in the 1980s: The Issue of Geographic Restrictions," *Antitrust Bulletin,* Spring 1983.

Hope, N. and Klein, T., "Issues in External Debt Management," *Finance and Development,* September 1983.

Kane, E. J., "Policy Implementations of Structural Changes in Financial Markets," *American Economic Review,* May 1983.

Kareken, J. H., "The First Step in Bank Deregulation: What About the FDIC?" *American Economic Review,* May 1983.

Longstreth, B. (then member of the Securities and Exchange Commission), "In Search of a Safety Net for the Financial Services Industry," *Bankers Magazine,* July/August, 1983.

Rhoades, S. A. (Staff of the Board of Governors of the Federal Reserve System), *The Implications for Bank Merger Policy of Financial Deregulation, Interstate Banking, and Financial Supermarkets,* February 1984.

Roosa, R. V., "International Financial Crisis?" *Remarks* at Southern Methodist University, November 10, 1982.

Silber, W. L., "The Process of Financial Innovation," *American Economic Review,* May 1983.

Talley, S. H. (Staff of the Board of Governors of the Federal Reserve System), *Bank Capital Trends and Financing,* February 1983.

Teeters, N. H. (then member of the Board of Governors of the Federal Reserve System), and Terrell, H. S., "The Role of Banks in the International Financial System," *Federal Reserve Bulletin,* September 1983.

Wallis, A. (Under Secretary of State for Economic Affairs), "Bankers and the Debt Crisis: An International Melodrama?" *Address* before the International Summer School of the American Bankers Association, August 25, 1983.

Federal Regulators

Comptroller General of the U.S., "Federal Financial Institutions Examination Council Has Made Limited Progress Toward Accomplishing Its Mission," *Report* to the Congress, February 3, 1984.

Conover, C. T. (Comptroller of the Currency), *Statement* (on S. 2181, the Financial Services Competitive Equity Act), before the Committee on Banking, Housing and Urban Affairs, U.S. Senate, March 21, 1984.

_____, "Boom or Doom: What's In The Cards for Commercial Banks?" *Remarks* at Reserve City Bankers Convention, April 3, 1984.

Isaac, W. M. (Chairman of the Federal Deposit Insurance Corporation), "International and Domestic Implications of U.S. Commercial Lending to Foreign Governments and Corporations," *Statement* presented to Subcommittee on International Finance and Monetary Policy, Committee on Banking, Housing and Urban Affairs, U.S. Senate, February 17, 1983.

_____, *Statement* (on S. 2181, the Financial Services Competitive Equity Act and S. 2134, the Depository Institutions Holding Company Act Amendments of 1983), presented to Committee on Banking, Housing and Urban Affairs, March 21, 1984.

Volcker, P. A. (Chairman of the Board of Governors of the Federal Reserve System), *Statement* (on IMF legislation and international lending by banks), before the Committee on Banking, Housing and Urban Affairs, U.S. Senate, April 11, 1983.

_____, *Statement* (on basic rules to guide development of the banking system), before the Committee on Banking, Housing and Urban Affairs, U.S. Senate, January 16, 1984.

Laws and Regulations

Board of Governors of the Federal Reserve System, *Federal Regulatory Service* (updated periodically).

Comptroller of the Currency, *Comptroller's Manual for National Banks* (completely revised August 1983).

_____, *Comptroller's Handbook for National Bank Examiners* (revised periodically).

_____, *Annual Reports*.

Federal Deposit Insurance Corporation, *Rules and Regulations*.
———, *Annual Reports*.
———, *Deposit Insurance in a Changing Environment*, April 15, 1983.
Federal Financial Institutions Examination Council, *Annual Reports*.

Periodicals

Bankers Magazine.
Bankers News Weekly (American Bankers Association).
Banking, Journal of the American Bankers Association.
Board of Governors of the Federal Reserve System, *Federal Reserve Bulletin*.
Burroughs Clearing House.
Comptroller of the Currency, *Quarterly Journal*.
Federal Reserve Banks, *Monthly Reviews*.
Journal of Bank Research.
Journal of Commercial Bank Lending.
Solomon Bros. Bank Stock Weekly.
M. A. Schapiro & Co., Inc., *Bank Stock Quarterly*.

Newspaper

American Banker (New York).

Exhibit A
Securities and Exchange Commission, Article 9 of Regulation S-X, revised.

STATEMENT OF CASH RECEIPTS AND
DISBURSEMENTS [1]—Continued

RECEIPTS

SUMMARY

Cash balance at beginning of period..
Add total receipts ....   _____

  Total...
Deduct total disbursements ....   _____

    Cash balance at close of period [4] ....

[1] If statements are required for different periods the statements shall be presented in columnar form, if practicable.
[2] Include under this caption only advances to be reimbursed by the Committee. Under each of the two subcaptions state separately amounts received from (a) banks, (b) original underwriters of issues called for deposit (c) individuals, (d) committee members, and (e) others (specify).
[3] Such expenses shall be specified in reasonable detail either here or in a schedule herein referred to, indicating amounts for clerical, statistical, and other expenses paid to (a) original underwriters of issues called for deposit and any affiliates of such underwriters and (b) affiliates of committee members.
[4] The cash balance at the close of the most recent period shall agree with the cash shown in the statement of assets and liabilities as of the same date.

BANK HOLDING COMPANIES

SOURCE: Sections 210.9–01 to 210.9–07 appear at 48 FR 11107, Mar. 16, 1983, unless otherwise noted.

§ 210.9–01 Application of §§ 210.9–01 to 210.9–07

This article is applicable to consolidated financial statements filed for bank holding companies and to any financial statements of banks that are included in filings with the Commission.

§ 210.9–02 General requirement.

The requirements of the general rules in §§ 210.1 to 210.4 (Articles 1, 2, 3, 3A and 4) should be complied with where applicable.

§ 210.9–03 Balance sheets.

The purpose of this rule is to indicate the various items which, if applicable, should appear on the face of the balance sheets or in the notes thereto.

ASSETS

1. *Cash and due from banks.* The amounts in this caption should include all noninterest bearing deposits with other banks.

(a) Any withdrawal and usage restrictions (including requirements of the Federal Reserve to maintain certain average reserve balances) or compensating balance requirements should be disclosed (see § 210.5-02-1).

2. Interest-bearing deposits in other banks.

3. *Federal funds sold and securities purchased under resale agreements of similar arrangements.* These amounts should be presented gross and not netted against Federal funds purchased and securities sold under agreement to repurchase as reported in Caption 13.

4. *Trading account assets.* Include securities or any other investments held for trading purposes only.

5. Other short-term investments.

6. *Investment securities* Include securities held for investment only. Disclose the aggregate book value of investment securities; show on the balance sheet the aggregate market value at the balance sheet date. The aggregate amounts should include securities pledged, loaned or sold under repurchase agreements and similar arrangements; borrowed securities and securities purchased under resale agreements or similar arrangements should be excluded.

(a) Disclose in a note the carrying value and market value of securities of (1) the U.S. Treasury and other U.S. Government agencies and corporations; (2) states of the U.S. and political subdivisions; and (3) other securities.

7. *Loans.* Disclose separately (1) total loans, (2) the related allowance for losses and (3) unearned income.

(a) Disclose on the balance sheet or in a note the amount of total loans in each of the following categories:

(1) Commercial, financial and agricultural
(2) Real estate—construction
(3) Real estate—mortgage
(4) Installment loans to individuals
(5) Lease financing
(6) Foreign
(7) Other (State separately any other loan category regardless of relative size if necessary to reflect any unusual risk concentration).

(b) A series of categories other than those specified in (a) above may be used to present details of loans if considered a more appropriate presentation.

(c) The amount of foreign loans must be presented if the disclosures provided by § 210.9–05 are required.

(d) For each period for which an income statement is required, furnish in a note a statement of changes in the allowance for loan losses showing the balances at beginning and end of the period provision charged to income, recoveries of amounts charged off and losses charged to the allowance.

(e)(1)(i) As of each balance sheet date, disclose in a note the aggregate dollar amount of loans (exclusive of loans to any such persons which in the aggregate do not exceed $60,000 during the latest year) made by the registrant or any of its subsidiaries to directors, executive officers, or principal holders of equity securities (§ 210.1–02) of the registrant or any of its significant subsidiaries (§ 210.1–02), or to any associate of such persons. For the latest fiscal year, an analysis of activity with respect to such aggregate loans to related parties should be provided. The analysis should include the aggregate amount at the beginning of the period, new loans, repayments, and other changes. (Other changes, if significant, should be explained.)

(ii) This disclosure need not be furnished when the aggregate amount of such loans at the balance sheet date (or with respect to the latest fiscal year, the maximum amount outstanding during the period) does not exceed 5 percent of stockholders equity at the balance sheet date.

(2) If a significant portion of the aggregate amount of loans outstanding at the end of the fiscal year disclosed pursuant to (e)(1)(i) above relates to nonperforming loans, so state and disclose the aggregate amount of such nonperforming loans along with such other information necessary to an understanding of the effects of the transactions on the financial statements.

See, Industry Guide 3, Statistical Disclosure by Bank Holding Companies for definition of "nonperforming loans."

(3) Notwithstanding the aggregate disclosure called for by (e)(1) above, if any loans were not made in the ordinary course of business during any period for which an income statement is required to be filed, provide an appropriate description of each such loan (See § 210.4–08(L)(3)).

(4) Definition of terms. For purposes of this rule, the following definitions shall apply:

"Associate" means (i) a corporation, venture or organization of which such person is a general partner or is, directly or indirectly, the beneficial owner of 10 percent or more of any class of equity securities; (ii) any trust or other estate in which such person has a substantial beneficial interest or for which such person serves as trustee or in a similar capacity and (iii) any member of the immediate family or any of the foregoing persons.

"Executive officers" means the president, any vice president in charge of a principal business unit, division or function (such as loans, investments, operations, administration or finance), and any other officer or person who performs similar policymaking functions.

"Immediate Family" means such person's spouse; parents; children; siblings; mothers and fathers-in-law; sons and daughters-in-law; and brothers and sisters-in-law.

"Ordinary course of business" means those loans which were made on substantially the same terms, including interest rate and collateral, as those prevailing at the same time for comparable transactions with unrelated persons and did not involve more than the normal risk of collectibility or present other unfavorable features.

8. *Premises and equipment.*

9. *Due from customers on acceptances.* Include amounts receivable from customers on unmatured drafts and bills of exchange that have been accepted by a bank subsidiary or by other banks for the account of a subsidiary and that are outstanding—that is, not held by a subsidiary bank, on the reporting date. (If held by a bank subsidiary, they should be reported as "loans" under § 210.9–03.7.)

10. *Other assets.* Disclose separately on the balance sheet or in a note thereto any of the following assets or any other asset the amount of which exceeds thirty percent of stockholders equity. The remaining assets may be shown as one amount.

(1) Excess of cost over tangible and identifiable intangible assets acquired (net of amortization).

(2) Other intangible assets (net of amortization).

(3) Investments in and indebtness of affiliates and other persons.

(4) Other real estates.

(a) Disclose in a note the basis at which other real estate is carried. An reduction to fair market value from the carrying value of the related loan at the time of acquisition shall be accounted for as a loan loss. Any allowance for losses on other real estate which has been established subsequent to acquisition should be deducted from other real estate. For each period for which an income statement is required, disclosures should be made in a note as to the changes in the allowances, including balance at beginning and end of period, provision charged to income, and losses charged to the allowance.

11. Total assets.

LIABILITIES AND STOCKHOLDERS' EQUITY

Liabilities.

12. *Deposits.* Disclose separately the amounts of noninterest bearing deposits and interest bearing deposits.

(a) The amount of noninterest bearing deposits and interest bearing deposits in foreign banking offices must be presented if the disclosure provided by § 210.0–05 are required.

13. *Short-term borrowing.* Disclosure separately on the balance sheet or in a note, amounts payable for (1) Federal funds purchased and securities sold under agreements to repurchase; (2) commercial paper, and (3) other short-term borrowings.

(a) Disclose any unused lines of credit for short-term financing: (§ 210.5–02.19(b)).

14. *Bank acceptances outstanding.* Disclose the aggregate of unmatured drafts and bills of exchange accepted by a bank subsidiary, or by some other bank as its agent, less the amount of such acceptances acquired by the bank subsidiary through discount or purchase.

15. *Other liabilities.* Disclose separately on the balance sheet or in a note any of the following liabilities or any other items which are individually in excess of thirty percent of stockholders' equity (except that amounts in excess of 5 percent of stockholders' equity should be disclosed with respect to item (4)). The remaining items may be shown as one amount.

(1) Income taxes payable.

(2) Deferred income taxes.

(3) Indebtedness to affiliates and other persons the investments in which are accounted for by the equity method.

(4) Indebtedness to directors, executive officers, and principal holders of equity securities of the registrant or any of its significant subsidiaries (the guidance in ·§ 210.9-03.7(e) shall be used to identify related parties for purposes of this disclosure).

(5) Accounts payable and accrued expenses.

16. *Long-term debt.* Disclose in a note the information required by § 210.5-02.22.

17. *Commitments and contingent liabilities.*

18. *Minority interest in consolidated subsidiaries.* The information required by § 210.5-02.27 should be disclosed if applicable.

REDEEMABLE PREFERRED STOCKS

19. *Preferred stocks subject to mandatory redemption requirements or whose redemption is outside the control of the issuer.* See § 210.5-02.28.

Non-redeemable Preferred Stocks

20. *Preferred stocks which are not redeemable or are redeemable solely at the option of the issuer.* See § 210.5-02.29.

Common Stocks

21. *Common stocks.* See § 210.5-02.30.

Other Stockholders' Equity

22. *Other stockholders' equity.* See § 210.5-02.31.

23. *Total liabilities and stockholders' equity.*

§ 210.9–04 Income statements.

The purpose of this rule is to indicate the various items which, if applicable, should appear on the face of the income statement or in the notes thereto.

1. *Interest and fees on loans.* Include commitment and origination fees, late charges and current amortization of premium and accretion of discount on loans which are related to or are an adjustment of the loan interest rate.

2. *Interest and dividends on investment securities.* Disclosure separately (1) taxable interest income, (2) nontaxable interest income, and (3) dividends.

3. *Trading account interest.*

4. *Other interest income.*

5. *Total interest income.*

6. *Interest on deposits.*

7. *Interest on short-term borrowings.*

8. *Interest on long-term debt.*

9. *Total interest expense.*

10. *Net interest income.*

11. *Provision for loan losses.*

12. *Net interest income after provision for loan losses.*

13. *Other income.* Disclose separately any of the following amounts, or any other item of other income, which exceed one percent of the aggregate of total interest income and other income. The remaining amounts may be shown as one amount, except for investment securities gains or losses which shall be shown separately regardless of size.

(a) Commissions and fees and fiduciary activities.

(b) Commissions, broker's fees and markups on securities underwriting and other securities activities.

(c) Insurance commissions, fees and premiums.

(d) Fees for other customer services.

(e) Profit or loss on transactions in securities in dealer trading account.

(f) Equity in earnings of unconsolidated subsidiaries and 50 percent or less owned persons.

(g) Gains or losses on disposition of equity in securities of subsidiaries or 50 percent or less owned persons.

(h) Investment securities gains or losses. The method followed in determining the cost of investments sold (e.g., "average cost," "first-in, first-out," or "identified certificate) and related income taxes shall be disclosed.

14. *Other expenses.* Disclose separately any of the following amounts, or any other item of other expense, which exceed one percent of the aggregate of total interest income and other income. The remaining amounts may be shown as one amount.

(a) Salaries and employee benefits.

(b) Net occupancy expense of premises.

(c) Goodwill amortization.

(d) Net cost of operation of other real estate (including provisions for real estate losses, rental income and gains and losses on sales of real estate).

(e) Minority interest in income of consolidated subsidiaries.

14. *Bank acceptances outstanding.* Disclose the aggregate of unmatured drafts and bills of exchange accepted by a bank subsidiary, or by some other bank as its agent, less the amount of such acceptances acquired by the bank subsidiary through discount or purchase.

15. *Other liabilities.* Disclose separately on the balance sheet or in a note any of the following liabilities or any other items which are individually in excess of thirty percent of stockholders' equity (except that amounts in excess of 5 percent of stockholders' equity should be disclosed with respect to item (4)). The remaining items may be shown as one amount.

(1) Income taxes payable.

(2) Deferred income taxes.

(3) Indebtedness to affiliates and other persons the investments in which are accounted for by the equity method.

(4) Indebtedness to directors, executive officers, and principal holders of equity securities of the registrant or any of its significant subsidiaries (the guidance in § 210.9-03.7(e) shall be used to identify related parties for purposes of this disclosure).

(5) Accounts payable and accrued expenses.

16. *Long-term debt.* Disclose in a note the information required by § 210.5-02.22.

17. *Commitments and contingent liabilities.*

18. *Minority interest in consolidated subsidiaries.* The information required by § 210.5-02.27 should be disclosed if applicable.

REDEEMABLE PREFERRED STOCKS

19. *Preferred stocks subject to mandatory redemption requirements or whose redemption is outside the control of the issuer.* See § 210.5-02.28.

Non-redeemable Preferred Stocks

20. *Preferred stocks which are not redeemable or are redeemable solely at the option of the issuer.* See § 210.5-02.29.

Common Stocks

21. *Common stocks.* See § 210.5-02.30.

Other Stockholders' Equity

22. *Other stockholders' equity.* See § 210.5-02.31.

23. *Total liabilities and stockholders' equity.*

§ 210.9-04 Income statements.

The purpose of this rule is to indicate the various items which, if applicable, should appear on the face of the income statement or in the notes thereto.

1. *Interest and fees on loans.* Include commitment and origination fees, late charges and current amortization of premium and accretion of discount on loans which are related to or are an adjustment of the loan interest rate.

2. *Interest and dividends on investment securities.* Disclosure separately (1) taxable interest income, (2) nontaxable interest income, and (3) dividends.

3. *Trading account interest.*

4. *Other interest income.*

5. *Total interest income.*

6. *Interest on deposits.*

7. *Interest on short-term borrowings.*

8. *Interest on long-term debt.*

9. *Total interest expense.*

10. *Net interest income.*

11. *Provision for loan losses.*

12. *Net interest income after provision for loan losses.*

13. *Other income.* Disclose separately any of the following amounts, or any other item of other income, which exceed one percent of the aggregate of total interest income and other income. The remaining amounts may be shown as one amount, except for investment securities gains or losses which shall be shown separately regardless of size.

(a) Commissions and fees and fiduciary activities.

(b) Commissions, broker's fees and markups on securities underwriting and other securities activities.

(c) Insurance commissions, fees and premiums.

(d) Fees for other customer services.

(e) Profit or loss on transactions in securities in dealer trading account.

(f) Equity in earnings of unconsolidated subsidiaries and 50 percent or less owned persons.

(g) Gains or losses on disposition of equity in securities of subsidiaries or 50 percent or less owned persons.

(h) Investment securities gains or losses. The method followed in determining the cost of investments sold (e.g., "average cost," "first-in, first-out," or "identified certificate) and related income taxes shall be disclosed.

14. *Other expenses.* Disclose separately any of the following amounts, or any other item of other expense, which exceed one percent of the aggregate of total interest income and other income. The remaining amounts may be shown as one amount.

(a) Salaries and employee benefits.

(b) Net occupancy expense of premises.

(c) Goodwill amortization.

(d) Net cost of operation of other real estate (including provisions for real estate losses, rental income and gains and losses on sales of real estate).

(e) Minority interest in income of consolidated subsidiaries.

15. *Income or loss before income tax expense.*

16. *Income tax expense.* The information required by § 210.4-08(h) should be disclosed.

17. *Income or loss before extraordinary items and cumulative effects of changes in accounting principles.*

18. *Extraordinary items, less applicable tax.*

19. *Cumulative effects of changes in accounting principles.*

20. *Net income or loss.*

21. *Earnings per share data.*

§ 210.9-05   Foreign activities.

(a) *General requirement.* Separate disclosure concerning foreign activities shall be made for each period in which either (1) assets, or (2) revenue, or (3) income (loss) before income tax expense, or (4) net income (loss), each as associated with foreign activities, exceeded ten percent of the corresponding amount in the related financial statements.

(b) *Disclosures.* (1) Disclose total identifiable assets (net of valuation allowances) associated with foreign activities.

(2) For each period for which an income statement is filed, state the amount of revenue, income (loss) before taxes, and net income (loss) associated with foreign activities. Disclose significant estimates and assumptions (including those related to the cost of capital) used in allocating revenue and expenses to foreign activities; describe the nature and effects of any changes in such estimates and assumptions which have a significant impact on interperiod comparability.

(3) The information in paragraph (b) (1) and (2) of this section shall be presented separately for each significant geographic area and in the aggregate for all other geographic areas not deemed significant.

(c) *Definitions.* (1) "Foreign activities" include loans and other revenues producing assets and transactions in which the debtor or customer, whether an affiliated or unaffiliated person, is domiciled outside the United States.

(2) The term "revenue" includes the total of the amount reported at §§ 210.9-04.5 and 210.9-04.13.

(3) A "significant geographic area" is one in which assets or revenue or income before income tax or net income exceed 10 percent of the comparable amount as reported in the financial statements.

§ 210.9-06   Condensed financial information of registrant.

The information prescribed by § 210.12-04 shall be presented in a note to the financial statements when the restricted net assets (§ 210.4-08(e)(3)) of consolidated subsidiaries exceed 25 percent of consolidated net assets as of the end of the most recently completed fiscal year. The investment in and indebtedness of and to bank subsidiaries shall be stated separately in the condensed balance sheet from amounts for other subsidiaries; the amount of cash dividends paid to the registrant for each of the last three years by bank subsidiaries shall be stated separately in the condensed income statement from amounts for other subsidiaries. For purposes of the above test, restricted net assets of consolidated subsidiaries shall mean that amount of the registrant's proportionate share of net assets of consolidated subsidiaries (after intercompany eliminations) which as of the end of the most recent fiscal year may not be transferred to the parent company by subsidiaries in the form of loans, advances or cash dividends without the consent of a third party (i.e., lender, regulatory agency, foreign government, etc.). Where restrictions on the amount of funds which may be loaned or advanced differ from the amount restricted as to transfer in the form of cash dividends, the amount least restrictive to the subsidiary shall be used. Redeemable preferred stocks (§ 210.5-02.28) and minority interests shall be deducted in computing net assets for purposes of this test.

§ 210.9-07   Schedules.

(a) The following schedules, which should be examined by an independent accountant, should be filed unless the required information is not applicable or is presented in the related financial statements.

Schedule I—Indebtedness to Related Parties. The schedule prescribed by § 210.12-05 should be filed for each period for which an income statement is required in support of the amounts required to be reported by § 210.9-03.15(4) unless such aggregate amount does not exceed 5 percent of stockholders' equity at either the beginning or the end of the period.

Schedule II—Guarantees of Securities of Other Issuers. The schedule prescribed by § 210.12-08 should be filed as of the date of the most recent audited balance sheet with respect to any guarantees of securities of other issuers by the person for which the statements are being filed.

INTERIM FINANCIAL STATEMENTS

§ 210.10-01 Interim financial statements.

(a) *Condensed statements.* Interim financial statements shall follow the general form and content of presentation prescribed by the other sections of this Regulation with the following exceptions:

(1) Interim financial statements required by this rule need only be provided as to the registrant and its subsidiaries consolidated and may be unaudited. Separate statements of other entities which may otherwise be required by this regulation may be omitted.

(2) Interim balance sheets shall include only major captions (i.e., numbered captions) prescribed by the applicable sections of this Regulation with the exception of inventories. Data as to raw materials, work in process and finished goods inventories shall be included either on the face of the balance sheet or in the notes to the financial statements, if applicable. Where any major balance sheet caption is less than 10% of total assets, and the amount in the caption has not increased or decreased by more than 25% since the end of the preceding fiscal year, the caption may be combined with others.

(3) Interim statements of income shall also include major captions prescribed by the applicable sections of this Regulation. When any major income statement caption is less than 15% of average net income for the most recent three fiscal years and the amount in the caption has not increased or decreased by more than 20% as compared to the corresponding interim period of the preceding fiscal year, the caption may be combined with others. In calculating average net

income, loss years should be excluded. If losses were incurred in each of the most recent three years, the average loss shall be used for purposes of this test. Notwithstanding these tests, Rule 4-02 of Regulation S-X applies and de minimis amounts therefore need not be shown separately.

(4) The statement of changes in financial position may be abbreviated, starting with a single figure of funds provided by operations and showing other changes individually only when they exceed 10% of the average of funds provided by operations for the most recent three years. Notwithstanding this test, Rule 4-02 of Regulation S-X applies and de minimis amounts therefore need not be shown separately.

(5) The interim financial information shall include disclosures either on the face of the financial statements or in accompanying footnotes sufficient so as to make the interim information presented not misleading. Registrants may presume that users of the interim financial information have read or have access to the audited financial statements for the preceding fiscal year and that the adequacy of additional disclosure needed for a fair presentation, except in regard to material contingencies, may be determined in that context. Accordingly, footnote disclosure which would substantially duplicate the disclosure contained in the most recent annual report to security holders or latest audited financial statements, such as a statement of significant accounting policies and practices, details of accounts which have not changed significantly in amount or composition since the end of the most recently completed fiscal year, and detailed disclosures prescribed by Rule 4-08 of this Regulation, may be omitted. However, disclosure shall be provided where events subsequent to the end of the most recent fiscal year have occurred which have a material impact on the registrant. Disclosures should encompass for example, significant changes since the end of the most recently completed fiscal year in such items as: accounting principles and practices; estimates inherent in the preparation of financial statements; status of long-term contracts; capital-

Exhibit B
Securities and Exchange Commission, Revision of Industry Guide Disclosures for Bank Holding Companies

component installations) located on Federal property under the control of other agencies will coordinate their action with appropriate officials of the other agencies concerned.

§ 1204.1003 Procedures.

(a) All entrances to NASA installations will be conspicuously posted with the following notice:

PURSUANT TO NASA REGULATIONS THE ENTRANCE OF INDIVIDUALS TO, OR THEIR CONTINUED PRESENCE ON, THIS INSTALLATION IS CONDITIONED UPON THEIR CONSENT TO INSPECTION OF THEIR PERSONS, AND OF PROPERTY IN THEIR POSSESSION OR CONTROL.

(b) Inspection pursuant to this subpart will be conducted only by NASA security personnel or members of the installation security patrol or guard force. Such inspections will be conducted in accordance with guidelines established by the Chief, NASA Security Office, NASA Headquarters.

(c) If an individual does not consent to an inspection, it will not be carried out, and the individual will be denied admission to, or be escorted from, the installation.

(d) If, during an inspection, an individual is found to be in unauthorized possession of items believed to represent a threat to the safety or security of the installation, the individual will be denied admission to, or be escorted from, the installation and appropriate law enforcement authorities will be notified immediately.

(e) If, during an inspection conducted pursuant to this subpart, an individual is in possession of U.S. Government property without proper authorization, that person will be required to relinquish the property to the security representative conducting the inspection pending proper authorization for the possession of the property or its removal from the installation. The individual relinquishing the property will be given a receipt therefor.

James M. Beggs,
Administrator.

[FR Doc. 83–22791 Filed 8–18–83; 8:45 am]
BILLING CODE 7510–01–M

SECURITIES AND EXCHANGE COMMISSION

17 CFR Parts 210, 229, 231 and 241

[Release Nos. 33–6478; 34–20068; FR–13; File S7–970]

Revision of Industry Guide Disclosures for Bank Holding Companies

AGENCY: Securities and Exchange Commission.

ACTION: Final amendments.

SUMMARY: The Commission authorizes final amendments to its guidelines concerning disclosure by bank holding companies with respect to information about nonaccrual, past due and restructured loans, potential problem loans, foreign outstandings and loan concentrations. The amendments revise the current guidelines dealing with nonperforming loans to focus more broadly on the various risk elements involved in lending activities.

EFFECTIVE DATE: The revisions adopted herein are applicable to filings containing financial statements for fiscal years ending on or after December 31, 1983. Early adoption of these guidelines is encouraged. Upon adoption, the information called for by Item III.C.3. need not be provided for any reported periods ending prior to December 31, 1983 if it is impracticable to do so. Also, the information called for by Item III.C.1. may be presented in accordance with the previous guidelines in Item III.C. for reported periods ending prior to December 31, 1983.

FOR FURTHER INFORMATION CONTACT: Edmund Coulson or Michael P. McLaughlin (202–272–2130), Office of the Chief Accountant, or Howard P. Hodges, Jr. or Henry J. Velsor (202–272–2553), Division of Corporation Finance, Securities and Exchange Commission, Washington, D.C. 20549.

SUPPLEMENTARY INFORMATION:

Executive Summary

This release amends the existing Item III.C., "Nonperforming Loans," of the Industry Disclosure Guides for Bank Holding Companies ("Guide 3") to establish a new section—"Risk Elements."[1] The terminology "nonperforming loans" is no longer utilized in Guide 3. This risk elements section calls for four categories of disclosure:

• Nonaccrual, past due and restructured loans.
• Potential problem loans.
• Foreign outstandings.
• Loan concentrations.

The above information does not have to be set forth in a single table.

The first of the four risk categories contains three of the four classifications of loans which are designated as nonperforming loans in the current Item III.C. of Guide 3, except that the Commission's existing criterion for

determining a restructured loan is being replaced by the criteria of Statement of Financial Accounting Standards No. 15 ("FAS 15")[2] for troubled debt restructurings. A significant change in the amended guidelines for disclosure of nonaccrual, past due and restructured loans is the exclusion of certain instructions present in the current Guide which allowed for the use of different criteria, and permitted exclusion of certain loans. This change has the effect of enhancing comparability of disclosures among registrants. Users of this information, particularly financial analysts, have stressed the importance of comparability in this area.

The second category, potential problem loans, is currently the fourth existing criterion for classification of loans as nonperforming (i.e., "serious doubts" loans). These are loans which are not disclosed as part of the first category described above, but where information known by management indicates that the borrower may not be able to comply with present payment terms.

The third category calls for "foreign outstandings" disclosures. This new category is a codification of the substance of the alternative table disclosures of Staff Accounting Bulletin No. 49 ("SAB 49"), "Disclosures by Bank Holding Companies about Certain Foreign Loans" [47 FR 49627, November 2, 1982]. The threshold for disclosure provided in SAB 49, however, has been changed and certain additional disclosures are called for. Certain implementation guidance has also been provided.

The fourth category calls for disclosure of "loan concentrations" which are defined as amounts loaned to a multiple number of borrowers engaged in similar activities which would cause them to be similarly impacted by economic or other conditions. A disclosure threshold of 10% of total loans has been provided.

The Commission believes that these revised guidelines will improve the utility of disclosures by bank holding companies by focusing more broadly on the various risk elements involved in lending activities. Since they require more uniformity in the preparation of the disclosures, the revisions should improve comparability of disclosures among registrants, a factor important to analysts and other users of the data in assessing risk.

---

[1] The Commission solicited public comments on the proposed revision of Guide 3 in Release No. 33–6462 (April 15, 1983) [48 FR 18826, April 26, 1983]. Forty-nine comment letters were received in response to this proposal.

[2] Financial Accounting Standards Board Statement of Financial Accounting Standards No. 15 "Accounting by Debtors and Creditors for Troubled Debt Restructurings" (June 1977).

As a result of a coordinated effort by the Commission and the Federal banking agencies, the amended guidelines pertaining to "nonaccrual, past due and restructured loans" as well as "foreign outstanding" are consistent with the present and planned disclosure requirements of the Federal banking agencies. Uniformity in the bases for presenting information by bank holding companies in Commission filings and by banks in supplementary disclosures for bank regulatory purposes will reduce compliance burdens and enhance the usefulness of the disclosure reports by investors and the public.

Risk Elements Disclosure

The final guidelines contain a revised format for "Risk Element" disclosures which includes four categories: (1) Non-accrual, past due and restructured loans; (2) potential problem loans; (3) foreign outstandings; and (4) loan concentrations.

A majority of the commentators expressed concerns about the perceived requirement for a tabular format. They were concerned that investors might add all of the amounts disclosed in such a presentation and equate the total to the previously reported "nonperforming loan" amount, and conclude that the risk had increased. The Commission did not intend that the proposed disclosures necessarily be presented in a single tabular format. Registrants may present this data in a manner deemed appropriate to their facts and circumstances provided that such presentation is not misleading.

Rather than adopting the proposal that would have required a breakdown of each of the risk element disclosures by type of loan as set forth in Item III.A. of Guide 3 (loan categories), the final guidelines call for separate disclosure of aggregate foreign and domestic loan amounts only. The proposed display was intended to provide information for assessing relative risks based on the classification of the loan and on the nature of the borrower. This change was made in response to commentators' concerns that such detailed disclosure would be burdensome and complex. However, as discussed later under "Foreign Outstandings," the final amendments call for disclosure of foreign outstandings by type of borrower.

The Commission has adopted a provision for disclosure of potential problem loans which are not reported as "nonaccrual, past due or restructured," but where known information causes management to have serious doubts as to the ability of the borrowers to comply with the present loan repayment terms.

"Potential problem loan" information is only required to be presented for the latest reported period. Some commentators asserted that this provision was unnecessary because many such loans may already be reported as nonaccrual in accordance with the registrant's policies. While the Commission understands that the amounts of potential problem loans may not be significant for most registrants because they may place such loans on nonaccrual status, it recognizes there may be difficult judgments as to classification of certain loans and believes that potential problem loans represent material information to investors.

These final amendments add the "foreign outstandings" disclosures to the matters encompassed in the risk elements section in the proposing release. The Commission determined that it is appropriate to include foreign outstandings in the risk elements section in order to embody all risk related disclosure guidelines in one section of the Guide and to emphasize the risks present in cross-border lending activities.

In response to commentators' concerns, the final amendments include a disclosure provision, as an instruction to the "foreign outstandings" category, concerning foreign borrowers whose economic and political conditions are expected to have a material impact on the timely payment of interest or principal. The proposal would have required that "any loans to private and public sector borrowers in foreign countries experiencing economic and political conditions which have created liquidity problems which may have a material impact on the timing of interest or principal payments" be included in the "serious doubts" category. The majority of respondents to the proposal expressed concern that including liquidity-impaired foreign loans in a category of loans which typically comprises credit-impaired loans may be misleading because of the dissimilarity of respective risks. These respondents asserted that any discussion of foreign loans where borrowers may be adversely affected by liquidity problems are best made in the context of disclosures about foreign lending activities.

Many respondents did not concur with the Commission's characterization of industry loan concentrations as a "risk element" because they believed it was inappropriate to present loan concentrations with nonaccrual, past due and restructured loans and other loans as to which there are serious doubts about the ability of the borrower

to comply with loan repayment terms. As noted above, loan concentration data would not necessarily have to be presented together with data called for by the other categories of risk elements. The Commission recognizes that the nature of the risks associated with each of the four categories may vary but believes that this can be effectively communicated in registrant filings.

Determination of Certain Risk Elements

The final amendments do not include the substance of certain instructions in the existing Item III.C. which allowed registrants to use different criteria and exclude certain loans in the classification of loans as "nonperforming." The Commission has determined that uniformity in the presentation of this data, and thus comparability among registrants, is important to investors.

Many respondents urged the Commission to retain the substance of the existing Instruction 5 to Item III.C. which provides that "the registrant may use different criteria and may present quantitative information in a different manner than described above if such presentation more effectively identifies and communicates the present risk elements in the loan portfolio.[3] Some respondents urged the Commission to include a similar instruction to provide necessary flexibility in communicating the diversity of lending risks.

Many respondents also urged the Commission to retain the current Instruction 1 to Item III.C. for presentation of past due, nonaccrual and restructured loans. That instruction provided that installment loans to individuals and lease financing amounts may be excluded if the total amount of such loans does not exceed 10% of total loans. These respondents contended that the specific 10% materiality threshold for exclusion should be retained and that data on delinquent consumer loans, if material, should be presented and analyzed separately from data on troubled commercial loans. These persons asserted that consumer delinquencies are not indicative of the same sort of risks as commercial loans because of the nature of the loans and the fact that the accounting convention of automatic charge-off when installment loans reach a certain

[3] The genesis of Instruction 5 to Section III.C. was the initial adoption in 1976 of Guide 3. The intent of this instruction was to provide flexibility in reporting what was then new information about risk elements in the loan portfolio. This instruction was provided since there were varying opinions as to the most appropriate method of determining such elements and the disclosures were in a sense experimental.

delinquency mitigates much of the uncertainty, and therefore risk, normally associated wtih commerical loans.

The Commission is concerned that there has been disparity of practice among registrants in disclosing non-performing loans thereby impacting the comparability of that data. Users who responded to the proposal indicated that risk elements were important indicators and that comparability among registrants is essential. Because the Commission agrees that consistency will enhance the utility of this information to investors, analysts and other users, the substance of Instruction 5 has not been included in the final admendments, and an instruction has been added to the revised Item III.C.1. to specifically prohibit any exclusions. Varying risk elements associated with the types of loans included in the past due, nonaccrual and restructured loan categories may be described in narrative discussions setting forth the reasons for and impact of such factors.

Foregone Interest on Certain Loans

The final guidelines reflect the proposed amendment to include disclosure of interest income that would have been earned under the original loan terms for nonaccrual and restructured loans, and the amounts actually recognized. The proposing release indicated that the amount of interest earned and the amount actually recognized on troubled debt restructurings is an existing financial statement disclosure requirement of FAS 15. The additional disclosure of such amounts related to nonaccrual loans should supplement the disclosures required under generally accepted accounting principles ("GAAP").

Over half of the respondents addressing this point agreed with the proposed disclosures and financial analysts stated that this disclosure was particularly important. Other commentators raised various conceptual objections to any presentation of information representing hypothetical interest that would have been earned by the registrant if the loan had been current. This amendment was adopted because it communicates an element of the cost of carrying certain problem loans, provides supplemental data for nonaccrual loans similar to information already required under GAAP and is an important factor in the estimation of current and potential earning power. Registrants may supplement these disclosures by appropriate textual discussions to the extent they believe necessary to explain the impact of such loans on their operations.

Foreign Outstandings

The Commission has codified the substance of SAB 49's alternative table disclosure for foreign outstandings. Information about foreign outstandings is required for a three-year period rather than the proposed five-year period.

A majority of the commentators responding to the proposal to disclose outstandings to foreign countries in excess of 1% of consolidated outstandings urged retention of the alternatives provided by SAB 49. SAB 49 allows either a tabular presentation of foreign outstandings exceeding 1% or identification of outstandings to foreign countries in excess of 1% where economic or political conditions may impact the timely payment of principal or interest. Many commentators believed that it is not appropriate to require disclosure of outstandings in each country where outstandings exceed 1% of total outstandings because the reader of financial statements could inappropriately interpret this total amount as an unusual risk. Although these commentators generally agreed that there is an additional risk that a foreign government may impose restrictions on funds leaving the country or that foreign exchange may not be available to make timely payments of interest or principal, they did not believe that these risks warranted the type of disclosure proposed by the Commission.

The Commission has carefully considered the views of commentators and has concluded that the proposed table disclosure approach is preferable to one that focuses only on certain countries that are currently experiencing liquidity problems. The amendments adopted herein identify the registrant's significant cross-border exposures in foreign countries and allow investors to arrive at their own conclusions as to any potential or actual transfer risks involved.

The final guidelines call for certain additional disclosures when a foreign country is experiencing liquidity problems because of economic or political conditions which *are expected to have* a material impact on timely payment. This standard implies a greater degree of certainty in determining the impact of such conditions than that of the proposal, viz. when such conditions *may have* an impact on timely payment. The adopted standard should result in greater consistency of disclosures among registrants.

The revised guidelines utilize a disclosure threshold based on total assets. In response to the Commission's inquiry with respect to the propriety of the proposed disclosure threshold of 1%

of outstandings, approximately half the respondents stated that the Commission should retain the "consolidated outstandings" threshold measurement for disclosure; slightly less than half of the respondents felt the measurement should be based on consolidated assets; and the remainder believed that the threshold should be based on a percentage of registrants' equity.

The Commission has determined that the use of a threshold based on 1% of total assets has the merit of simplicity of calculation since the total assets amount is readily obtainable from a registrant's balance sheet. In contrast, outstandings typically can not be computed unless supplemental data is furnished. Also, disclosures using a 1% of total assets threshold will be similar to disclosures made pursuant to SAB 49. Finally, in addition to disclosures about individual countries whose outstandings exceed 1% of total assets, the final guidelines (Instruction 7 to Item III.C.3.) call for aggregate disclosures for countries where outstandings are between .75% and 1% of total assets. This disclosure format is consistent with that proposed in the Federal banking agencies' Country Exposure Report.[*]

The proposed separate disclosure of private and public-sector cross-border outstandings has been revised to call for disclosure of outstandings by the types of borrowers specified in Item III.A., i.e., governments and official institutions, banks and other financial institutions, commercial and industrial, and other. Registrants have presented breakdowns similar to that adopted, and users have commented that this level of disclosure is important in assessing a registrant's exposure in certain countries.

The final amendments call for disclosure of outstandings which are repayable in dollars or other non-local currency; they do not require that gross amounts repayable in *local* currency be disclosed. Many commentators asserted that most loans repayable in local currency are substantially funded by local operations and that any net unfunded amounts normally do not reflect significant transfer risk since they generally are not material. The revised guide provides that any material amounts of local currency outstandings which are not hedged or are not funded by local currency borrowings should be reflected in cross-border outstandings.

---

[*]The Federal banking agencies have announced their intention to provide for increased and more timely disclosures about banks' country exposures. These disclosures would be based on the information called for by the revised Item III.C. of Guide 3 and would be available to the public upon request.

An instruction to Item III.C.3. allows any legally enforceable written guarantees of principal or interest by domestic or other non-local third parties to be netted against the amounts of foreign outstandings presented. The Commission agrees with those respondents who asserted that, when the source of repayment of outstandings is assured by third parties, and the registrant is clearly not exposed to transfer risk because of this recourse, presentation of amounts net of such guarantees more appropriately reflects the registrant's exposure to transfer risks. The amendments also allow collateral values to be netted against the cross-border outstandings of a foreign country in certain limited circumstances.

Several commentators queried whether commitments to lend additional dollar amounts, such as through irrevocable letter of credit agreements, should be included in the determination of "outstandings." Under the revised guide, such commitments would not be included in outstandings, but they would be separately disclosed if material.

In the proposing release, the Commission requested specific comment as to whether a loan to a foreign branch of a foreign bank was or should be reflected as a loan to the foreign country in which the parent bank is located. A substantial majority of those commenting stated that such interbank loans should be reflected as a loan of the parent of the foreign branch. Accordingly, the final amendments include an instruction which indicates that loans made to a branch of a foreign bank located outside the foreign bank's home country may be classified based on the parent's geographic location.

Loan Concentrations

The Commission believes that information about loan concentrations is material information to investors. Accordingly, the final amendments include a requirement to disclose, as of the most recent reported period, any concentration of loans exceeding 10% of total loans. The substance of the concentration disclosure requirement was transferred from the instructions to Item III.A. which calls for disclosure of the categories of loans in the registrant's portfolio. However, concentration disclosures do not have to be made pursuant to the amended Item III.C. if the substance of such disclosures is otherwise made pursuant to Item III.A.

While not intended to indicate levels of prudent lending, the 10% threshold for disclosure of concentrations is intended to provide useful information to investors in evaluating lending portfolios. A 10% threshold has been

utilized in other areas in Guide 3 and in Article 9 of Regulation S–X [17 CFR 210.9] for purposes of specifying materiality levels for disclosure purposes.[5]

. General guidance is provided in a definition of loan concentrations which states that concentrations are considered to exist when there are amounts loaned to a multiple number of borrowers engaged in similar activities which would cause them to be similarly impacted by economic or other conditions. The definition reflects the objective of this category, i.e., to highlight potential risks when economic or other conditions may result in an adverse impact on the financial condition of the registrant due to concentrated levels of lending activities to borrowers with common characteristics.

As with the other revised guidelines, the Commission staff will monitor disclosures in this area and assess whether additional guidance of a different threshold is appropriate.

Other Matters

The final amendments implement a new Item III.D., which calls for the disclosure of any material amounts of other interest bearing assets (interest bearing deposits with other banks, municipal bonds, etc.) which would be required to be disclosed as past due, nonaccrual or restructured loans, or potential problem loans, if such interest bearing assets were loans.

The final amendments make conforming amendments to Article 9 of Regulation S–X 17 CFR Part 210 and Item 404 of Regulation S–K [17 CFR 229.404] to replace references to "nonperforming" loans with references to those loans described in Item III.C.1. or 2. of Guide 3.

Codification Update

The "Codification of Financial Reporting Policies" announced in Financial Reporting Release No. 1 (April 15, 1982) [47 FR 21028, May 17, 1982] is updated to:

1. Add a new Section 401.08 entitled "Risk Elements Involved in Lending Activities."

2. Include in Section 401.08 the sections of this release entitled "Executive Summary," "Risk Elements Disclosure," "Determination of Certain Risk Elements," "Forgone Interest on Certain Loans," "Foreign Outstandings" and "Loan Concentrations" numbered as specified below:

a. Executive Summary.

---

[5] E.g., *see* 210.9–05(c)(3). Items III.C. and V.A. of Guide 3.

b. Risk Elements Disclosure.

c. Determination of Certain Risk Elements.

d. Forgone Interest on Certain Loans.

e. Foreign Outstandings.

f. Loan Concentrations.

This codification is a separate publication issued by the Commission. It will not be published in the **Federal Register**/Code of Federal Regulations System.

List of Subjects in 17 CFR Parts 210, 229, 231 and 241

Accounting, Reporting and recordkeeping requirements, Securities.

The Commission hereby amends 17 CFR Chapter II as follows:

PART 210—FORM AND CONTENT OF AND REQUIREMENTS FOR FINANCIAL STATEMENTS, SECURITIES ACT OF 1933, SECURITIES EXCHANGE ACT OF 1934, PUBLIC UTILITY HOLDING COMPANY ACT OF 1935, INVESTMENT COMPANY ACT OF 1940, AND ENERGY POLICY AND CONSERVATION ACT OF 1975

1. By revising paragraph 7(e)(2) of § 210.9–03 to read as follows:

§ 210.9–03   Balance sheets.

*   *   *   *   *

7. *Loans.* * * *

(e) * * *

(2) If a significant portion of the aggregate amount of loans outstanding at the end of the fiscal year disclosed pursuant to (e)(1)(i) above relates to loans which are disclosed as nonaccrual, past due, restructured or potential problems (see Item III.C. 1. or 2. of Industry Guide 3, Statistical Disclosure by Bank Holding Companies), so state and disclose the aggregate amounts of such loans along with such other information necessary to an understanding of the effects of the transactions on the financial statements.

*   *   *   *   *

PART 229—STANDARD INSTRUCTIONS FOR FILING UNDER SECURITIES ACT OF 1933, SECURITIES EXCHANGE ACT OF 1934 AND ENERGY POLICY AND CONSERVATION ACT OF 1975— REGULATION S–K

2. By revising Instruction 3 to paragraph (c) of § 229.404 as follows:

§ 229.404 Item 404.   Certain relationships and related transactions.

*   *   *   *   *

Instructions to Paragraph (c) of Item 404

*   *   *   *   *

3. If the lender is a bank, savings and loan association, or broker-dealer extending credit under Federal Reserve Regulation T [12 CFR Part 220] and the loans are not disclosed as

nonaccrual, past due, restructured or potential problems (see Item III.C. 1. and 2. of Industry Guide 3. Statistical Disclosure by Bank Holding Companies), disclosure may consist of a statement, if such is the case, that the loans to such persons (A) were made in the ordinary course of business, (B) were made on substantially the same terms, including interest rates and collateral, as those prevailing at the time for comparable transactions with other persons, and (C) did not involve more than the normal risk of collectibility or present other unfavorable features.

. . . . .

PART 231—INTERPRETIVE RELEASES RELATING TO THE SECURITIES ACT OF 1933 AND GENERAL RULES AND REGULATIONS THEREUNDER

3. By revising Securities Act Industry Guide 3 [Statistical Disclosure by Bank Holding Companies] of Part 231 by revising the requirements and instructions of Items III.A. and III.C., and by adding new Item III.D.

. . . . .

III. Loan Portfolio.

. . . . .

A. *Types of Loans.*

. . . . .

Instructions. A series of categories other than those specified above may be used to present details of loans if considered a more appropriate presentation.

. . . . .

B. *Maturities and Sensitivities of Loans to Changes in Interest Rates.*

. . . . .

C. *Risk Elements.*
1. *Nonaccrual, Past Due and Restructured Loans.* As of the end of each reported period, state separately the aggregate amount of loans in each of the following categories:
(a) Loans accounted for on a nonaccrual basis:
(b) Accruing loans which are contractually past due 90 days or more as to principal *or* interest payments; and,
(c) Loans not included above which are "troubled debt restructurings" as defined in Statement of Financial Accounting Standards No. 15 ("FAS 15"), "Accounting by Debtors and Creditors for Troubled Debt Restructurings."
Instructions. (1) The information required by this Item should be provided separately for domestic and for foreign loans for each reported period.
(2) As of the most recent reported period, state separately as to foreign and domestic loans included in (a) and (c) above the following information: (i) the gross interest income that would have been recorded in the period then ended if the loans had been current in accordance with their original terms and had been outstanding throughout the period or since origination, if held for part of the period; and (ii) the amount of interest income on those loans that was included in net income for the period.

(3) A discussion of the registrant's policy for placing loans on nonaccrual status should be provided.
(4) No loans shall be excluded from the amounts presented. Supplemental disclosures may be made to facilitate understanding of the aggregate amounts reported. These disclosures may include, for example, information as to the nature of the loans, any guarantees, the extent of collateral, or amounts in process of collection.
2. *Potential Problem Loans.* As of the end of the most recent reported period, describe the nature and extent of any loans which are not now disclosed pursuant to Item III.C.1. above, but where known information about possible credit problems of borrowers (which are not related to transfer risk inherent in cross-border lending activities) causes management to have serious doubts as to the ability of such borrowers to comply with the present loan repayment terms and which may result in disclosure of such loans pursuant to Item III.C.1.
3. *Foreign Outstandings.* As of the end of each of the last three reported periods, state the name of the country and aggregate amount of cross-border outstandings to borrowers in each foreign country where such outstandings exceed 1% of total assets.
Instructions. (1) Cross-border outstandings are defined as loans (including accrued interest), acceptances, interest-bearing deposits with other banks, other interest-bearing investments and any other monetary assets which are denominated in dollars or other non-local currency. To the extent that material local currency outstandings are not hedged or are not funded by local currency borrowings, such amounts should be included in cross-border outstandings. Commitments such as irrevocable letters of credit should not be included in outstandings; however, where such items are material, the amounts should be separately disclosed.
(2) Disclose separately the amounts of cross-border outstandings by type of foreign borrower as set forth in Item III.A. above.
(3) If a material amount of the outstandings to any foreign country disclosed herein is included in the amounts disclosed pursuant to Item III.C.1. or 2. identify each such country and the related amounts disclosed pursuant to those Items.
(4) Amounts of any legally enforceable, written guarantees of principal or interest by domestic or other non-local third parties may be netted against cross-border outstandings of a country. If such a guarantee is made by a foreign guarantor, the guarantee amount shall be reflected as an outstanding of such guarantor. The value of any tangible, liquid collateral may also be netted against cross-border outstandings of a country if it is held and realizable by the lender outside of the borrower's country.
(5) For purposes of determining the amount of outstandings to be reported, loans made to, or deposits placed with, a branch of a foreign bank located outside the foreign bank's home country should be considered as loans to, or deposits with, the foreign bank.
(6) Where current conditions in a foreign country give rise to liquidity problems which are expected to have a material impact on the timely payment of interest or principal on

that country's private or public sector debt, disclosure of the nature and impact of such developments should be made.
(7) For countries whose outstandings are between .75% and 1% of total assets, disclose the names of the countries and the aggregate amount of outstandings attributable to all such countries.
(8) The disclosure threshold set forth in this Item is for disclosure guidance and is not intended as an indicator of a prudent level of lending to any one country by an individual bank.
4. *Loan Concentrations.* As of the end of the most recent reported period, describe any concentration of loans exceeding 10% of total loans which are not otherwise disclosed as a category of loans pursuant to Item III.A. of this Guide. Loan concentrations are considered to exist when there are amounts loaned to a multiple number of borrowers engaged in similar activities which would cause them to be similarly impacted by economic or other conditions. *Instructions.*
(1) If a material amount of the loan concentrations disclosed herein or pursuant to Item III.3A. is included in the amounts disclosed pursuant to Item III.C.1. or 2., that fact should be discussed.
(2) The disclosure threshold in this Item is for disclosure guidance and is not intended as an indicator of a prudent level of lending.
D. *Other Interest Bearing Assets.* As of the end of the most recent reported period, disclose the nature and amounts of any other interest bearing assets that would be required to be disclosed under Item III.C.1. or 2. if such assets were loans.

4. By amending Part 231 by adding this release number to the list of interpretive releases set forth thereunder.

PART 241—INTERPRETIVE RELEASES RELATING TO THE SECURITIES EXCHANGE ACT OF 1934 AND GENERAL RULES AND REGULATIONS THEREUNDER

5. By conforming Exchange Act Industry Guide 3 [Statistical Disclosure by Bank Holding Companies] to the amendments for Securities Act Industry Guide 3.

6. By amending Part 241 by adding this release number to the list of interpretive releases set forth thereunder.

Authority: These rules are being adopted pursuant to the authority in Sections 7, 19a, and Schedule A (25) and (26) of the Securities Act of 1933, 15 U.S.C. 77g, 77s(a), 77nn (25) and (26); and Sections 12, 13, 14, 15(d), and 23(n) of the Securities Exchange Act of 1934, 15 U.S.C. 78l, 78m, 78n, 78o(d), 78w(a).

By the Commission.
Dated: August 11, 1983.
George A. Fitzsimmons,
Secretary.

[FR Doc. 83-22786 Filed 8-18-83; 8:45 am]
BILLING CODE 8010-01-M

Exhibit C
Citicorp, 1983 Annual Report.

Exhibit C   165

FINANCIAL REPORTING RESPONSIBILITY

The accompanying financial statements have been prepared by the management of Citicorp in conformity with generally accepted accounting principles appropriate in the circumstances. Where amounts must be based on estimates and judgments, they represent the best estimates and judgments of management. The financial information appearing throughout this annual report is consistent with that in the financial statements.

The financial control system of Citicorp is designed to provide reasonable assurance that the financial records are reliable for preparing financial statements and maintaining accountability for assets and that assets are safeguarded against loss from unauthorized use or disposition. The system in use at Citicorp provides such reasonable assurance, supported by the careful selection and training of staff, the establishment of organizational structures providing an appropriate and well-defined division of responsibilities, and the communication of policies and standards of business conduct throughout the institution.

The accounting policies and system of internal accounting controls are under the general oversight of the Citicorp and Citibank Boards of Directors, acting through the Audit and Examining Committees described on page 65. These committees are comprised entirely of directors who are not officers or employees of Citicorp. The Chief Auditor of Citicorp, who reports directly to the Board of Directors, conducts an extensive program of audits and risk asset reviews worldwide, carried out by a staff of resident inspectors and reviewers and traveling teams. In addition, Peat, Marwick, Mitchell & Co., independent certified public accountants, is engaged to examine our financial statements.

Peat, Marwick, Mitchell & Co. obtains and maintains an understanding of our accounting and financial controls and conducts such tests and other auditing procedures as they consider necessary in the circumstances to express the opinion in their report that follows. Peat, Marwick, Mitchell & Co. has free access to the Audit and Examining Committees, with no members of management present, to discuss their examination and their findings as to the integrity of Citicorp's financial reporting and the adequacy of the system of internal accounting controls.

REPORT OF INDEPENDENT AUDITORS

 Peat, Marwick, Mitchell & Co.
Certified Public Accountants

The Board of Directors and Stockholders of Citicorp:

We have examined the consolidated balance sheet of Citicorp and subsidiaries as of December 31, 1983 and 1982, the related consolidated statements of income, changes in stockholders' equity and changes in financial position for each of the years in the three-year period ended December 31, 1983, and the consolidated balance sheet of Citibank, N. A. and subsidiaries as of December 31, 1983 and 1982. Our examinations were made in accordance with generally accepted auditing standards and, accordingly, included such tests of the accounting records and such other auditing procedures as we considered necessary in the circumstances.

In our opinion, the aforementioned consolidated financial statements present fairly the financial position of Citicorp and subsidiaries at December 31, 1983 and 1982, and the results of their operations and the changes in their financial position for each of the years in the three-year period ended December 31, 1983, and the financial position of Citibank, N. A. and subsidiaries at December 31, 1983 and 1982, in conformity with generally accepted accounting principles applied on a consistent basis.

Peat, Marwick, Mitchell & Co.

New York, New York
January 17, 1984

CONSOLIDATED STATEMENT OF INCOME

CITICORP AND SUBSIDIARIES

IN MILLIONS OF DOLLARS EXCEPT PER SHARE AMOUNTS

	1983	1982	1981
Interest Revenue			
Interest and Fees on Loans	**$12,018**	$12,591	$12,680
Interest on Deposits with Banks	**1,074**	1,619	1,906
Interest on Federal Funds Sold and Securities Purchased Under Resale Agreements	**757**	520	441
Interest and Dividends on Investment Securities (Note 1)	**531**	562	741
Interest on Trading Account Assets	**459**	515	556
Lease Financing Revenue	**358**	366	334
	$15,197	$16,173	$16,658
Interest Expense			
Interest on Deposits	**$ 6,894**	$ 8,505	$ 9,591
Interest on Other Borrowed Money (Notes 5 and 6)	**4,002**	3,837	4,253
Interest on Long-Term Debt and Convertible Notes (Notes 7 and 8)	**258**	305	335
	$11,154	$12,647	$14,179
NET INTEREST REVENUE	**$ 4,043**	$ 3,526	$ 2,479
Loan Loss Expense			
Provision for Possible Losses on Commercial Loans (Note 2)	**$ 293**	$ 284	$ 102
Consumer Credit Loss Expense (Note 3)	**$ 227**	$ 189	$ 203
NET INTEREST REVENUE AFTER LOAN LOSS EXPENSE	**$ 3,523**	$ 3,053	$ 2,174
Fees, Commissions and Other Revenue			
Fees and Commissions	**$ 1,288**	$ 1,109	$ 1,001
Trading Account	**82**	125	88
Foreign Exchange	**274**	241	265
Investment Securities Transactions	**11**	(46)	(43)
Other Revenue (Note 11)	**185**	166	263
	$ 1,840	$ 1,595	$ 1,574
Other Operating Expense			
Salaries	**$ 1,507**	$ 1,407	$ 1,225
Staff Benefits (Note 12)	**337**	309	264
Total Staff Expense	**$ 1,844**	$ 1,716	$ 1,489
Net Premises Expense (Notes 4 and 17)	**344**	306	268
Equipment Expense (Notes 4 and 17)	**331**	287	225
Other Expense	**1,238**	1,089	954
	$ 3,757	$ 3,398	$ 2,936
Income Before Taxes	**$ 1,606**	$ 1,250	$ 812
Applicable Income Taxes (Note 13)	**746**	527	281
NET INCOME	**$ 860**	$ 723	$ 531
Earnings Per Share (Note 14)			
On Common and Common Equivalent Shares	**$6.48**	$5.60	$4.20
Assuming Full Dilution	**$6.15**	$5.33	$4.02

Accounting policies and explanatory notes on pages 38-51 form an integral part of the financial statements.

Exhibit C   167

CONSOLIDATED BALANCE SHEET   CITICORP AND SUBSIDIARIES

IN MILLIONS OF DOLLARS	December 31 1983	December 31 1982
Assets		
Cash and Due from Banks	$ 4,166	$ 4,660
Deposits at Interest with Banks	11,268	10,915
Investment Securities (Market value $5,805 and $4,792 in 1983 and 1982, respectively) (Note 1)	5,834	4,771
Trading Account Assets	3,790	3,592
Federal Funds Sold and Securities Purchased Under Resale Agreements	3,596	3,292
Loans and Lease Financing, Net (Notes 2 and 3)		
Commercial (Net of allowance for possible losses on loans of $540 and $490 and unearned discount of $386 and $463 in 1983 and 1982, respectively)	$ 59,702	$ 62,028
Consumer (Net of allowance for credit losses of $226 and $190 and unearned discount of $4,030 and $4,093 in 1983 and 1982, respectively)	28,769	23,015
Lease Financing (Net of allowance for credit losses of $5 and $7 in 1983 and 1982, respectively)	1,812	1,848
Total Loans and Lease Financing, Net	$ 90,283	$ 86,891
Customers' Acceptance Liability	8,681	9,317
Premises and Equipment (Note 4)	1,849	1,553
Interest and Fees Receivable	2,109	2,034
Other Assets	3,079	2,972
TOTAL	**$134,655**	**$129,997**
Liabilities		
Non-Interest-Bearing Deposits in Domestic Offices	$ 7,836	$ 7,389
Interest-Bearing Deposits in Domestic Offices	21,091	18,191
Non-Interest-Bearing Deposits in Overseas Offices	2,505	3,071
Interest-Bearing Deposits in Overseas Offices	48,362	47,887
Total Deposits	$ 79,794	$ 76,538
Purchased Funds and Other Borrowings (Note 5)	22,299	22,857
Acceptances Outstanding	8,816	9,414
Accrued Taxes and Other Expenses (Note 13)	2,619	2,556
Other Liabilities	3,135	3,251
Intermediate-Term Debt (Original maturities from one to 15 years) (Note 6)	9,372	7,709
Long-Term Debt (Original maturities of 15 years or more) (Note 7)	2,460	2,467
Convertible Notes (Note 8)	349	350
Redeemable Preferred Stock (Note 9)	40	40
Stockholders' Equity		
Preferred Stock (Without Par Value) (Note 10)	$ 540	$ —
Common Stock ($4.00 Par) (Note 11)	549	542
Issued Shares: 137,152,815 in 1983; 135,525,454 in 1982		
Surplus	911	875
Retained Earnings	4,129	3,579
Common Stock in Treasury, at Cost	(358)	(181)
Shares: 12,577,465 in 1983; 8,303,810 in 1982		
Total Stockholders' Equity	$ 5,771	$ 4,815
TOTAL	**$134,655**	**$129,997**

Accounting policies and explanatory notes on pages 38-51 form an integral part of the financial statements.

CONSOLIDATED STATEMENT OF CHANGES IN STOCKHOLDERS' EQUITY

CITICORP AND SUBSIDIARIES

IN MILLIONS OF DOLLARS

	1983	1982	1981
Preferred Stock (Note 10)			
Issuance of Stock	$ 550	$ —	$ —
Purchase and Retirement of Stock	(10)	—	—
BALANCE AT END OF YEAR	$ 540	$ —	$ —
Common Stock (Note 11)			
Balance at Beginning of Year	$ 542	$ 534	$ 522
Shares: 135,525,454 in 1983; 133,419,092 in 1982; and 130,378,410 in 1981			
Issuance of Stock in Exchange for Outstanding Debt (2,000,000 shares)	—	—	8
Issuance of Stock under Savings Incentive, Stock Option and Stock Purchase Plans and Conversion of Convertible Notes (Notes 8 and 12)	7	8	4
Shares: 1,627,361 in 1983; 2,106,362 in 1982; and 1,040,682 in 1981			
BALANCE AT END OF YEAR	$ 549	$ 542	$ 534
Shares: 137,152,815 in 1983; 135,525,454 in 1982; and 133,419,092 in 1981			
Surplus			
Balance at Beginning of Year	$ 875	$ 829	$ 772
Preferred Stock Issuance Cost	(10)	—	—
Issuance of Stock in Exchange for Outstanding Debt (Note 11)	—	—	38
Issuance of Stock under Savings Incentive, Stock Option, Stock Purchase and Executive Incentive Compensation Plans and Conversion of Convertible Notes (Notes 8 and 12)	45	46	19
Gain on Purchase and Retirement of Preferred Stock	1	—	—
BALANCE AT END OF YEAR	$ 911	$ 875	$ 829
Retained Earnings			
Balance at Beginning of Year	$3,579	$3,093	$2,760
Accumulated Foreign Currency Translation at January 1, 1982	—	(2)	—
Net Income	860	723	531
Cash Dividends Declared (including preferred dividends of $33 in 1983, and redeemable preferred dividends of $4 in 1983, 1982 and 1981)	(271)	(222)	(198)
Foreign Currency Translation	(39)	(13)	—
BALANCE AT END OF YEAR	$4,129	$3,579	$3,093
Common Stock in Treasury, at Cost			
Balance at Beginning of Year	$ (181)	$ (175)	$ (163)
Shares: 8,303,810 in 1983; 8,131,341 in 1982; and 7,743,083 in 1981			
Treasury Stock Transactions, at Cost	(177)	(6)	(12)
Shares: 4,273,655 in 1983; 172,469 in 1982; and 388,258 in 1981			
BALANCE AT END OF YEAR	$ (358)	$ (181)	$ (175)
Shares: 12,577,465 in 1983; 8,303,810 in 1982; and 8,131,341 in 1981			
Total Stockholders' Equity			
Balance at Beginning of Year	$4,815	$4,281	$3,891
Changes during the Year, Net	956	534	390
BALANCE AT END OF YEAR	$5,771	$4,815	$4,281

Accounting policies and explanatory notes on pages 38-51 form an integral part of the financial statements.

Exhibit C   169

CONSOLIDATED STATEMENT OF CHANGES IN FINANCIAL POSITION		CITICORP AND SUBSIDIARIES		
IN MILLIONS OF DOLLARS		1983	1982	1981
Funds Provided				
Net Income		$ 860	$ 723	$ 531
Increase in				
Deposits		3,256	4,413	354
Purchased Funds and Other Borrowings Net of Federal Funds Sold and Securities Purchased Under Resale Agreements		—	51	227
Intermediate-Term Debt		1,663	2,123	2,235
Long-Term Debt		—	—	270
Preferred Stock		540	—	—
Decrease in				
Cash and Due from Banks and Deposits at Interest with Banks		141	—	3,519
Investment Securities and Trading Account Assets		—	1,168	1,096
Other, Net		—	567	—
TOTAL		**$6,460**	$9,045	$8,232
Funds Used				
Cash Dividends Declared		$ 271	$ 222	$ 198
Increase in				
Cash and Due from Banks and Deposits at Interest with Banks		—	328	—
Investment Securities and Trading Account Assets		1,261	—	—
Federal Funds Sold and Securities Purchased Under Resale Agreements		304	—	—
Loans and Lease Financing, Net		3,392	8,292	7,170
Premises and Equipment		296	184	146
Decrease in				
Purchased Funds and Other Borrowings		558	—	—
Long-Term Debt		7	19	—
Other, Net		371	—	718
TOTAL		**$6,460**	$9,045	$8,232

Accounting policies and explanatory notes on pages 38-51 form an integral part of the financial statements.

CONSOLIDATED BALANCE SHEET   CITIBANK, N.A. AND SUBSIDIARIES

IN MILLIONS OF DOLLARS	DECEMBER 31 1983	December 31 1982
Assets		
Cash and Due from Banks	$ 3,881	$ 4,435
Deposits at Interest with Banks	11,043	10,433
Investment Securities (Market value $5,118 and $3,966 in 1983 and 1982, respectively)	5,100	3,906
Trading Account Assets	2,266	2,308
Federal Funds Sold and Securities Purchased Under Resale Agreements	4,091	4,191
Loans and Lease Financing	$ 71,568	$ 71,897
Less: Allowance for Loan and Lease Financing Losses	(569)	(511)
Unearned Discount on Loans	(1,595)	(1,858)
Loans and Lease Financing, Net	$ 69,404	$ 69,528
Customers' Acceptance Liability	9,082	9,843
Premises and Equipment	1,452	1,214
Interest and Fees Receivable	1,734	1,720
Other Assets	2,562	2,377
TOTAL	**$110,615**	$109,955
Liabilities		
Non-Interest-Bearing Deposits in Domestic Offices	$ 7,147	$ 6,956
Interest-Bearing Deposits in Domestic Offices	17,007	15,556
Non-Interest-Bearing Deposits in Overseas Offices	2,449	3,090
Interest-Bearing Deposits in Overseas Offices	50,735	48,547
Total Deposits	$ 77,338	$ 74,149
Purchased Funds and Other Borrowings	13,049	14,108
Acceptances Outstanding	9,219	9,941
Accrued Taxes and Other Expenses	2,054	2,424
Other Liabilities	1,406	1,782
Intermediate-Term and Long-Term Debt	1,625	2,066
Stockholder's Equity (Note 18)		
Capital Stock ($20.00 par)	$ 751	$ 751
Outstanding Shares: 37,534,553 in both years		
Surplus	1,073	1,066
Retained Earnings	4,100	3,668
Total Stockholder's Equity	$ 5,924	$ 5,485
TOTAL	**$110,615**	$109,955

Accounting policies and explanatory notes on pages 38-51 form an integral part of the financial statements.

Exhibit C   171

BASIS OF PRESENTATION

The consolidated financial statements include the accounts of Citicorp, its wholly-owned subsidiary, Citibank, N.A. and their majority-owned subsidiaries, after the elimination of all material intercompany transactions.

Affiliates which are 20%- to 50%-owned are carried under the equity method of accounting and the pro rata share of their income (loss) is included in other revenue. Income from investments in less than 20%-owned companies is recognized when dividends are received.

Gains and losses on disposition of branches, subsidiaries, affiliates and other equity investments (including venture capital investments) and charges for management's estimate of permanent impairment in value, are included in other revenue.

Beginning in 1983, financial results are reported using the single-step income statement format required by the Securities and Exchange Commission, which eliminates the caption "Income Before Securities Transactions." Gains and losses on investment securities transactions are now included as a component of fees, commissions and other revenue. Financial statements for prior periods have been reclassified to conform with the new presentation.

Foreign currency translation, which represents the effects of translating into US dollars, at current exchange rates, financial statements of overseas operations with a primary or functional currency other than the US dollar, is included in retained earnings in the accompanying consolidated balance sheet, along with related hedge and tax effects.

The effects of translating foreign currency financial statements of those overseas operations with the US dollar as the primary or functional currency, including those operating in a highly inflationary environment, are included in foreign exchange revenue, along with related hedge effects. Foreign exchange trading positions, including spot and forward contracts, are valued monthly at prevailing market rates and the resulting gains and losses are included in foreign exchange revenue.

INVESTMENT SECURITIES AND TRADING ACCOUNT ASSETS

Investment securities are carried at cost adjusted for amortization of premiums to call date and accretion of discounts to maturity. Gains and losses on sales of investment securities are computed on a specific identified cost basis.

Beginning in 1983, money market instruments held for trading purposes, previously reported as deposits at interest with banks and loans, are now reported as trading account assets in accordance with a new Securities and Exchange Commission rule. Financial statements for prior periods have been reclassified to conform with the new presentation.

Trading account assets, consisting of securities and money market instruments, are presented net of obligations to deliver assets sold but not yet purchased and, along with related futures and forward transactions, are valued at market. Interest on trading account assets, net, is included in interest revenue. Gains and losses from all trading activities, both realized and unrealized, are included in trading account revenue.

No transfers are made between investment securities and the trading account.

COMMERCIAL LOANS

Commercial loans are stated at their face amount, net of unearned discount and the allowance for possible losses on commercial loans.

Additions to the allowance are made by means of the provision for possible losses on commercial loans charged to expense. Loan losses are deducted from the allowance and subsequent recoveries are added. The level of net loan losses for the year is a significant factor in determining the appropriate level for the provision for possible losses on commercial loans. Based on management's judgment as to the appropriate level of the allowance for possible losses, the amount actually provided may be greater or less than the net loan losses for the year. The determination of the amount by which the provision should exceed or be less than net loan losses is based on management's current evaluation of the anticipated impact of domestic and international economic conditions, changes in the character and size of the portfolio, past and expected future loss experience and other pertinent indicators.

When it is determined as a result of evaluation procedures that the payment of interest or principal on a commercial loan is doubtful of collection, the loan is placed on a nonaccrual basis. In any case where interest or principal is past due for 90 days or more, the loan is automatically placed on nonaccrual basis unless an affirmative determination is made by senior credit management that the condition is not indicative of doubt as to the collectibility of principal or interest. Any interest accrued on a loan placed on a nonaccrual basis is reversed and charged against current earnings. Interest on nonaccrual loans is thereafter included in earnings only to the extent actually received in cash.

CONSUMER LOANS

Consumer loans are stated at their face amount, net of unearned discount and the allowance for consumer credit losses.

Consumer loans are written off upon reaching a predetermined number of days past due on a contractual basis. The number of days is set at an appropriate level by loan product and by country so as to result in the recognition of losses on a basis which makes the likelihood of subsequent recovery of those losses fall between 20% to 30%. Consumer credit loss expense is charged to earnings in an amount that results in an allowance sufficient to cover anticipated losses based on the mix of the portfolio, past and expected future loss experience, and economic conditions and trends.

Interest on discount loans is accrued on a declining basis which results in an approximate level rate of return over the term of the loan. Interest accrued on nondiscount loans is based on the principal amount of loans outstanding.

LEASE FINANCING

Lease financing represents Citicorp's share of aggregate rentals on lease financing transactions and residual values net of related unearned income.

Lease financing transactions substantially represent direct financing leases and also include leveraged leases. Unearned income is amortized under a method which substantially results in an approximate level rate of return when related to the unrecovered lease investment.

Gains and losses from sales of residual values of leased equipment are included in other revenue.

STAFF BENEFITS AND EARNINGS PER SHARE

Staff benefits expense includes prior and current service costs of retirement plans which are accrued on a current basis, contributions under the savings incentive plan, awards under the executive incentive compensation plan and costs of other staff benefits. No charges are reflected in earnings due to the granting or exercise of options under the stock option plans or the subscription for or purchase of stock under the stock purchase plans.

Common equivalent shares are included in the calculation of earnings per share representing shares issuable under the executive incentive compensation plan and the dilutive effect of options and subscriptions to purchase shares under the stock option and stock purchase plans. Options and subscriptions may be for either market value or book value stock. Market value stock is Citicorp common stock that is not restricted by Citicorp as to resale but can be sold by the staff member in the market. Book value stock is Citicorp common stock that is issued at a price equal to book value per share and can be resold only to Citicorp at the per share book value at the time of sale but which has the same voting, dividend and liquidation rights as market value stock. For outstanding options and subscriptions involving only market value shares, common equivalent shares are computed using the treasury stock method.

Under the stock option and stock purchase plans, options are also granted in tandem and subscription agreements are also entered into that give the staff member the alternative to purchase either market value or book value shares up to the end of the option or subscription period at exercise or purchase prices fixed at the date of grant or subscription.

If circumstances are such that purchase of market value shares clearly represents the economically preferable alternative to the staff member, the earnings per share calculation includes common equivalent shares representing the dilutive effect, computed by the treasury stock method, of the market value shares under option or subscription. If circumstances indicate that purchase of book value shares is the staff member's preferable alternative, the book value shares under option or subscription enter into the earnings per share calculation according to the two-class method. This method recognizes the fact that there are effectively two classes of stock participating in earnings: one, outstanding shares of stock which share in all earnings, and another, book value shares under option or subscription which share only in undistributed earnings.

After issuance, book value shares are included in the weighted average number of shares of common stock outstanding used to calculate earnings per share.

Upon issuance of shares under the savings incentive, stock option and stock purchase plans, proceeds received in excess of par value are credited to surplus. Upon issuance of treasury shares under the executive incentive compensation plan, the excess of the amount of the awards over the average cost of treasury shares is credited to surplus.

INCOME TAXES

Provision for deferred taxes is made for items of revenue and expense reported in the financial statements in different years than for tax purposes, including an appropriate provision for taxes on undistributed income of subsidiaries and affiliates.

Investment tax credits on leased equipment are recognized over a period of time related to the recovery of the lease investment which gives rise to such credits. Other investment tax credits are recognized in the year the asset is acquired.

Exhibit C 173

1. INVESTMENT SECURITIES

	1983		1982	
IN MILLIONS OF DOLLARS AT YEAR END	CARRYING VALUE	MARKET VALUE	CARRYING VALUE	MARKET VALUE
U.S. Treasury and Federal Agencies	$2,823	$2,735	$2,017	$2,017
State and Municipal				
New York City and Municipal Assistance Corporation	278	247	388	323
All other	199	136	258	175
Other	2,534	2,687	2,108	2,277
TOTAL	$5,834	$5,805	$4,771	$4,792

Interest and Dividends on Investment Securities

IN MILLIONS OF DOLLARS FOR THE YEAR	1983	1982	1981
U.S. Treasury and Federal Agencies	$257	$264	$431
State and Municipal (substantially all exempt from federal income tax)	36	56	54
Other	238	242	256
TOTAL	$531	$562	$741

2. COMMERCIAL LOANS

Commercial Loans Outstanding

IN MILLIONS OF DOLLARS AT YEAR END	1983	1982
In Domestic Offices		
Commercial and industrial[1]	$14,910	$17,817
Mortgage and real estate[2]	3,975	2,915
Loans to financial institutions[3]	2,341	2,623
	$21,226	$23,355
In Overseas Offices		
Commercial and industrial[1]	$27,592	$29,590
Mortgage and real estate[2]	1,822	2,745
Loans to financial institutions	5,914	4,151
Governments and official institutions	4,074	3,140
	$39,402	$39,626
	$60,628	$62,981
Unearned discount	(386)	(463)
Allowance for possible losses on commercial loans	(540)	(490)
COMMERCIAL LOANS, NET	$59,702	$62,028

(1)Includes loans not otherwise separately categorized.
(2)Includes only loans secured primarily by real estate.
(3)Includes loans to governments and official institutions of $475 million and $243 million in 1983 and 1982, respectively.

CHANGES IN THE ALLOWANCE FOR POSSIBLE LOSSES ON COMMERCIAL LOANS

IN MILLIONS OF DOLLARS	1983	1982	1981
Balance at Beginning of Year	**$490**	$400	$359
Deductions			
Loan losses	**$292**	$245	$127
Less loan recoveries	**(51)**	(53)	(67)
Net loan losses	**$241**	$192	$ 60
Additions			
Provision for possible losses on commercial loans	**$293**	$284	$102
Other (principally adjustments relating to the translation of overseas allowance balances)	**(2)**	(2)	(1)
	$291	$282	$101
BALANCE AT END OF YEAR	**$540**	$490	$400

Citicorp's nonaccrual and renegotiated commercial loans amounted to $2,110 million, $1,662 million and $1,036 at December 31, 1983, 1982 and 1981, respectively. Renegotiated loans are those commercial loans on which the rate of interest has been reduced as a result of the inability of the borrower to meet the original terms of the loan. Foregone revenue from nonaccrual and renegotiated commercial loans was as follows:

IN MILLIONS OF DOLLARS FOR THE YEAR	1983	1982	1981
Interest income that would have been accrued at original contractual rates[1]	**$297**	$192	$160
Amount recognized as interest income[2]	**256**	132	87
FOREGONE REVENUE	**$ 41**	$ 60	$ 73

(1) $65 million, $86 million and $86 million in domestic offices; $232 million, $106 million and $74 million in overseas offices in 1983, 1982 and 1981, respectively.
(2) Represents interest collected on nonaccrual loans and interest accrued at reduced rates on renegotiated loans. $41 million, $35 million and $51 million in domestic offices; $215 million, $97 million and $36 million in overseas offices in 1983, 1982 and 1981, respectively.

3. CONSUMER LOANS

The consumer loan category represents loans managed by Citicorp's Individual Banking business. This is generally defined as including loans to individual consumers in major countries throughout the world, to meet their borrowing requirements for housing, automobiles and other personal and family purposes. The consumer category also includes indirect types of consumer finance such as dealer floor plan lending.

CONSUMER LOANS OUTSTANDING

IN MILLIONS OF DOLLARS AT YEAR END	1983	1982
In Domestic Offices		
Mortgage and real estate[1]	**$10,751**	$ 9,261
Installment, revolving credit and other consumer loans	**15,418**	11,213
	$26,169	$20,474
In Overseas Offices		
Mortgage and real estate[1]	**$ 2,370**	$ 1,735
Installment, revolving credit and other consumer loans	**4,486**	5,089
	$ 6,856	$ 6,824
	$33,025	$27,298
Unearned discount	**(4,030)**	(4,093)
Allowance for consumer credit losses	**(226)**	(190)
CONSUMER LOANS, NET	**$28,769**	$23,015

(1) Includes only loans secured primarily by real estate.

CHANGES IN THE ALLOWANCE FOR CONSUMER CREDIT LOSSES

IN MILLIONS OF DOLLARS	1983	1982	1981
Balance at Beginning of Year	**$190**	$173	$147
Deductions			
Loan losses	**$283**	$266	$270
Less loan recoveries	**(87)**	(82)	(74)
Net loan losses	**$196**	$184	$196
Additions			
Consumer credit loss expense	**$227**	$189	$203
Other additions (principally allowance balances of acquired companies)	**5**	12	19
	$232	$201	$222
BALANCE AT END OF YEAR	**$226**	$190	$173

Exhibit C   175

4. PREMISES AND EQUIPMENT

Depreciation and amortization of premises and equipment was $199 million in 1983, $179 million in 1982 and $148 million in 1981. Generally, depreciation and amortization are computed on the straight-line basis over the estimated useful life of the asset or the lease term.

5. PURCHASED FUNDS AND OTHER BORROWINGS

Purchased Funds and Other Borrowings, Original Maturities of Less Than One Year

	1983			1982		
IN MILLIONS OF DOLLARS	AMOUNT OUTSTANDING AT YEAR END	AVERAGE OUTSTANDING DURING YEAR	MAXIMUM OUTSTANDING AT ANY MONTH END	AMOUNT OUTSTANDING AT YEAR END	AVERAGE OUTSTANDING DURING YEAR	MAXIMUM OUTSTANDING AT ANY MONTH END
Federal funds purchased and securities repurchase agreements (in domestic offices) [1]	$ 8,596	$8,379	$10,096	$ 9,719	$9,331	$10,674
Commercial paper [2]	4,087	$3,766	$ 4,578	5,352	$4,859	$ 5,517
Other funds borrowed	9,616	$8,498	$10,139	7,786	$6,367	$ 7,786
TOTAL	$22,299			$22,857		

(1) Weighted average interest rate was 9.66% during 1983 and 11.76% during 1982.
(2) Weighted average interest rate was 9.14% during 1983 and 12.64% during 1982; 9.87% at year-end 1983 and 9.38% at year-end 1982.

6. INTERMEDIATE-TERM DEBT

Intermediate-Term Debt, Original Maturities From One to 15 Years

IN MILLIONS OF DOLLARS AT YEAR END	DUE WITHIN 1 YEAR	DUE 1-5 YEARS	DUE 6-10 YEARS	DUE 11-15 YEARS	1983[1] TOTAL	1982 TOTAL
Parent Company						
10¼% notes due 1984	$ 200	$ —	$ —	$ —	$ 200	$ 200
Various notes due 1986 (interest rates 9¼% to 16.45%)	250	604	—	—	854	606
Various notes due 1987 (interest rates 11¼% to 16%)	—	409	—	—	409	378
Various notes due 1988 (interest rates 11.79% to 12.15%)	—	271	—	—	271	—
12% notes due 1990	—	—	300	—	300	—
Various notes due 1993 (interest rates 12¼% to 12½%)	—	—	310	—	310	—
11.30% notes due 1995	—	250	—	—	250	—
Floating rate notes due 1985	—	100	—	—	100	100
Floating rate notes due 1987	—	150	—	—	150	150
Floating rate notes due 1989	109	100	—	—	209	219
Floating rate notes due 1992	—	900	—	—	900	—
Floating rate notes due 1995	—	200	150	—	350	—
Floating rate notes due 1998	—	275	—	—	275	—
Other	59	24	—	—	83	193
	$ 618	$3,283	$ 760	$ —	$4,661	$1,846
Subsidiaries						
Debentures and other borrowings by Citicorp Australia Holdings Limited	$ 256	$ 339	$ 5	$ —	$ 600	$ 935
Promissory notes issued by Citicorp Savings	15	1	—	—	16	930
15½% notes due 1984	171	—	—	—	171	175
Various notes due 1986 (interest rates 10% to 16¾%)	—	676	—	—	676	683
12% notes due 1987	—	200	—	—	200	200
11½% notes due 1988	—	100	—	—	100	—
Various notes due 1990 (interest rates 10⅜% to 11¾%)	—	—	200	—	200	—
Floating rate notes due 1983	—	—	—	—	—	300
Floating rate notes due 1984	370	—	—	—	370	370
Floating rate notes due 1992	100	—	—	—	100	100
Floating rate notes due 1997	—	125	—	—	125	125
Floating rate notes without stated maturity	85	—	—	—	85	132
Promissory notes due 1990	—	—	300	—	300	—
Promissory notes due 1996	—	—	—	100	100	100
Zero coupon notes due 1985	—	129	—	—	129	113
Other	317	1,026	192	4	1,539	1,700
	$1,314	$2,596	$ 697	$104	$4,711	$5,863
TOTAL	$1,932	$5,879[2]	$1,457	$104	$9,372	$7,709

(1) Maturity distribution is based upon contractual maturities or earlier dates at which debt is repayable at the option of the holder or requires mandatory sinking fund payments.
(2) Maturity distribution-consolidated: 1985-$1,161; 1986-$3,130; 1987-$914; 1988-$674. Parent Company: 1985-$475; 1986-$1,978; 1987-$559; 1988-$271.

The interest rates on the floating rate note issues and promissory notes shown in the accompanying table are determined periodically by formulas based on certain money market rates or, in certain instances, by minimum interest rates as specified in the agreements governing the respective issues. Interest rates on floating rate note issues and promissory notes at December 31, 1983 were as follows: parent company issues due 1985-10.30% (9.25% in 1982), 1987-10.30% (9.25% in 1982), 1989-9.90% and 10.30% (9.20% and 9.25% in 1982), 1992-10.05% and 10.30%, 1995-10.15% and 10.20% and 1998-10.02%; issues of subsidiaries due 1984-10.125% and 9.75% (9.875% and 9.375% in 1982), 1992-15.0% (15.0% in 1982), 1997-15.5% (15.5% in 1982) and without stated maturity—9.56% (11.00% in 1982); promissory notes due 1990-10.20% and 1996-10.425% (9.375% in 1982).

Citicorp Australia Holdings Limited (CAHL) issues debentures periodically at various interest rates and maturities which are secured by the assets of CAHL and certain of its consolidated subsidiaries. At December 31, 1983, the debentures had an average interest rate of 13.22% and an average maturity of 1.3 years. At December 31, 1982, the average interest rate was 14.86%.

The zero coupon notes due 1985 were issued at a discount resulting in an effective interest yield of 14.57%. Principal payable at maturity is $150 million.

Citicorp guarantees substantially all the intermediate-term debt issued by its subsidiaries except for CAHL.

Certain of the agreements under which these notes and debentures were issued prohibit Citicorp, under certain conditions, from paying dividends in shares of Citibank capital stock and from creating encumbrances on such shares.

Exhibit C 177

7. LONG-TERM DEBT

Long-Term Debt, Original Maturities of 15 Years or More

IN MILLIONS OF DOLLARS AT YEAR END	DUE WITHIN 1 YEAR	DUE 1-5 YEARS	DUE 6-10 YEARS	DUE 11-15 YEARS	DUE 15 YEARS & OVER	1983[1] TOTAL	1982 TOTAL
Parent Company							
8½% notes due 2002	$ —	$ 46	$ 57	$ 58	$ 89	**$ 250**	$ 250
8.45% notes due 2007	—	27	83	84	150	**344**	344
8⅛% notes due 2007	—	—	—	26	140	**166**	166
10⅞% notes due 2010	—	—	36	59	155	**250**	250
Floating rate notes due 1998	—	—	100	100	—	**200**	200
Floating rate notes due 2004	—	70	132	142	156	**500**	500
Other	60	—	—	—	—	**60**	60
	$60	$143	$408	$ 469	$690	**$1,770**	$1,770
Subsidiaries							
Promissory notes due 1996	$ —	$ —	$ —	$ 500	$ —	**$ 500**	$ 500
Floating rate notes due 1994[2]	—	—	—	100	—	**100**	100
Other[2]	2	6	77	5	—	**90**	97
	$ 2	$ 6	$ 77	$ 605	$ —	**$ 690**	$ 697
TOTAL	$62	$149[3]	$485	$1,074	$690	**$2,460**	$2,467

(1) Maturity distribution is based upon contractual maturities or earlier dates at which debt is repayable at the option of the holder or requires mandatory sinking fund payments.
(2) Guaranteed by Citicorp.
(3) Maturity distribution: 1985—$31; 1986—$29; 1987—$41; 1988—$48.

The interest rates on floating rate note issues and promissory notes are determined periodically during the year by formulas based on certain money market rates and are subject to certain minimum per annum interest rates as specified in the agreements governing the respective issues. Interest rates on floating rate note issues at December 31, 1983 were 11.1% (12.55% in 1982) for the 1998 issue, 10.35% (9.75% in 1982) for the 2004 issue and 10.375% (9.69% in 1982) for the 1994 issue. The interest rate on the promissory notes due 1996 was 10.30% at December 31, 1983 (9.25% in 1982).

Certain of the agreements under which these notes and bonds were issued prohibit Citicorp, under certain conditions, from paying dividends in shares of Citibank capital stock and from creating encumbrances on such shares.

8. CONVERTIBLE NOTES

At December 31, 1983 and 1982, outstanding 5¾% convertible subordinated notes due in 2000 were $349 million and $350 million, respectively. The notes are unsecured obligations of Citicorp, convertible at the option of the holder into Citicorp common stock at a conversion price of $41 per share, subject to adjustment in certain events, and are also redeemable at the option of Citicorp at prices decreasing from 103.45% in 1984 to 100% in 1995 and thereafter. The liability on the notes is subordinated to obligations to other creditors.

9. REDEEMABLE PREFERRED STOCK

At December 31, 1983 and 1982, 400,000 shares of non-voting redeemable preferred stock were outstanding, subject to redemption at a price of $100 per share through a mandatory sinking fund beginning in 1990 which would retire all of the stock by 2013. Dividends, which are cumulative, are payable semiannually at an annual rate of $11 per share until 1985 and thereafter at a rate determined periodically by a formula based on certain money market rates. Citicorp may be required to repurchase the preferred stock at $100 per share if loans are not extended to the preferred stockholder under certain circumstances.

10. PREFERRED STOCK

IN MILLIONS OF DOLLARS AT YEAR END	1983
Adjustable Rate Preferred Stock, Second Series 3,900,000 shares	**$390**
Adjustable Rate Preferred Stock, Third Series, 1,500,000 shares	150
	$540

Dividends on both series of preferred stock are cumulative and payable quarterly at rates determined quarterly, by formulas based on interest rates of certain U.S. Treasury obligations, subject to certain minimum and maximum rates as specified in the agreements governing the respective instruments. The dividend rates on the second and third series were 7.875% and 9.50%, respectively, at December 31, 1983.

Citicorp may, at its option, redeem the Second Series on or after February 28, 1988 at $103 per share through February 28, 1993 and at $100 per share thereafter and may, at its option, redeem the Third Series on or after September 1, 1988 at $103 per share until August 31, 1989 and at amounts declining thereafter to $100 per share beginning September 1, 1992.

Both series rank prior to Common Stock as to dividends and liquidation and do not have general voting rights.

At December 31, 1983 and 1982, authorized preferred stock (issuable as either redeemable or nonredeemable) was 10 million shares, of which a total of 5.4 million shares of nonredeemable preferred stock were issued and outstanding at December 31, 1983 and 400,000 shares of redeemable preferred stock were issued and outstanding at December 31, 1983 and 1982. Additionally, 100,000 shares of nonredeemable preferred stock were issued and retired during 1983.

11. CITICORP COMMON STOCK

At December 31, 1983 and 1982, authorized common stock was 200 million shares. The outstanding shares at December 31, 1983 and 1982 include 1.9 million and 1.7 million book value shares, respectively, issued in connection with certain staff benefit plans. Under the terms of the plans the payment for book value shares sold back to Citicorp can be settled in cash or in market value shares at the option of Citicorp.

At December 31, 1983, shares were reserved for issuance as follows: on conversion of convertible notes, 8.5 million shares; under the savings incentive plan, 13.4 million book value shares; under the 1973 stock option plan, under which options may be granted in tandem, a maximum of 5.4 million shares if issued at market value and a maximum of 6.8 million shares if issued at book value; under the 1983 stock option plan, under which options may be granted in tandem, a maximum of 10.0 million shares if issued at market value and a maximum of 15.0 million shares if issued at book value; under the stock purchase plan, 7.2 million shares; and under the executive incentive compensation plan, 425 thousand shares.

During 1981, Citicorp exchanged 2,000,000 newly issued shares of common stock for $88 million par value of Citicorp's outstanding 8⅛% notes and 8.45% notes, both due 2007. These notes will be used to meet future sinking fund requirements, and this transaction resulted in a nontaxable gain of $41 million which is included in Other Revenue.

12. STAFF BENEFITS

Retirement Plans. There are a number of pension plans covering substantially all staff members. The cost of the principal plan amounted to $44 million in 1983, $41 million in 1982 and $29 million in 1981. The costs of all benefits under the plan are accrued and funded on a current basis.

A comparison of the actuarial value of accumulated plan benefits and plan net assets for the principal benefit plan as of the most recent actuarial valuation date is presented below.

	JANUARY 1,	
IN MILLIONS OF DOLLARS	**1983**	1982
Retirement benefits earned by employees		
Vested	**$384**	$363
Non-vested	**49**	43
	$433	$406
Plan Net Assets Available for Benefits at market	**$771**	$596

Retirement benefits earned by employees represent the present value of accumulated benefits earned based upon years of service. The amount was determined using a rate of return of 8% for both 1983 and 1982.

Savings Incentive Plan. Effective January 1, 1982, the savings incentive plan replaced the staff incentive plan. The expense associated with the plan amounted to $36 million in 1983 and $31 million in 1982.

Under the plan, eligible staff members receive awards equal to 3% of their covered salary. Staff members have the option of receiving their award in cash or deferring some or all of it in various investment funds. Citicorp grants an additional award equal to the amount deferred by the employee. Several investment options are available including Citicorp market value shares, which the fund acquires in the open market, and book value shares issued by Citicorp.

The expense associated with the previous staff incentive plan amounted to $37 million in 1981.

Exhibit C   179

Stock Option Plans. During 1983, the shareholders of Citicorp approved a new stock option plan which became effective March 31, 1983. No further options may be granted pursuant to previous stock option plans. Options previously granted under a stock option plan that became effective April 2, 1973 and was extended and amended effective April 1, 1977 do not fully expire until 1992. Under both the 1983 plan and 1973 plan, as extended and amended, options have been granted to key staff members for terms up to 10 years to purchase common stock at not less than the fair market value of the shares at the date of grant. In addition, the 1983 plan and 1973 plan, as extended and amended, provide for the granting in tandem of options to purchase market value shares of common stock at not less than the market value at the date of grant or a proportionate number of book value shares of common stock at not less than the book value per share at the date of grant. Such a proportionate number of book value shares is determined based on the ratio of market value to book value per share at the date of grant. Under the 1983 plan and 1973 plan, 50% of the options granted are exercisable beginning on the first anniversary and 50% beginning on the second anniversary of the date of grant.

In the accompanying table in the captions shares under option and options granted, options granted in tandem are included on the basis that represents the economically preferable alternative to the staff member.

At December 31, 1983, options to purchase 4,032,821 shares were exercisable. At that date, 8,404,450 shares were available to grant options to purchase market value shares and 7,430,703 shares (a proportionate number based on the price ratio of book value shares to market value shares) were available to grant options to purchase book value shares. Additional shares may become available for options to purchase market value shares under the plan to the extent presently outstanding options under the 1983 plan terminate or expire unexercised. As the number of market value shares available for options so increases, or if the price ratio of market value shares to book value shares increases, the number of book value shares available for options will increase proportionately, subject to a maximum of 15 million shares.

Stock Purchase Plan. The plan permits all eligible staff members (two years employment with Citicorp or its subsidiaries) to purchase shares within a specified period not to exceed 24 months under agreements entered into with all such staff members from time to time at the fair market value or book value per share at the dates of the agreements.

Agreements aggregating $44 million were entered into at June 30, 1982. Outstanding subscriptions, which aggregated $22 million at December 31, 1983 and $35 million at December 31, 1982, may be used for the purchase of market value shares at $25.125 per share, book value shares at $35.637 per share, or a combination of both. In 1983, 474,637 market value shares and 306 book value shares were purchased by staff members, and in 1982, 289,043 market value shares and 461 book value shares were purchased by staff members under the terms of the June 30, 1982 agreements.

Under agreements entered into on March 31, 1980 for the purchase of market value shares at $18.125 per share and book value shares at $29.414 per share, 905,273 market value and 67,724 book value shares were purchased in 1982 and 430,662 market value and 1,796 book value shares were purchased in 1981. These agreements expired on March 31, 1982.

Executive Incentive Compensation Plan. Under the Executive Incentive Compensation Plan, awards are made to key staff members, payable at the election of the participants, in cash, or in market value or book value shares of Citicorp common stock, in three installments or on a deferred basis.

The aggregate amount of the awards was approximately $17 million in 1983 and 1982 and $6 million in 1981.

CHANGES IN OPTIONS AND SHARES UNDER OPTION

	NUMBER OF SHARES	OPTION PRICE PER SHARE
Shares under option at		
December 31, 1983	6,273,571	$18 to $42
December 31, 1982	5,608,439	$18 to $42
Options granted		
1983	1,635,364	$36 to $39
1982	1,444,600	$25 to $33
1981	1,184,775	$23 to $27
Options exercised		
1983	827,318	$18 to $42
1982	473,296	$18 to $38
1981	313,575	$18 to $32

13. APPLICABLE INCOME TAXES

IN MILLIONS OF DOLLARS FOR THE YEAR	1983	1982	1981
Domestic			
Current			
Federal*	$ 20	$ 4	$ 8
State and local	27	11	4
	$ 47	$ 15	$ 12
Deferred			
Federal	$ 80	$ 7	$(135)
State and local	7	4	14
	$ 87	$ 11	$(121)
Total domestic	$134	$ 26	$(109)
Foreign (substantially current)	612	501	390
TOTAL PROVISION	$746	$527	$ 281

The total provision includes $6 million for 1983, and reductions for tax benefits of $22 million and $19 million for the years 1982 and 1981, respectively, resulting from investment securities transactions.

Although not affecting the total provision, current income tax payments may differ from the amounts shown as current as a result of the final determination as to the timing of certain deductions and credits, and will differ because of the availability of investment tax credits.

As a U.S. corporation, all of Citicorp's foreign pre-tax earnings are subject to domestic taxation currently if earned by a foreign branch, or when earnings are effectively repatriated, if earned by a foreign subsidiary or affiliate. For 1983, foreign pre-tax earnings represented 73% of consolidated pre-tax income (approximately 100% in 1982 and 1981). In addition, certain of Citicorp's domestic income is subject to foreign income tax where the payor of such income is domiciled overseas.

Deferred taxes result from timing differences in the recognition of revenue and expense for tax and financial accounting purposes.

Components of Deferred Taxes

IN MILLIONS OF DOLLARS FOR THE YEAR	1983	1982	1981
Lease financing transactions	$(4)	$29	$ 28
Loan loss deduction	(27)	(7)	(8)
Interest income	(1)	(4)	(19)
Domestic taxes on overseas income:			
Foreign tax credits	34	55	(89)
Other	(43)	(38)	(41)
Investment tax credits	63	(15)	(28)
Other	65	(9)	36
TOTAL	$87	$ 11	$(121)

Analysis of Effective Rate

FOR THE YEAR	1983	1982	1981
U.S. federal income tax rate	46.0%	46.0%	46.0%
Changes from statutory rate resulting from:			
Tax-exempt interest income	(2.6%)	(4.1%)	(5.6%)
Equity-for-Debt Exchange	—	—	(2.3%)
Income subject to tax at capital gains rates	(.9%)	(.5%)	(1.8%)
State and local income taxes, net of U.S. federal income tax benefit	1.1%	.6%	1.3%
Taxes on income of overseas subsidiaries	1.8%	3.5%	1.0%
Income from 20%- to 50%-owned affiliates included on an after-tax basis	(1.7%)	(.9%)	(.7%)
Translation loss on foreign branch taxes	3.8%	—	—
Other	(1.0%)	(2.4%)	(3.2%)
TOTAL*	46.5%	42.2%	34.7%

*U.S. Federal income taxes in these analyses do not include amounts which, in the opinion of management, represent a de facto additional Federal tax burden that is paid currently. Banks effectively incur this tax in the form of earnings remitted to the U.S. Treasury by the Federal Reserve, representing the Fed's investment earnings on the non-interest bearing reserves that banks are required to maintain with Federal Reserve Banks. For Citicorp, it is estimated that this de facto additional tax approximated $66 million, $82 million and $91 million for the years 1983, 1982 and 1981, respectively, based on average reserve deposits of $866 million, $955 million and $1,074 million in 1983, 1982 and 1981, respectively. The total effective tax rate for such years, adjusted for these amounts and including an equivalent adjustment to increase income before income tax, would be 48.6%, 45.7% and 41.3%, respectively. The de facto additional tax is calculated based on Citicorp's bank subsidiaries' average reserve deposits as a percentage of average total Federal Reserve assets, applied to the earnings remitted to the U.S. Treasury by the Federal Reserve. While no single method can precisely quantify this additional Federal tax burden, Citicorp believes the foregoing method is an appropriate estimate of such tax burden.

Not included above is the effect of investments in tax-exempt state and municipal securities, assets which yield lower rates of interest than would be the case if the income was taxable.

Exhibit C   181

14. EARNINGS PER SHARE

The accompanying table shows the calculation of earnings per share on common and common equivalent shares for net income after deduction of dividends on redeemable preferred stock and preferred stock. Shares issuable under stock option grants and stock purchase plan subscriptions which give staff members the alternative to purchase either market value or book value shares are either included as common equivalent shares or enter into the earnings per share calculation according to the two-class method based upon the economically preferable alternative to staff members, as further described in the Statement of Accounting Policies.

Calculation of Earnings Per Share

IN MILLIONS OF DOLLARS, EXCEPT PER SHARE AMOUNTS	1983	1982	1981
Net Income Available for Common Stockholders			
a. Distributed portion (dividends)	$234	$217	$193
b. Undistributed portion	589	502	334
TOTAL	$823	$719	$527
Shares			
Weighted average common shares outstanding—Market value	123.1	124.7	121.8
Weighted average common shares outstanding—Book value	1.7	1.4	1.4
Common stock equivalents[1]	1.2	.4	.4
c. Shares applicable to distributed portion	126.0	126.5	123.6
Book value shares issuable under stock option and stock purchase plans	1.5	2.7	2.1
d. Shares applicable to undistributed portion	127.5	129.2	125.7
Earnings Per Share			
a÷c Distributed portion	$1.86	$1.72	$1.56
b÷d Undistributed portion	4.62	3.88	2.64
TOTAL	$6.48	$5.60	$4.20

[1] Common stock equivalents represent shares issuable under the executive incentive compensation plan and the dilutive effect of market value shares issuable under stock option and stock purchase plans computed using the treasury stock method.

The fully diluted calculation assumes conversion of all outstanding convertible notes. The number of shares issuable on conversion (8.5 million in 1983, 1982 and 1981) is added to the number of shares included in the calculation (resulting in a total of 136.0 million shares in 1983, 137.7 million shares in 1982 and 134.2 million in 1981), and the related after-tax interest expense ($10.8 million in 1983 and $10.9 million in 1982 and 1981) is eliminated.

15. PLEDGED ASSETS

IN MILLIONS OF DOLLARS AT YEAR END	1983
U.S. Treasury and federal agency securities	$ 6,681
State and municipal securities	493
Other	3,786
TOTAL	$10,960

Certain investment securities, trading account assets and other assets are subject to repurchase agreements and are pledged to secure public and trust deposits and for other purposes.

16. GEOGRAPHIC DISTRIBUTION OF REVENUE, EARNINGS AND ASSETS

Citicorp attributes its net interest and other operating revenue, income before taxes, net income and average total assets to operations based on the domicile of the customer. U.S. possessions are included in their respective geographic areas.

Because of the integration of global activities, it is not practicable to make a precise separation, and various assumptions must be made in arriving at allocations and adjustments to be used in presenting this data.

The principal allocations and adjustments are: (1) charges for all funds employed that are not generated locally are calculated on the amount and nature of the assets and based on a marginal cost of funds concept; Citicorp stockholders' equity is treated as generated and earning based on each area's percentage of total assets; (2) allocation of expenses incurred by one area on behalf of another, including administrative costs, based on methods intended to reflect services provided; (3) allocation of tax expenses at statutory U.S. tax rates, with appropriate adjustments for certain items that are not subject to tax or are taxed at different rates; and (4) allocation of the difference between actual net loan losses and loan loss expense.

Certain components of the corporation's activities are not allocated to geographical areas and are presented in aggregate in the "Other" category. These items primarily include: (1) general corporate expenses, such as corporate-level staff costs (other than those charged to the core businesses), costs associated with corporate-level assets and other expenses not charged to the core businesses (Institutional Banking, Individual Banking and the Capital Markets Group); (2) the earnings and funding costs related to the investment securities portfolio that is managed at the corporate level; and (3) tax expenses retained at the corporate level after the allocation for tax expenses discussed above.

The Securities and Exchange Commission requires that an allowance for loan losses applicable to loans related to foreign activities be disclosed in a note to the financial statements. Citicorp makes no such allocation, and no portion of the allowance for possible losses on commercial loans or allowance for consumer credit losses is restricted to any individual loans or groups of loans. For the purpose of meeting the requirement under generally accepted accounting principles to calculate earnings and assets attributable to foreign operations, $301 million at December 31, 1983, $251 million at December 31, 1982 and $194 million at December 31, 1981 of such allowances is allocated to foreign operations. In the judgment of management, such allocation is not meaningful, since the entire amount of each allowance is available to absorb losses with respect to both domestic and foreign loans.

Geographic Distribution of Revenue, Earnings and Assets[5]

IN MILLIONS OF DOLLARS	TOTAL REVENUE[1]			INCOME BEFORE TAXES			NET INCOME						AVERAGE TOTAL ASSETS
	1983	1982	1981	1983	1982	1981	1983	1982	1981	1983	1982	1981	
North America[2]	**$2,992**	$2,386	$1,953	**$ 685**[4]	$ 354[4]	$294[4]	**$411**	$218	$183	**$ 55,021**	$ 46,923	$ 41,863	
Caribbean, Central and South America[3]	**1,018**	1,017	835	**490**	463	363	**282**	268	216	**18,516**	18,682	17,820	
Europe, Middle East and Africa	**1,182**	1,253	915	**347**	487	319	**204**	270	184	**30,461**	30,813	32,539	
Asia/Pacific	**718**	649	595	**346**	323	283	**191**	180	162	**22,438**	20,404	16,517	
Other	**(27)**	(184)	(245)	**(262)**	(377)	(447)	**(228)**	(213)	(214)	**1,487**	4,660	7,156	
TOTAL	**$5,883**	$5,121	$4,053	**$1,606**	$1,250	$812	**$860**	$723	$531	**$127,923**	$121,482	$115,895	

(1) Includes Net Interest Revenue and Fees, Commissions and Other Revenue.
(2) Includes amounts attributed to United States operations (in 1983, 1982 and 1981, respectively) as follows: total revenue, $2,915 million, $2,339 million and $1,935 million; income before taxes, $649 million, $343 million and $302 million; net income, $392 million, $215 million and $185 million; and average total assets, $52,370 million, $44,456 million and $39,744 million.
(3) Includes amounts attributed to Brazil operations (in 1983, 1982 and 1981, respectively) as follows: total revenue, $401 million, $452 million and $344 million; income before taxes, $297 million, $322 million and $222 million; net income, $168 million, $174 million and $124 million; and average total assets denominated in cruzeiros and other currencies, $6,058 million, $5,591 million and $4,858 million.
(4) In North America, income before taxes includes approximately $69 million in 1983, $95 million in 1982 and $117 million in 1981 of tax-exempt income, reducing the federal income tax provision attributed to the United States.
(5) Prior years' amounts have been reclassified to conform to the 1983 presentation.

Exhibit C 183

17. COMMITMENTS AND CONTINGENT LIABILITIES

In the normal course of business there are outstanding various commitments and contingent liabilities, such as lease commitments, commitments to extend credit, future foreign exchange contracts, letters of credit and guarantees, which are not reflected in the financial statements. Management of Citicorp does not anticipate any material loss as a result of these transactions.

Standby letters of credit, issued primarily by Citibank for the account of major customers, are obligations to make payments for customers' accounts under certain conditions to meet contingencies related to customers' obligations, including performance of contractual commitments. At December 31, 1983, outstanding standby letters of credit participated to other financial institutions or supported by collateral, primarily marketable securities, totalled approximately $6,615 million. Other standby letters of credit totalled approximately $10,658 million. Approximately 49% of total outstanding standby letters of credit as of December 31, 1983 had been issued on behalf of domestic customers and 51% had been issued on behalf of overseas customers.

Citicorp and its subsidiaries are obligated under a number of noncancelable leases for premises and equipment, most of which have renewal or purchase options. Minimum rental commitments on noncancelable leases are $104 million in 1984, $95 million in 1985, $86 million in 1986, $78 million in 1987, $75 million in 1988 and $400 million thereafter, totaling $838 million. Rental expense was $194 million in 1983, $177 million in 1982 and $141 million in 1981.

Various legal proceedings are pending against Citicorp and its subsidiaries. Management of Citicorp considers that the aggregate liability, if any, resulting from these proceedings will not be material.

18. STOCKHOLDER'S EQUITY OF CITIBANK, N.A.

Authorized capital stock of Citibank was 40 million shares at December 31, 1983, 1982 and 1981.

Changes in Stockholder's Equity

IN MILLIONS OF DOLLARS	1983	1982	1981
Balance at Beginning of Year	**$5,485**	$4,871	$4,438
Additions			
Net income	$ 756	$ 883	$ 674
Other additions, net	7	26	4
	$ 763	$ 909	$ 678
Deductions			
Dividends declared	$ 272	$ 252	$ 231
Foreign currency translation	30	9	—
Write-off of intangibles associated with acquisition of subsidiaries and affiliates.	22	34	14
	$ 324	$ 295	$ 245
BALANCE AT END OF YEAR	**$5,924**	$5,485	$4,871

The Board of Governors of the Federal Reserve System requires that investments by Citibank in overseas subsidiaries and affiliates be carried at a value not in excess of underlying book value. Citibank charges retained earnings with the amount of goodwill associated with these investments to the extent required. In accordance with generally accepted accounting principles, such charges are not reflected in the Citicorp financial statements, and the related amounts, net of amortization, aggregating $101 million, $70 million and $77 million at December 31, 1983, 1982, and 1981, respectively, are included in other assets in the Citicorp consolidated balance sheet. Citicorp's equity investment in Citibank amounted to $6,025 million, $5,555 million and $4,948 million at December 31, 1983, 1982 and 1981, respectively.

19. CITICORP (Parent Company Only)

Condensed Balance Sheet

IN MILLIONS OF DOLLARS	DECEMBER 31 1983	DECEMBER 31 1982
Assets		
Deposits with Subsidiary Banks, principally interest bearing	$ 5,521	$ 1,687
Investment Securities at Cost (Market value $207 and $321 in 1983 and 1982, respectively)	232	331
Investments in and Advances to Subsidiaries Other Than Banks	11,359	11,255
Investments in and Advances to Citibank, N.A. and Other Subsidiary Banks	6,860	6,291
Other Assets	203	148
TOTAL	**$24,175**	$19,712
Liabilities and Stockholders' Equity		
Purchased Funds and Other Borrowings	$ 8,036	$ 7,381
Advances from Subsidiaries	2,551	2,691
Other Liabilities	997	819
Debt, Convertible Notes and Redeemable Preferred Stock (Notes 6, 7, 8 and 9)	6,820	4,006
Stockholders' Equity	5,771	4,815
TOTAL	**$24,175**	$19,712

Condensed Statement of Income

IN MILLIONS OF DOLLARS	1983	1982	1981
Revenue			
Dividends from Bank Subsidiaries	$ 272	$ 252	$ 231
Dividends from Other Subsidiaries	—	—	66
Interest from Subsidiaries	1,094	1,103	1,230
Other (principally interest on investment securities)	58	55	259
	$1,424	$1,410	$1,786
Expense			
Interest on Other Borrowed Money	$1,074	$1,092	$1,352
Interest and Fees Paid to Subsidiaries	358	414	356
Interest on Long-Term Debt and Convertible Notes	191	234	247
Other Expense	7	10	7
	$1,630	$1,750	$1,962
Loss before Taxes and Equity in Undistributed Income of Subsidiaries	$ (206)	$ (340)	$ (176)
Applicable Income Tax Benefit—Current	202	211	285
Equity in Undistributed Net Income of Subsidiaries	864	852	422
NET INCOME	**$ 860**	$ 723	$ 531

Condensed Statement of Changes in Financial Position

IN MILLIONS OF DOLLARS	1983	1982	1981
Funds Provided			
Net Income	$ 860	$ 723	$ 531
Deduct Equity in Undistributed Net Income of Subsidiaries	864	852	422
Funds Derived from Operations	$ (4)	$ (129)	$ 109
Decrease in			
Deposits with Subsidiary Banks	—	835	4
Investment Securities	99	1,367	79
Investments in and Advances to Subsidiaries	191	—	—
Increase in			
Purchased Funds and Other Borrowings	655	—	504
Advances from Subsidiaries	—	431	692
Debt, Convertible Notes and Redeemable Preferred Stock	2,814	478	839
Preferred Stock	540	—	—
Other, Net	—	33	7
TOTAL	**$4,295**	$3,015	$2,234
Funds Used			
Cash Dividends Declared	$ 271	$ 222	$ 198
Investments in and Advances to Subsidiaries	—	2,007	2,036
Increase in Deposits with Subsidiary Banks	3,834	—	—
Decrease in Purchased Funds and Other Borrowings	—	786	—
Advances from Subsidiaries	140	—	—
Other, Net	50	—	—
TOTAL	**$4,295**	$3,015	$2,234

Various legal restrictions limit the extent to which certain subsidiaries of Citicorp can supply funds to Citicorp or its other subsidiaries and affiliates. In addition, the approval of the Comptroller of the Currency is required if total dividends declared by a national bank in any calendar year exceed the bank's net profits (as defined) for that year combined with its retained net profits for the preceding two calendar years. Under the formula as it applies to Citicorp's national bank subsidiaries (which at December 31, 1983 have combined net assets of approximately $6.7 billion), Citicorp can receive dividends from such bank subsidiaries in 1984 without approval of the Comptroller of the Currency of approximately $1.2 billion, plus an additional amount equal to their net profits for 1984 up to the date of any such dividend declaration.

Exhibit C   185

The accompanying data have been prepared according to guidelines issued by the Financial Accounting Standards Board to illustrate certain aspects of how inflation affects Citicorp. The data are intended to supplement, but not replace, the basic historical financial statements. The audited financial statements and other traditional financial data included in this report continue to represent Citicorp's actual operating results. The inflation-adjusted data reflect the effects of general inflation using the historical cost/constant dollar method, with the U.S. Consumer Price Index for All Urban Consumers being used to show data in average 1983 dollars. Because Citicorp does not have significant amounts of fixed assets and inventories, current cost information showing the effect of changing prices of specific goods and services does not differ significantly from the constant dollar data and has not been presented.

The assets and liabilities of a financial institution are primarily monetary in nature. As such, they represent obligations to pay or receive fixed and determinable amounts of money which are not affected by future changes in prices. During periods of inflation, monetary assets lose value in terms of purchasing power, while monetary liabilities have corresponding purchasing power gains. The assets of a financial institution also include items such as trading account assets and premises and equipment that are considered nonmonetary and, therefore, do not give rise to purchasing power losses in the inflation-adjusted data. As a result of these nonmonetary assets increasing over the past five years, purchasing power losses from earlier years have changed to purchasing power gains in the past two periods. And, as the accompanying table shows, revenue, earnings and net assets grew over the past five years even after adjusting for the effects of inflation during that period.

1983 CONSTANT DOLLAR DATA

IN MILLIONS OF DOLLARS

Net income, as reported in the consolidated statement of income	$860
Adjustment to restate depreciation for the effects of general inflation[1]	(79)
NET INCOME, ADJUSTED FOR GENERAL INFLATION	**$781**
Purchasing power gain on net monetary liabilities in 1983[1]	$ 16

FINANCIAL DATA RESTATED FOR THE EFFECTS OF GENERAL INFLATION

IN MILLIONS, EXCEPT PER SHARE DATA;
RESTATED AMOUNTS ARE IN AVERAGE
1983 DOLLARS

	1983	1982	1981	1980	1979
Total Revenue[2]					
As reported	$5,883	$5,121	$4,053	$3,702	$3,311
Restated	5,883	5,286	4,440	4,476	4,545
Net Income					
As reported	$ 860	$ 723	$ 531	$ 499	$ 541
Restated	781	676	509	532	673
Net Assets at Year-End					
As reported	$5,771	$4,815	$4,281	$3,891	$3,598
Restated[3]	6,480	5,927	5,445	5,336	5,474
Purchasing Power Gain (Loss) on Net Monetary Liabilities (Assets)[3][4]	$ 16	$ 41	0	$ (98)	$ (164)
Per Share					
Net Income[5]					
As reported	$ 6.48	$ 5.60	$ 4.20	$ 4.02	$ 4.34
Restated	5.86	5.23	4.04	4.28	5.39
Cash Dividends Declared					
As reported	1.88	1.72	1.56	1.42	1.30
Restated	1.88	1.78	1.71	1.72	1.78
Market Price at Year-End					
As reported	37.12	32.50	25.25	24.25	23.75
Restated	36.50	33.17	26.77	28.00	30.83
Average Consumer Price Index (1967=100)	298.4	289.1	272.4	246.8	217.4

(1) Adjustments reflecting the effects of general inflation do not assume any income tax benefit or cost.
(2) Restated in accordance with single step income statement format required by the Securities and Exchange Commission.
(3) Reflects effects of a balance sheet reclassification of certain trading assets previously held in monetary classifications to net trading account assets which is a non-monetary classification. Years 1980 and 1979 were not restated for the effect as the information was not readily available.
(4) Premises and equipment and net trading account assets, among other items, are treated as nonmonetary items.
(5) On common and common equivalent shares.

EARNINGS BY QUARTER

CITICORP AND SUBSIDIARIES

IN MILLIONS OF DOLLARS EXCEPT PER SHARE AMOUNTS	1983				1982			
	4th	3rd	2nd	1st	4th	3rd	2nd	1st
Net Interest Revenue	$1,097	$ 959	$. 971	$1,016	$ 984	$ 941	$ 799	$ 802
Fees, Commissions and								
Other Revenue	471	483	451	435	437	408	335	415
TOTAL REVENUE	$1,568	$1,442	$1,422	$1,451	$1,421	$1,349	$1,134	$1,217
Provision for Possible Losses on								
Commercial Loans	$ 134	$ 30	$ 45	$ 84	$ 113	$ 86	$ 40	$ 45
Consumer Credit Loss Expense	62	59	54	52	55	49	40	45
Operating Expense	1,021	943	914	879	917	856	834	791
TOTAL EXPENSE	$1,217	$1,032	$1,013	$1,015	$1,085	$ 991	$ 914	$ 881
Income before Taxes	$ 351	$ 410	$ 409	$ 436	$ 336	$ 358	$ 220	$ 336
Income Taxes	150	189	199	208	143	159	83	142
NET INCOME	$ 201	$ 221	$ 210	$ 228	$ 193	$ 199	$ 137	$ 194
Per Share[1]								
Net Income								
On Common and Common								
Equivalent Shares	$1.49	$1.66	$1.59	$1.74	$1.49	$1.54	$1.06	$1.51
Assuming Full Dilution	$1.41	$1.58	$1.51	$1.65	$1.42	$1.46	$1.01	$1.44
TOTAL ASSETS	$134,655	$130,542	$130,193	$128,276	$129,997	$128,430	$120,095	$117,332

(1) On net income available for common stockholders after deducting total preferred stock dividends of $12 million in the fourth quarter of 1983, $10 million in the third quarter of 1983, $11 million in the second quarter of 1983, and $4 million in the first quarter of 1983 and $1 million in each quarter of 1982.

COMMON DIVIDENDS

	1983	1982	1981
Cash Dividends Declared (Millions)	$234	$217	$193
Cash Dividends Declared Per Share	$1.88	$1.72	$1.56
Dividends Per Share as a Percentage of Net Income Per Share	29.0%	30.7%	37.1%

COMMON DIVIDENDS BY QUARTER

	1983				1982			
	4th	3rd	2nd	1st	4th	3rd	2nd	1st
Cash Dividends Declared (Millions)	$59	$58	$58	$59	$55	$54	$54	$54
Cash Dividends Declared Per Share	.47	.47	.47	.47	.43	.43	.43	.43

CITICORP COMMON STOCK PRICE RANGE

	1983				1982		
QUARTER	HIGH	LOW	CLOSE	QUARTER	HIGH	LOW	CLOSE
4th	37¹/₂	30¹/₂	37¹/₈	4th	40	27³/₈	32¹/₂
3rd	40¹/₂	34⁵/₈	35⁷/₈	3rd	27⁷/₈	21¹/₂	27¹/₂
2nd	46¹/₈	37⁷/₈	39¹/₂	2nd	29⁵/₈	24¹/₄	25¹/₈
1st	42¹/₂	32¹/₂	41¹/₄	1st	27⁵/₈	23³/₈	25⁷/₈

Exhibit C 187

AVERAGE BALANCES AND INTEREST RATES

TAXABLE EQUIVALENT BASIS

CITICORP AND SUBSIDIARIES

IN MILLIONS OF DOLLARS	1983 AVERAGE VOLUME	INTEREST	% AVERAGE RATE	1982 AVERAGE VOLUME	INTEREST	% AVERAGE RATE	1981 AVERAGE VOLUME	INTEREST	% AVERAGE RATE
INTEREST REVENUE									
Loans and Lease Financing (Net of Unearned Discount)									
Commercial Loans[1]									
In Domestic Offices									
Commercial and Industrial	$ 16,285	$ 1,960	12.04	$ 16,287	$ 2,409	14.79	$ 14,352	$ 2,489	17.34
Mortgage and Real Estate	3,421	372	10.86	2,742	359	13.09	2,385	369	15.49
Loans to Financial Institutions	2,198	234	10.63	1,394	180	12.91	1,254	188	15.00
In Overseas Offices	38,677	5,703	14.75	38,387	6,589	17.17	36,876	7,078	19.20
Total Commercial Loans	$ 60,581	$ 8,269	13.65	$ 58,810	$ 9,537	16.22	$ 54,867	$10,124	18.45
Consumer Loans[1]									
In Domestic Offices	$ 19,616	$ 2,847	14.51	$ 14,585	$ 2,121	14.54	$ 11,799	$ 1,671	14.16
In Overseas Offices	5,307	938	17.68	5,208	970	18.63	4,909	916	18.67
Total Consumer Loans	$ 24,923	$ 3,785	15.19	$ 19,793	$ 3,091	15.62	$ 16,708	$ 2,587	15.48
Total Loans	$ 85,504	$12,054	14.10	$ 78,603	$12,628	16.07	$ 71,575	$12,711	17.76
Lease Financing	1,774	362	20.39	1,793	370	20.64	1,851	340	18.36
Total Loans and Lease Financing	$ 87,278	$12,416	14.23	$ 80,396	$12,998	16.17	$ 73,426	$13,051	17.77
Funds Sold and Resale Agreements	$ 4,297	$ 757	17.62	$ 3,169	$ 520	16.41	$ 2,555	$ 441	17.26
Investment Securities									
In Domestic Offices									
U.S. Treasury and Federal Agencies	$ 2,187	$ 245	11.18	$ 2,168	$ 250	11.53	$ 3,901	$ 425	10.89
State and Municipal	454	59	13.00	691	96	13.89	683	92	13.53
Other	382	26	6.76	402	39	9.70	397	40	10.09
In Overseas Offices (Principally local government issues)	1,924	232	12.06	1,835	224	12.21	1,946	230	11.79
Total	$ 4,947	$ 562	11.35	$ 5,096	$ 609	11.95	$ 6,927	$ 787	11.36
Trading Account Assets									
U.S. Treasury and Federal Agencies	$ 749	$ 78	10.43	$ 1,243	$ 161	12.95	$ 1,804	$ 251	13.93
State and Municipal	218	26	11.99	195	29	14.87	147	23	15.74
Other (Principally in overseas offices)	2,228	366	16.43	1,776	339	19.06	1,594	293	18.35
Total	$ 3,195	$ 470	14.72	$ 3,214	$ 529	16.45	$ 3,545	$ 567	15.99
Interest-Bearing Deposits (Principally in overseas offices)	$ 10,702	$ 1,074	10.04	$ 11,950	$ 1,619	13.55	$ 12,569	$ 1,906	15.17
Total Earning Assets	$110,419	$15,279	13.84	$103,825	$16,275	15.68	$ 99,022	$16,752	16.92
Non-Interest Earning Assets	17,504			17,657			16,873		
TOTAL ASSETS	$127,923			$121,482			$115,895		
INTEREST EXPENSE									
Deposits									
In Domestic Offices									
Savings Deposits	$ 6,252	$ 479	7.66	$ 2,062	$ 105	5.09	$ 1,983	$ 99	5.01
Negotiable Certificates of Deposit	3,525	326	9.26	4,699	593	12.62	2,762	428	15.49
Other Time Deposits	9,808	1,008	10.27	8,136	1,042	12.81	6,639	952	14.34
Total Domestic Interest-Bearing Deposits	$ 19,585	$ 1,813	9.26	$ 14,897	$ 1,740	11.68	$ 11,384	$ 1,479	13.00
In Overseas Offices	47,735	5,081	10.65	48,578	6,765	13.93	48,697	8,112	16.66
Total	$ 67,320	$ 6,894	10.24	$ 63,475	$ 8,505	13.40	$ 60,081	$ 9,591	15.96
Funds Borrowed									
In Domestic Offices									
Purchased Funds and Other Borrowings									
Federal Funds Purchased and Securities Sold Under Agreements to Repurchase	$ 8,379	$ 809	9.66	$ 9,331	$ 1,097	11.76	$ 10,936	$ 1,738	15.89
Commercial Paper	3,766	344	9.14	4,859	614	12.64	4,867	803	16.51
Other Purchased Funds	4,951	483	9.75	2,609	337	12.92	1,912	280	14.63
Intermediate-Term Debt	3,868	449	11.62	1,739	248	14.26	922	143	15.51
Long-Term Debt and Convertible Notes	2,620	241	9.20	2,620	283	10.80	2,654	309	11.63
Total in Domestic Offices	$ 23,584	$ 2,326	9.86	$ 21,158	$ 2,579	12.19	$ 21,291	$ 3,273	15.37
In Overseas Offices	7,976	1,934	24.24	8,440	1,563	18.52	7,713	1,315	17.05
Total	$ 31,560	$ 4,260	13.50	$ 29,598	$ 4,142	13.99	$ 29,004	$ 4,588	15.82
Total Interest-Bearing Liabilities	$ 98,880	$11,154	11.28	$ 93,073	$12,647	13.59	$ 89,085	$14,179	15.92
Demand Deposits in Domestic Offices	6,867			6,675			8,615		
Other Non-Interest-Bearing Liabilities	16,824			17,191			14,168		
Total Stockholders' Equity	5,352			4,543			4,027		
TOTAL LIABILITIES AND STOCKHOLDERS' EQUITY	$127,923			$121,482			$115,895		
NET INTEREST REVENUE AS A PERCENTAGE OF AVERAGE INTEREST-EARNING ASSETS		$ 4,125	3.74		$ 3,628	3.49		$ 2,573	2.60
Average Common Stockholders' Equity as a Percentage of Average Total Assets		3.9%			3.7%			3.5%	

(1) Loan fees are included in appropriate loan categories; such fees were $416 in 1983, $358 in 1982 and $315 in 1981.
(2) The taxable equivalent adjustment is based on the marginal tax rate of 46%.

ANALYSIS OF CHANGES IN NET INTEREST REVENUE
TAXABLE EQUIVALENT BASIS

| | 1983 vs. 1982 | | | 1982 vs. 1981 | | |
| | INCREASE (DECREASE) DUE TO CHANGE IN: | | | INCREASE (DECREASE) DUE TO CHANGE IN: | | |
IN MILLIONS OF DOLLARS	AVERAGE VOLUME	AVERAGE RATE	NET CHANGE*	AVERAGE VOLUME	AVERAGE RATE	NET CHANGE*
Loans—Commercial	$ 297	$(1,565)	$(1,268)	$ 859	$(1,446)	$ (587)
Loans—Consumer	776	(82)	694	481	23	504
Lease Financing	(4)	(4)	(8)	(11)	41	30
Funds Sold & Resale Agreements	197	40	237	114	(35)	79
Investment Securities	(17)	(30)	(47)	(221)	43	(178)
Trading Account Assets	(3)	(56)	(59)	(54)	16	(38)
Interest-Bearing Deposits	(157)	(388)	(545)	(91)	(196)	(287)
TOTAL INTEREST REVENUE	$1,089	$(2,085)	$ (996)	$1,077	$(1,554)	$ (477)
Deposits	$ 556	$(2,167)	$(1,611)	$ 591	$(1,677)	$(1,086)
Funds Borrowed	251	(133)	118	96	(542)	(446)
TOTAL INTEREST EXPENSE	$ 807	$(2,300)	$(1,493)	$ 687	$(2,219)	$(1,532)
NET INTEREST REVENUE	$ 282	$ 215	$ 497	$ 390	$ 665	$ 1,055

(1) Rate/Volume variance is allocated based on the percentage relationship of changes in volume and changes in rate to the total "Net Change."

INVESTMENT SECURITIES
CARRYING VALUE AND YIELD** BY MATURITY DATE AS OF DECEMBER 31, 1983

| | U.S. TREASURY | | FEDERAL AGENCIES | | STATE AND MUNICIPAL | | OTHER (PRINCIPALLY IN OVERSEAS OFFICES) | |
IN MILLIONS OF DOLLARS	AMOUNT	YIELD	AMOUNT	YIELD	AMOUNT	YIELD	AMOUNT	YIELD
Due Within 1 Year	$ 813	10.36%	$ 78	9.94%	$ 4	3.50%	$1,297	*
After 1 but Within 5 Years	820	10.73%	266	11.47%	21	3.86%	865	*
After 5 but Within 10 Years	153	11.30%	16	11.88%	77	6.52%	314	*
After 10 Years	158	12.37%	519	9.97%	375	6.86%	58	*
TOTAL	$1,944	10.76%	$ 879	10.52%	$477	6.67%	$2,534	*
Carrying Value and Yield** As of December 31, 1982	$1,004	12.46%	$1,013	11.50%	$646	6.86%	$2,108	*
Carrying Value and Yield** As of December 31, 1981	$2,531	11.05%	$ 908	11.47%	$786	7.36%	$2,294	*

*Yield information not readily available.
**Computed by dividing annual interest (net of amortization of premium or accretion of discount) by the carrying value of the respective investment securities at December 31, 1983, 1982 and 1981.

Exhibit C 189

LOANS AND LEASE FINANCING OUTSTANDING

IN MILLIONS OF DOLLARS AT YEAR END	1983	1982	1981	1980	1979
Commercial					
In Domestic Offices					
Commercial and Industrial[1]	$14,910	$17,817	$16,104	$14,340	$13,243
Mortgage and Real Estate[2]	3,975	2,915	2,635	2,057	1,436
Loans to Financial Institutions	2,341	2,623	1,287	1,425	1,369
	$21,226	$23,355	$20,026	$17,822	$16,048
In Overseas Offices					
Commercial and Industrial[1]	$27,592	$29,590	$29,462	$26,603	$24,745
Mortgage and Real Estate[2]	1,822	2,745	2,659	2,402	2,053
Loans to Financial Institutions	5,914	4,151	3,403	2,790	2,024
Governments and Official Institutions	4,074	3,140	3,635	5,066	4,917
	$39,402	$39,626	$39,159	$36,861	$33,739
	$60,628	$62,981	$59,185	$54,683	$49,787
Unearned Discount	(386)	(463)	(423)	(407)	(270)
Allowance for Possible Losses on Commercial Loans	(540)	(490)	(400)	(359)	(328)
Commercial Loans, Net	$59,702	$62,028	$58,362	$53,917	$49,189
Consumer					
In Domestic Offices					
Mortgage and Real Estate[2]	$10,751	$ 9,261	$ 5,925	$ 4,317	$ 3,195
Installment, revolving credit and other[1]	15,418	11,213	9,556	8,435	7,542
	$26,169	$20,474	$15,481	$12,752	$10,737
In Overseas Offices	6,856	6,824	6,806	6,116	5,188
	$33,025	$27,298	$22,287	$18,868	$15,925
Unearned Discount	(4,030)	(4,093)	(3,759)	(3,057)	(2,448)
Allowance for Consumer Credit Losses	(226)	(190)	(173)	(147)	(129)
Consumer Loans, Net	$28,769	$23,015	$18,355	$15,664	$13,348
Lease Financing					
Lease Financing, Net of Unearned Income	$ 1,817	$ 1,855	$ 1,891	$ 1,855	$ 1,553
Allowance for Lease Losses	(5)	(7)	(8)	(7)	(4)
Lease Financing, Net	$ 1,812	$ 1,848	$ 1,883	$ 1,848	$ 1,549
TOTAL LOANS AND LEASE FINANCING, NET	$90,283	$86,891	$78,600	$71,429	$64,086

(1) Includes loans not otherwise separately categorized.
(2) Includes only loans secured primarily by real estate.

LOAN MATURITIES AND SENSITIVITY TO CHANGES IN INTEREST RATES

THE MATURITIES OF THE GROSS COMMERCIAL LOAN PORTFOLIO AS OF DECEMBER 31, 1983 ARE AS FOLLOWS: IN MILLIONS OF DOLLARS	DUE WITHIN 1 YEAR	OVER 1 BUT WITHIN 5 YEARS	OVER 5 YEARS	TOTAL
In Domestic Offices				
Commercial and Industrial Loans	$10,354	$ 2,651	$1,905	**$14,910**
Mortgage and Real Estate	1,899	895	1,181	**3,975**
All Other Loans	1,582	450	309	**2,341**
In International Offices	24,143	10,264	4,995	**39,402**
TOTAL	$37,978	$14,260	$8,390	**$60,628**
The following table represents the sensitivity of the above loans due after one year to changes in interest rates:				
Loans at Predetermined Interest Rates		$ 5,178	$3,890	
Loans at Floating or Adjustable Interest Rates		9,082	4,500	
TOTAL		$14,260	$8,390	

DETAIL OF COMMERCIAL LOAN LOSS EXPERIENCE

IN MILLIONS OF DOLLARS	1983	1982	1981	1980	1979
ALLOWANCE FOR POSSIBLE LOSSES ON COMMERCIAL LOANS AT BEGINNING OF YEAR	**$490**	$400	$359	$328	$304
Deductions					
Gross Loan Losses					
Domestic Real Estate	$ **3**	$ 4	$ 6	$ 2	$ 20
International Real Estate	**11**	8	4	1	—
Governments and Official Institutions	**47**	11	—	—	—
Loans to Financial Institutions	**23**	—	3	2	2
Commercial and Industrial:					
Domestic	**81**	91	46	66	42
International	**127**	131	68	38	55
	$292	$245	$127	$109	$119
Loan Recoveries					
Domestic Real Estate	$ **10**	$ 11	$ 12	$ 19	$ 2
International Real Estate	**1**	1	12	8	8
Governments and Official Institutions	**—**	—	—	—	—
Loans to Financial Institutions	**8**	9	8	8	2
Commercial and Industrial:					
Domestic	**11**	3	16	10	17
International	**21**	29	19	15	30
	$ **51**	$ 53	$ 67	$ 60	$ 59
Net Loan Losses					
Domestic	$ **55**	$ 72	$ 19	$ 31	$ 43
International	**186**	120	41	18	17
	$241	$192	$ 60	$ 49	$ 60
Additions					
Provision for Possible Losses on Commercial Loans	**$293**	$284	$102	$ 86	$ 83
Other Additions (Deductions) (Principally from sale of companies and adjustments relating to the translation of international balances)	**(2)**	(2)	(1)	(6)	1
	$291	$282	$101	$ 80	$ 84
ALLOWANCE FOR POSSIBLE LOSSES ON COMMERCIAL LOANS AT END OF YEAR	**$540**	$490	$400	$359	$328
Excess of Provision over Net Loan Losses	$ **52**	$ 92	$ 42	$ 37	$ 23
Cumulative Excess of Provision over Net Loan Losses (since 1978)	**$246**	$194	$102	$ 60	$ 23
Cumulative Increase in Allowance (since 1978)	**$236**	$186	$ 96	$ 55	$ 24

Exhibit C   191

DETAIL OF CONSUMER CREDIT LOSS EXPERIENCE[2]

IN MILLIONS OF DOLLARS	1983	1982	1981	1980	1979
ALLOWANCE FOR CONSUMER CREDIT LOSSES AT BEGINNING OF YEAR	**$190**	$173	$147	$129	$103

Deductions

Gross Loan Losses

Domestic	**$210**	$197	$207	$211	$160
International	**73**	69	63	51	45
	$283	$266	$270	$262	$205

Loan Recoveries

Domestic	**$ 67**	$ 62	$ 57	$ 47	$ 43
International	**20**	20	17	20	37
	$ 87	$ 82	$ 74	$ 67	$ 80

Net Loan Losses

Domestic	**$143**	$135	$150	$164	$117
International	**53**	49	46	31	8[1]
	$196	$184	$196	$195	$125

Additions

Consumer Credit Loss Expense	**$227**	$189	$203	$212	$151
Other Additions (Principally Balances of Acquired Companies)	**5**	12	19	—	—
	$232	$201	$222	$212	$151
ALLOWANCE FOR CONSUMER CREDIT LOSSES AT END OF YEAR	**$226**	$190	$173	$147	$129
Cumulative Excess of Consumer Credit Loss Expense over Net Loan Losses (since 1978)	**$ 86**	$ 55	$ 50	$ 43	$ 26
Cumulative Increase in Allowance (since 1978)	**$123**	$ 87	$ 70	$ 44	$ 26

(1) Includes a $25 million reduction to reflect a more realistic estimate of credit losses and recoveries of an overseas subsidiary.
(2) Consumer loan losses primarily relate to installment and revolving credit loans.

TIME DEPOSITS

IN DOMESTIC OFFICES ($100,000 OR MORE) IN MILLIONS OF DOLLARS AT YEAR END	CERTIFICATES OF DEPOSITS	OTHER TIME DEPOSITS
Under 3 months	$1,975	$1,638
3 to 6 months	1,254	140
6 to 12 months	401	148
Over 12 months	406	379

AVERAGE DEPOSIT LIABILITIES IN OVERSEAS OFFICES

	1983		1982		1981	
IN MILLIONS OF DOLLARS	AVERAGE BALANCE	% AVERAGE INTEREST RATE	AVERAGE BALANCE	% AVERAGE INTEREST RATE	AVERAGE BALANCE	% AVERAGE INTEREST RATE
Banks[1]	$19,352	10.38	$21,509	13.69	$24,430	16.12
Other demand deposits	6,667	4.25	5,364	6.95	5,486	8.58
Other time and savings deposits[1]	24,008	11.62	25,466	13.54	22,216	16.67
TOTAL	**$50,027**	**10.16**	$52,339	12.93	$52,132	15.56

(1) Primarily consists of time certificates of deposit and other time deposits in denominations of $100,000 or more.

PROPERTIES

The principal offices of Citicorp and Citibank, N.A. ("Citibank") are located at 399 Park Avenue, New York, New York, a 39-story building owned by Citibank. Citibank also owns Citicorp Center, a 59-story building located at 153 East 53rd Street across from 399 Park Avenue. Approximately 66% of the Citicorp Center and 399 Park Avenue complex is occupied by Citicorp. In addition, Citibank also owns other properties in New York, including 111 Wall Street which is totally occupied by Citicorp and its affiliates and 55 Wall Street, a 9-story building of which 35% is so occupied. Of the approximately 1,900 offices and other facilities of Citicorp located throughout the world, approximately 346 are owned and the balance are leased.

CONSENT OF INDEPENDENT AUDITORS

 PEAT MARWICK

Peat, Marwick, Mitchell & Co.
Certified Public Accountants

The Board of Directors
Citicorp:

We consent to incorporation by reference of our report dated January 17, 1984, relating to the consolidated balance sheet of Citicorp and subsidiaries as of December 31, 1983 and 1982 and the related consolidated statements of income, changes in stockholders' equity and changes in financial position for each of the years in the three-year period ended December 31, 1983 and the consolidated balance sheet of Citibank, N.A. and subsidiaries as of December 31, 1983 and 1982, which report appears on page 32 of the 1983 Citicorp Annual Report and Form 10-K, in the following Registration Statements: of Citicorp, Nos. 2-47648, 2-58678, 2-77058 and 2-82298 on Form S-8 and Nos. 2-80820, 2-89518 and 2-82265 on Form S-3; of Citicorp Homeowners, Inc. No. 2-75944 on Form S-11, and of Citibank, N.A. No. 2-80415 on Form S-11.

Peat, Marwick, Mitchell & Co.

New York, New York
March 2, 1984

EXHIBITS, FINANCIAL STATEMENT SCHEDULES, AND REPORTS ON FORM 8-K

Financial Statements Filed:
Citicorp and Subsidiaries:
Consolidated Statement of Income
Consolidated Balance Sheet
Consolidated Statement of Changes in
    Stockholders' Equity
Consolidated Statement of Changes in Financial Position

Citicorp filed no Form 8-K Current Report for any month in the year ended December 31, 1983.

Citicorp's significant subsidiaries (as defined) and their place of incorporation or organization include:

Citibank, N.A.	United States
Citibank (South Dakota), N.A.	United States
Citicorp Banking Corporation	Delaware

Other subsidiaries of Citicorp and their place of incorporation or organization include:

Citibank (Delaware)	Delaware
Citibank (New York State), N.A.	United States
Citicorp International Group, Inc.	Delaware

Citicorp's Articles of Incorporation and By-laws, Instruments Defining the Rights of Securities Holders, including Indentures and constituent instruments relating to various executive and staff benefit plans, have been previously filed with the Commission as Exhibits to various Citicorp registration statements.

Stockholders may obtain copies of such documents by writing Citicorp, Office of the Secretary, 399 Park Avenue, New York, New York 10043.

Exhibit C   193

SIGNATURES

Pursuant to the requirements of Section 13 or 15(d) of the Securities Exchange Act of 1934, the registrant has duly caused this report to be signed on its behalf by the undersigned, thereunto duly authorized.

CITICORP
(Registrant)

Paul Kolterjahn

Paul Kolterjahn
Senior Vice President—Secretary

March 2, 1984

Pursuant to the requirements of the Securities Exchange Act of 1934, this report has been signed on March 2, 1984 by the following persons in the capacities indicated.

D.S. Howard

Donald S. Howard
Executive Vice President
(Principal Financial Officer)

Thomas E. Jones

Thomas E. Jones
Senior Vice President and Chief Accounting Officer
(Principal Accounting Officer)

Walter B. Wriston (Citicorp's Principal Executive Officer) and the Directors of Citicorp (listed below) executed a power of attorney appointing Paul Kolterjahn their attorney-in-fact, empowering him to sign this report on their behalf.

Hans H. Angermueller
James H. Evans
Lawrence E. Fouraker
Arthur Furer
Clifton C. Garvin, Jr.
J. Peter Grace
Harry J. Gray
John W. Hanley
John P. Harbin
Robert S. Hatfield
Amory Houghton, Jr.
Juanita Kreps
C. Peter McColough
Roger Milliken
Charles M. Pigott
John S. Reed
Donald V. Seibert
Irving S. Shapiro
Eleanor H.B. Sheldon
Mario Henrique Simonsen
Darwin E. Smith
Thomas C. Theobald
Franklin A. Thomas
Walter B. Wriston

Exhibit D
Federal Financial Institutions Examination Council: Consolidated Reports
of Condition and Income,
with Supporting Schedules, Revised
Effective March 31, 1984

Consolidated Reports of Condition and Income for
A Bank With Domestic and Foreign Offices

Table of Contents

Board of Governors of the Federal Reserve System
Federal Deposit Insurance Corporation
Office of the Comptroller of the Currency

Consolidated Report of Condition for All Insured Commercial Banks

All schedules are to be reported in thousands of dollars. Unless otherwise indicated, report the amount outstanding as of the last business day of the quarter.

Schedule RC—Balance Sheet

Dollar Amounts in Thousands		Bil	Mil	Thou	
ASSETS					
1. Cash and balances due from depository institutions (from Schedule RC-A):					
a. Noninterest-bearing balances and currency and coin	RCON 0000				1.a.
b. Interest-bearing balances	RCON 0000				1.b.
2. Securities (from Schedule RC-B)	RCON 0000				2.
3. Federal funds sold and securities purchased under agreements to resell in domestic offices of the bank and of its Edge and Agreement subsidiaries, and in IBFs	RCON 0000				3.
4. Loans and lease financing receivables:					
a. Loans and leases, net of unearned income (from Schedule RC-C)	RCON 0000				4.a.
b. LESS: Allowance for loan and lease losses	RCON 0000				4.b.
c. Loans and leases, net of unearned income and allowance for losses					4.c.
5. Assets held in trading accounts	RCON 0000				5.
6. Premises and fixed assets (including capitalized leases)	RCON 0000				6.
7. Other real estate owned	RCON 0000				7.
8. Investments in unconsolidated subsidiaries and associated companies	RCON 0000				8.
9. Customers' liability to this bank on acceptances outstanding	RCON 0000				9.
10. Intangible assets	RCON 0000				10.
11. Other assets (from Schedule RC-F)	RCON 0000				11.
12. Total assets (sum of items 1 through 11)	RCON 0000				12.
LIABILITIES					
13. Deposits:					
a. In domestic offices (sum of totals of columns A and C, Schedule RC-E, part I)	RCON 0000				13.a.
(1) Noninterest-bearing	RCON 0000				13.a.(1)
(2) Interest-bearing	RCON 0000				13.a.(2)
b. In foreign offices, Edge and Agreement subsidiaries, and IBFs (from Schedule RC-E, part II)	RCON 0000				13.b.
(1) Noninterest-bearing	RCON 0000				13.b.(1)
(2) Interest-bearing	RCON 0000				13.b.(2)
14. Federal funds purchased and securities sold under agreements to repurchase in domestic offices of the bank and of its Edge and Agreement subsidiaries, and in IBFs	RCON 0000				14.
15. Demand notes issued to the U.S. Treasury	RCON 0000				15.
16. Other borrowed money	RCON 0000				16.
17. Mortgage indebtedness and obligations under capitalized leases	RCON 0000				17.
18. Bank's liability on acceptances executed and outstanding	RCON 0000				18.
19. Notes and debentures subordinated to deposits	RCON 0000				19.
20. Other liabilities (from Schedule RC-G)	RCON 0000				20.
21. Total liabilities (sum of items 13 through 20)	RCON 0000				21.
22. Limited-life preferred stock	RCON 0000				22.
EQUITY CAPITAL					
23. Perpetual preferred stock	RCON 0000				23.
24. Common stock	RCON 0000				24.
25. Surplus	RCON 0000				25.
26. Undivided profits and capital reserves	RCON 0000				26.
27. Cumulative foreign currency translation adjustments	RCON 0000				27.
28. Total equity capital (sum of items 23 through 27)	RCON 0000				28.
29. Total liabilities, limited-life preferred stock, and equity capital (sum of items 21, 22, and 28)	RCON 0000				29.

Schedule RC-A—Cash and Balances Due From Depository Institutions

Exclude assets held in trading accounts.

Dollar Amounts in Thousands	(Column A) Consolidated Bank			(Column B) Domestic Offices			
	Bil	Mil	Thou	Bil	Mil	Thou	
1. Cash items in process of collection, unposted debits, and currency and coin							1.
a. Cash items in process of collection and unposted debits							1.a.
b. Currency and coin							1.b.
2. Balances due from depository institutions in the U.S.							2.
a. U.S. branches and agencies of foreign banks (including their IBFs)							2.a.
b. Other depository institutions in the U.S. (including their IBFs) . . .							2.b.
3. Balances due from banks in foreign countries and foreign central banks							3.
a. Foreign branches of other U.S. banks							3.a.
b. Other banks in foreign countries and foreign central banks							3.b.
4. Balances due from Federal Reserve Banks							4.
5. Total (sum of items 1 through 4) (Total of column A must equal Schedule RC, item 1)							5.
Memorandum							
1. Noninterest-bearing balances due from commercial banks in the U.S. (included in item 2, column B above)							M.1.

Schedule RC-B—Securities

Exclude assets held in trading accounts.

Dollar Amounts in Thousands	Consolidated Bank						Domestic Offices			
	(Column A) Book Value			(Column B) Market Value[1]			(Column C) Book Value			
	Bil	Mil	Thou	Bil	Mil	Thou	Bil	Mil	Thou	
1. U.S. Treasury securities										1.
2. U.S. Government agency and corporation obligations:										
a. All holdings of U.S. Government-issued or -guaranteed certificates of participation in pools of residential mortgages										2.a.
b. All other										2.b.
3. Securities issued by states and political subdivisions in the U.S.										3.
4. Other domestic securities (debt and equity):										
a. All holdings of private (i.e., nongovernment-issued or -guaranteed) certificates of participation in pools of residential mortgages										4.a.
b. All other										4.b.
5. Foreign securities (debt and equity)										5.
6. Total (sum of items 1 through 5) (Total of column A must equal Schedule RC, item 2)										6.
Memorandum										
1. Pledged securities										M.1.

[1] See instructions for this schedule.

Schedule RC-C—Loans and Lease Financing Receivables

Net of unearned income and before adjustment for allowance for loan and lease losses. Exclude assets held in trading accounts.

Dollar Amounts in Thousands	(Column A) Consolidated Bank				(Column B) Domestic Offices			
		Bil	Mil	Thou		Bil	Mil	Thou
1. Loans secured by real estate									1.
a. Construction and land development									1.a.
b. Secured by farmland (including farm residential and other improvements)									1.b.
c. Secured by 1-4 family residential properties									1.c.
d. Secured by multifamily (5 or more) residential properties									1.d.
e. Secured by nonfarm nonresidential properties									1.e.
2. Loans to depository institutions:									
a. To commercial banks in the U.S.									2.a.
(1) To U.S. branches and agencies of foreign banks									2.a.(1)
(2) To other commercial banks in the U.S.									2.a.(2)
b. To other depository institutions in the U.S.									2.b.
c. To banks in foreign countries									2.c.
(1) To foreign branches of other U.S. banks									2.c.(1)
(2) To other banks in foreign countries									2.c.(2)
3. Loans to finance agricultural production and other loans to farmers									3.
4. Commercial and industrial loans:									
a. To U.S. addressees (domicile)									4.a.
b. To non-U.S. addressees (domicile)									4.b.
5. Acceptances of other banks:									
a. Of U.S. banks									5.a.
b. Of foreign banks									5.b.
6. Loans to individuals for household, family, and other personal expenditures (includes purchased paper)									6.
a. Credit cards and related plans									6.a.
b. Other									6.b.
7. Loans to foreign governments and official institutions (including foreign central banks)									7.
8. Obligations (other than securities) of states and political subdivisions in the U.S.:									
a. Nonrated industrial development obligations									8.a.
b. Other obligations (excluding securities)									8.b.
9. Other loans									9.
a. Loans for purchasing or carrying securities (secured and unsecured)									9.a.
b. All other loans									9.b.
10. Lease financing receivables (net of unearned income)									10.
a. Of U.S. addressees (domicile)									10.a.
b. Of non-U.S. addressees (domicile)									10.b.
11. LESS: Any unearned income on loans reflected in items 1-9 above.									11.
12. Total loans and leases, net of unearned income (sum of items 1 through 10 minus item 11)(Total of column A must equal Schedule RC, item 4.a.)									12.
Memorandum									
1. Commercial paper included in Schedule RC-C									M.1.

Schedule RC-D is to be completed only by banks with $1 billion or more in total assets.

Schedule RC-D—Assets Held in Trading Accounts in Domestic Offices Only

Dollar Amounts in Thousands	Domestic Offices			
		Bil	Mil	Thou
1. U.S. Treasury securities.....	RCON 0000				1.
2. U.S. Government agency and corporation obligations	RCON 0000				2.
3. Securities issued by states and political subdivisions in the U.S........................	RCON 0000				3.
4. Other bonds, notes, and debentures	RCON 0000				4.
5. Certificates of deposit	RCON 0000				5.
6. Commercial paper	RCON 0000				6.
7. Bankers acceptances	RCON 0000				7.
8. Other	RCON 0000				8.
9. Total (sum of items 1 through 8)	RCON 0000				9.

Schedule RC-E—Deposit Liabilities

I. Deposits in Domestic Offices

Dollar Amounts in Thousands	Transaction Accounts						Nontransaction Accounts			
	(Column A) Total transaction accounts			(Column B) Memo: Demand deposit component of total transaction accounts			(Column C) Total nontransaction accounts (including MMDAs)			
	Bil	Mil	Thou	Bil	Mil	Thou	Bil	Mil	Thou	
Deposits of:										
1. Individuals, partnerships, and corporations....	RCON 0000			RCON 0000			RCON 0000			1.
2. U.S. Government............................				RCON 0000			RCON 0000			2.
3. States and political subdivisions in the U.S....	RCON 0000			RCON 0000			RCON 0000			3.
4. Commercial banks in the U.S.	RCON 0000									4.
a. U.S. branches and agencies of foreign banks							RCON 0000			4.a.
b. Other commercial banks in the U.S.							RCON 0000			4.b.
5. Other depository institutions in the U.S.	RCON 0000			RCON 0000			RCON 0000			5.
6. Banks in foreign countries	RCON 0000			RCON 0000						6.
a. Foreign branches of other U.S. banks							RCON 0000			6.a.
b. Other banks in foreign countries							RCON 0000			6.b.
7. Foreign governments and official institutions (including foreign central banks).............	RCON 0000			RCON 0000			RCON 0000			7.
8. Certified and official checks				RCON 0000						8.
9. Total (sum of items 1 through 8) (sum of items 9, columns A and C, must equal Schedule RC, item 13.a.)				RCON 0000			RCON 0000			9.

Dollar Amounts in Thousands	Bil	Mil	Thou	
Memoranda				
1. Selected components of total deposits (i.e., sum of items 9, columns A and C):				
a. Total Individual Retirement Accounts (IRAs) and Keogh Plan accounts	RCON 0000			M.1.a.
b. Total brokered deposits	RCON 0000			M.1.b.
c. Total brokered retail deposits (included in memorandum item 1.b. above)............	RCON 0000			M.1.c.
2. Components of total nontransaction accounts (item 9, column C):				
a. Nontransaction savings deposits	RCON 0000			M.2.a.
b. Total time deposits of less than $100,000	RCON 0000			M.2.b.
c. Time certificates of deposit of $100,000 or more	RCON 0000			M.2.c.
d. Open-account time deposits of $100,000 or more	RCON 0000			M.2.d.
3. Deposits that are subject to *fixed* federal interest rate ceilings:				
a. Interest-bearing transaction accounts (included in item 9, column A)................	RCON 0000			M.3.a.
b. Nontransaction savings deposits (included in memorandum item 2.a. above)..........	RCON 0000			M.3.b.
c. Nontransaction time deposits (included in item 9, column C)	RCON 0000			M.3.c.

Schedule RC-E—Continued

II. Deposits in Foreign Offices (including Edge and
Agreement subsidiaries and IBFs)

Dollar Amounts in Thousands		Bil	Mil	Thou	
Deposits of:					
1. Individuals, partnerships, and corporations	RCON 0000				1.
2. U.S. banks (including IBFs and foreign offices of U.S. banks)	RCON 0000				2.
3. Foreign banks (including U.S. branches and agencies of foreign banks, including their IBFs)	RCON 0000				3.
4. Foreign governments and official institutions (including foreign central banks)	RCON 0000				4.
5. Certified and official checks	RCON 0000				5.
6. All other deposits	RCON 0000				6.
7. Total (sum of items 1 through 6) (must equal Schedule RC, item 13.b.)	RCON 0000				7.

Schedule RC-F—Other Assets

Dollar Amounts in Thousands		Bil	Mil	Thou	
1. Income earned, not collected on loans	RCON 0000				1.
2. Net deferred income taxes[1] (if *debit balance*)	RCON 0000				2.
3. Other (itemize amounts that exceed 25% of item 4 of this schedule)					3.
4. Total (sum of items 1 through 3) (must equal Schedule RC, item 11)	RCON 0000				4.

Schedule RC-G—Other Liabilities

Dollar Amounts in Thousands		Bil	Mil	Thou	
1. Expenses accrued and unpaid	RCON 0000				1.
2. Net deferred income taxes[1] (if *credit balance*)	RCON 0000				2.
3. Minority interest in consolidated subsidiaries	RCON 0000				3.
4. Other (itemize amounts that exceed 25% of item 5 of this schedule)	RCON 0000				4.
5. Total (sum of items 1 through 4) (must equal Schedule RC, item 20)	RCON 0000				5.

[1] See discussion of deferred income taxes in Glossary entry on "income taxes."

Schedule RC-H—Selected Balance Sheet Items for Domestic Offices

Dollar Amounts in Thousands	Domestic Offices			
		Bil	Mil	Thou
1. Customers' liability to this bank on acceptances outstanding.............................	RCON 0000				1.
2. Bank's liability on acceptances executed and outstanding...............................	RCON 0000				2.
3. Federal funds sold and securities purchased under agreements to resell	RCON 0000				3.
4. Federal funds purchased and securities sold under agreements to repurchase	RCON 0000				4.
5. Other borrowed money	RCON 0000				5.
EITHER				
6. Net due *from* own foreign offices, Edge and Agreement subsidiaries, and IBFs	RCON 0000				6.
OR				
7. Net due *to* own foreign offices, Edge and Agreement subsidiaries, and IBFs.............	RCON 0000				7.
8. Total assets	RCON 0000				8.
9. Total liabilities	RCON 0000				9.

Memorandum (*to be completed only by banks with IBFs and other "foreign" offices*)
EITHER

		Bil	Mil	Thou	
1. Net due *from* the IBF of the domestic offices of the reporting bank	RCON 0000				M.1.
OR				
2. Net due *to* the IBF of the domestic offices of the reporting bank......................	RCON 0000				M.2.

Schedule RC-I—Selected Assets and Liabilities of IBFs

To be completed only by banks with IBFs *and* other "foreign" offices.

Dollar Amounts in Thousands		Bil	Mil	Thou	
1. Total IBF assets of the consolidated bank (component of Schedule RC, item 12)	RCON 0000				1.
2. Total IBF loans and lease financing receivables (component of Schedule RC-C, item 12, column A)...	RCON 0000				2.
3. IBF commercial and industrial loans (component of Schedule RC-C, item 4, column A).....	RCON 0000				3.
4. Total IBF liabilities (component of Schedule RC, item 21)	RCON 0000				4.
5. IBF deposit liabilities due to banks, including other IBFs (component of Schedule RC-E, part II, items 2 and 3)	RCON 0000				5.
6. Other IBF deposit liabilities (component of Schedule RC-E, part II, items 1, 4, 5, and 6)	RCON 0000				6.

Schedule RC-J—Repricing Opportunities for Selected Balance Sheet Categories

The information required in this schedule represents the distribution across columns A through F of totals reported elsewhere in the Report of Condition (unless the bank's smallest foreign offices have been excluded). Through the December 31, 1984 report date, these *distributions* may be based on estimates reflecting a reasonable degree of accuracy, but the *totals* being distributed (recorded in column G) *must* match the amounts reported for the corresponding items elsewhere in the Report of Condition (unless the bank's smallest foreign offices have been excluded). The required matching for each line item is described in the instructions. For further assistance in the matching, a worksheet accompanies the report forms.

Dollar Amounts in Thousands

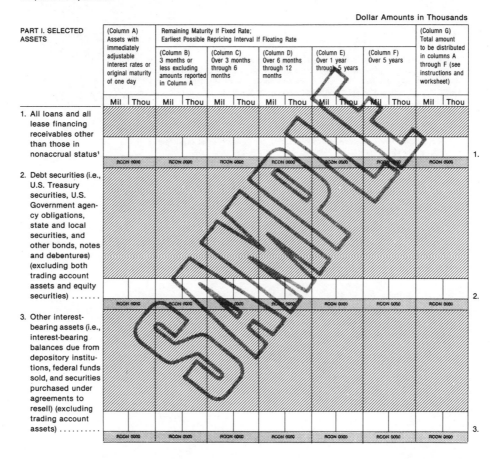

PART I. SELECTED ASSETS	(Column A) Assets with immediately adjustable interest rates or original maturity of one day		Remaining Maturity If Fixed Rate; Earliest Possible Repricing Interval If Floating Rate										(Column G) Total amount to be distributed in columns A through F (see instructions and worksheet)	
			(Column B) 3 months or less excluding amounts reported in Column A		(Column C) Over 3 months through 6 months		(Column D) Over 6 months through 12 months		(Column E) Over 1 year through 5 years		(Column F) Over 5 years			
	Mil	Thou	Mil	Thou	Mil	Thou	Mil	Thou	Mil	Thou	Mil	Thou	Mil	Thou
1. All loans and all lease financing receivables other than those in nonaccrual status[1]	RCON 0000		RCON 0000		RCON 0000		RCON 0000		RCON 0000		RCON 0000		RCON 0000		1.
2. Debt securities (i.e., U.S. Treasury securities, U.S. Government agency obligations, state and local securities, and other bonds, notes and debentures) (excluding both trading account assets and equity securities)	RCON 0000		RCON 0000		RCON 0000		RCON 0000		RCON 0000		RCON 0000		RCON 0000		2.
3. Other interest-bearing assets (i.e., interest-bearing balances due from depository institutions, federal funds sold, and securities purchased under agreements to resell) (excluding trading account assets)	RCON 0000		RCON 0000		RCON 0000		RCON 0000		RCON 0000		RCON 0000		RCON 0000		3.

[1] Amortizing real estate loans secured by 1 to 4 family residential properties in domestic offices and installment loans to individuals for household, family, and other personal expenditures (excluding credit cards and related plans) in domestic offices may be spread in item 1 of part I above by selecting one of two methods at the reporting bank's option: (1) by scheduled amortization, or (2) by final maturity for fixed rate loans and by earliest repricing opportunity for floating rate loans. The first method is preferred. The option may be exercised independently for such 1 to 4 family mortgages and for such consumer installment loans but must be followed consistently for all such loans within each category. When option (2) is selected, Memorandum item 2.a. or 2.b. or both must be reported as appropriate.

For floating rate loans, if option (1) is selected, the scheduled payments should be spread only to the earliest repricing opportunity, at which point the total remaining balance should be reported. If option (2) is selected, the entire balance of such loans should be reported by the earliest repricing opportunity.

Schedule RC-J—Continued

Memoranda

	Mil	Thou	
1. Fixed rate debt securities with remaining maturity of over 10 years (included in item 2, column F above)			M.1.
	RCON 0000		

2. Additional information required of banks that use the alternative reporting method for reporting certain multipayment loans in domestic offices in part I, item 1 above. [Banks that report amortizing 1-4 family real estate loans or consumer installment loans in item 1 of part 1 above on the basis of scheduled amortization must enter N/A in 2.a. or 2.b. below, as appropriate.]

	(Column A) Estimated regularly scheduled payments received during the calendar quarter ending with the report date		(Column B) Dollar amount outstanding as of the report date for loans for which aggregate payments received were reported in column A		
	Mil	Thou	Mil	Thou	
a. Amortizing real estate loans secured by 1 to 4 family residential properties in domestic offices					M.2.a.
	RCON 0000		RCON 0000		
b. Installment loans to individuals for household, family, and other personal expenditures (excluding credit cards and related plans) in domestic offices					M.2.b.
	RCON 0000		RCON 0000		

Schedule RC-J—Continued

Dollar Amounts in Thousands

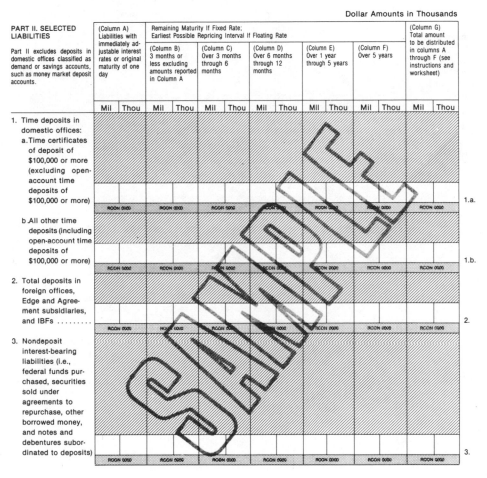

PART II. SELECTED LIABILITIES Part II excludes deposits in domestic offices classified as demand or savings accounts, such as money market deposit accounts.	(Column A) Liabilities with immediately adjustable interest rates or original maturity of one day		Remaining Maturity If Fixed Rate; Earliest Possible Repricing Interval If Floating Rate										(Column G) Total amount to be distributed in columns A through F (see instructions and worksheet)	
			(Column B) 3 months or less excluding amounts reported in Column A		(Column C) Over 3 months through 6 months		(Column D) Over 6 months through 12 months		(Column E) Over 1 year through 5 years		(Column F) Over 5 years			
	Mil	Thou	Mil	Thou	Mil	Thou	Mil	Thou	Mil	Thou	Mil	Thou	Mil	Thou
1. Time deposits in domestic offices: a. Time certificates of deposit of $100,000 or more (excluding open-account time deposits of $100,000 or more)															1.a.
b. All other time deposits (including open-account time deposits of $100,000 or more)															1.b.
2. Total deposits in foreign offices, Edge and Agreement subsidiaries, and IBFs															2.
3. Nondeposit interest-bearing liabilities (i.e., federal funds purchased, securities sold under agreements to repurchase, other borrowed money, and notes and debentures subordinated to deposits)															3.

Schedule RC-J—Continued

Dollar Amounts in Thousands

PART III. MATURITY OF DEBT SUBORDINATED TO DEPOSITS AND LIMITED-LIFE PREFERRED STOCK	Principal Amounts Due Within Specified Time Period From Report Date						(Column G) Total amount to be distributed in columns A through F (see instructions and worksheet)	
	(Column A) Less than 1 year	(Column B) 1 year to less than 2 years	(Column C) 2 years to less than 3 years	(Column D) 3 years to less than 4 years	(Column E) 4 years to less than 5 years	(Column F) 5 years or more		
	Mil	Thou	Mil	Thou	Mil	Thou	Mil	Thou	Mil	Thou	Mil	Thou	Mil	Thou
1. Notes and debentures subordinated to deposits (excluding mandatory convertible debt qualified for primary capital or equity capital equivalents)								RCON 0000	1.
2. Limited-life preferred stock	RCON 0000	RCON 0000	RCON 0000	RCON 0000	RCON 0000	RCON 0000	RCON 0000	2.

Memorandum
1. Mandatory convertible debt qualified for primary capital or equity capital equivalents................ M.1.

RCON 0000

Schedule RC-K—Quarterly Averages[1]

Dollar Amounts in Thousands		Bil	Mil	Thou	
ASSETS					
1. Interest-bearing balances due from depository institutions	RCON 0000				1.
2. U.S. Treasury securities and U.S. Government agency and corporation obligations	RCON 0000				2.
3. Securities issued by states and political subdivisions in the U.S.	RCON 0000				3.
4. Other securities (debt and equity)	RCON 0000				4.
5. Federal funds sold and securities purchased under agreements to resell in domestic offices of the bank and of its Edge and Agreement subsidiaries, and in IBFs	RCON 0000				5.
6. Loans:					
a. Loans in domestic offices:					
(1) Total loans	RCON 0000				6.a.(1)
(2) Loans secured by real estate	RCON 0000				6.a.(2)
(3) Loans to finance agricultural production and other loans to farmers[2]	RCON 0000				6.a.(3)
(4) Commercial and industrial loans	RCON 0000				6.a.(4)
(5) Loans to individuals for household, family, and other personal expenditures . . .	RCON 0000				6.a.(5)
(6) Obligations (other than securities) of states and political subdivisions in the U.S. . .	RCON 0000				6.a.(6)
b. Total loans in foreign offices, Edge and Agreement subsidiaries, and IBFs	RCON 0000				6.b.
7. Assets held in trading accounts	RCON 0000				7.
8. Earning assets	RCON 0000				8.
9. Total assets	RCON 0000				9.
LIABILITIES					
10. Time certificates of deposit of $100,000 or more in domestic offices	RCON 0000				10.
11. All other interest-bearing deposits *not* subject to fixed federal interest rate ceilings in domestic offices	RCON 0000				11.
12. Interest-bearing deposits in foreign offices, Edge and Agreement subsidiaries, and IBFs . .	RCON 0000				12.
13. Federal funds purchased and securities sold under agreements to repurchase in domestic offices of the bank and of its Edge and Agreement subsidiaries, and in IBFs	RCON 0000				13.
14. Other borrowed money	RCON 0000				14.

[1] For all items, banks have the option of reporting either (1) an average of daily figures for the quarter or (2) an average of 13 weekly figures (i.e., the Wednesday of each week of the quarter).
[2] Must be reported separately only if agricultural loans in domestic offices exceed five percent of total loans in domestic offices.

Schedule RC-L—Commitments and Contingencies

Please read carefully the instructions for the preparation of Schedule RC-L.

Dollar Amounts in Thousands		Bil	Mil	Thou	
1. Commitments to make or purchase loans or to extend credit in the form of lease financing arrangements (report only the unused portions of commitments that are fee paid or otherwise legally binding)	RCON 0000				1.
2. Futures and forward contracts (exclude contracts involving foreign exchange):					
a. Commitments to purchase	RCON 0000				2.a.
b. Commitments to sell	RCON 0000				2.b.
3. Standby contracts and other option arrangements:					
a. Obligations to purchase under option contracts	RCON 0000				3.a.
b. Obligations to sell under option contracts	RCON 0000				3.b.
4. Commitments to purchase foreign currencies and U.S. dollar exchange (spot and forward)	RCON 0000				4.
5. Standby letters of credit and foreign office guarantees:					
a. Standby letters of credit and foreign office guarantees:					
(1) To U.S. addressees (domicile)	RCON 0000				5.a.(1)
(2) To non-U.S. addressees (domicile)	RCON 0000				5.a.(2)
b. Amount of standby letters of credit in items 5.a.(1) and 5.a.(2) conveyed to others through participations	RCON 0000				5.b.
6. Commercial and similar letters of credit	RCON 0000				6.
7. Participations in acceptances (as described in the instructions) conveyed to others by the reporting (accepting) bank	RCON 0000				7.
8. Participations in acceptances (as described in the instructions) acquired by the reporting (nonaccepting) bank	RCON 0000				8.
9. Securities borrowed	RCON 0000				9.
10. Securities lent	RCON 0000				10.
11. Other significant commitments and contingencies (list below each component of this item over 25% of Schedule RC, item 28, "Total equity capital")	RCON 0000				11.

Memorandum

		Bil	Mil	Thou	
1. Loans originated by the reporting bank that have been sold or participated to others during the calendar quarter ending with the report date (exclude the portions of such loans retained by the reporting bank; see instructions for other exclusions)	RCON 0000				M.1.

Schedule RC-M—Memoranda

	Dollar Amounts in Thousands		Bil	Mil	Thou	
1. Extensions of credit by the reporting bank to its executive officers, principal shareholders, and their related interests as of the report date:						
a. Aggregate amount of all extensions of credit to all executive officers, principal shareholders, and their related interests	RCON 0000					1.a.
b. Number of executive officers and principal shareholders to whom the amount of all extensions of credit by the reporting bank (including extensions of credit to related interests) equals or exceeds the lesser of $500,000 or 5 percent of total capital as defined for this purpose in agency regulations	Number RCON 0000					1.b.
2. Federal funds sold and securities purchased under agreements to resell (Schedule RC, item 3) with U.S. branches and agencies of foreign banks	RCON 0000					2.
3. Amount of reserve balances actually passed through to the Federal Reserve by the reporting bank on behalf of its respondent depository institutions[1]	RCON 0000					3.
4. Amount of reserve balances actually passed through to the Federal Reserve on behalf of the reporting bank by its correspondent bank[1]	RCON 0000					4.
Item 5 is to be completed only by banks with $1 billion or more in total assets.						
5. Customers' liability to this bank on acceptances outstanding (Schedule RC, item 9):						
a. U.S. addressees (domicile)	RCON 0000					5.a.
b. Non-U.S. addressees (domicile)	RCON 0000					5.b.

[1] See Glossary entry for "pass-through reserve balances."

Schedule RC-N—Past Due, Nonaccrual, and Renegotiated Loans and Lease Financing Receivables

The FFIEC regards only information reported in Column A confidential.

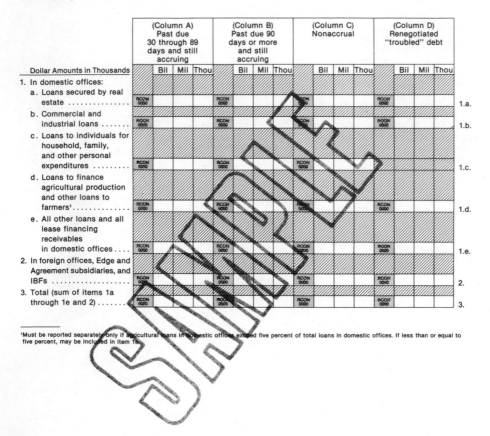

Dollar Amounts in Thousands	(Column A) Past due 30 through 89 days and still accruing			(Column B) Past due 90 days or more and still accruing			(Column C) Nonaccrual			(Column D) Renegotiated "troubled" debt			
	Bil	Mil	Thou	Bil	Mil	Thou	Bil	Mil	Thou	Bil	Mil	Thou	
1. In domestic offices:													
a. Loans secured by real estate													1.a.
b. Commercial and industrial loans													1.b.
c. Loans to individuals for household, family, and other personal expenditures													1.c.
d. Loans to finance agricultural production and other loans to farmers[1]..............													1.d.
e. All other loans and all lease financing receivables in domestic offices													1.e.
2. In foreign offices, Edge and Agreement subsidiaries, and IBFs													2.
3. Total (sum of items 1a through 1e and 2)													3.

[1] Must be reported separately only if agricultural loans in domestic offices exceed five percent of total loans in domestic offices. If less than or equal to five percent, may be included in item 1e.

Optional Submission of Narrative Statement Concerning the Figures Submitted on Schedule RC-N, Past Due, Nonaccrual, and Renegotiated Loans and Lease Financing Receivables

at close of business on _____ 19 ____

_____   _____,_____
Legal Title of Bank   City   State

The management of the reporting bank may, *if it wishes*, submit a brief narrative statement on the figures submitted on this schedule. This optional statement will be made available to the public, along with columns B, C, and D of this schedule and the Reports of Condition and Income, in response to any request for individual bank Report of Condition data or for this schedule. Banks choosing to submit the narrative statement should therefore ensure that the statement does not contain information that they are not willing to have made public or that would compromise the privacy of their customers.

The optional statement must be entered on this sheet. The statement should not exceed 100 words. Further, regardless of the number of words, the statement must not exceed 750 characters, including punctuation, indentation, and standard spacing between words and sentences. If any submission should exceed 750 characters, as defined, it will be truncated at 750 characters with no notice to the submitting bank and the truncated statement will appear as the bank's statement both on agency computerized records and in computer-file releases to the public.

All information furnished by the bank in the narrative statement must be accurate and not misleading. Appropriate efforts shall be taken by the submitting bank to ensure the statement's accuracy. The statement must be signed, in the space provided below, by a senior officer of the bank who thereby attests to its accuracy.

If, subsequent to the original submission, *material* changes are submitted for the data reported on this schedule, the existing narrative statement will be deleted from the files, and from disclosure; the bank, at its option, may replace it with a statement, under signature, appropriate to the amended data.

The optional narrative statement will appear in agency records and in release to the public exactly as submitted (or amended as described in the preceding paragraph) by the management of the bank (except for the truncation of overlength statements described above). THE STATEMENT WILL *NOT* BE EDITED OR SCREENED IN ANY WAY BY THE SUPERVISORY AGENCIES FOR ACCURACY OR RELEVANCE. DISCLOSURE OF THE STATEMENT SHALL NOT SIGNIFY THAT ANY FEDERAL SUPERVISORY AGENCY HAS VERIFIED OR CONFIRMED THE ACCURACY OF THE INFORMATION CONTAINED THEREIN. A STATEMENT TO THIS EFFECT WILL APPEAR ON ANY PUBLIC RELEASE OF THE OPTIONAL STATEMENT SUBMITTED BY THE MANAGEMENT OF THE REPORTING BANK.

Bank Management Statement (please type or print clearly):

_____   _____
Signature of Executive Officer of Bank   Date of Signature

Schedule RC-O—Other Data for Deposit Insurance Assessments

Dollar Amounts in Thousands		Bil	Mil	Thou	
1. Unposted debits:					
a. Actual amount of all unposted debits	RCON 0000				1.a.
OR					
b. Separate amount of unposted debits:					
(1) Actual amount of unposted debits to demand deposits	RCON 0000				1.b.(1)
(2) Actual amount of unposted debits to time and savings deposits	RCON 0000				1.b.(2)
2. Unposted credits (see instructions):					
a. Actual amount of all unposted credits	RCON 0000				2.a.
OR					
b. Separate amount of unposted credits:					
(1) Actual amount of unposted credits to demand deposits	RCON 0000				2.b.(1)
(2) Actual amount of unposted credits to time and savings deposits	RCON 0000				2.b.(2)
3. Uninvested trust funds (cash) held in bank's own trust department (not included in total deposits in domestic offices).	RCON 0000				3.
4. Deposits of consolidated subsidiaries in domestic offices (not included in total deposits in domestic offices):					
a. Demand deposits of consolidated subsidiaries	RCON 0000				4.a.
b. Time and savings deposits of consolidated subsidiaries	RCON 0000				4.b.
5. Deposits of insured branches in Puerto Rico and U.S. territories and possessions (included in Schedule RC-E, part II):					
a. Demand deposits in insured branches	RCON 0000				5.a.
b. Time and savings deposits in insured branches	RCON 0000				5.b.
Memorandum					
1. Total deposits in domestic offices of the bank (to be completed for the *June* report only):					
a. Amount of deposit accounts $100,000 or less.	RCON 0000				M.1.a.
b. Deposit accounts more than $100,000:					
(1) *Amount* outstanding	RCON 0000				M.1.b.(1)
(2) *Number* of accounts . . . . Number RCON 0000					M.1.b.(2)

Consolidated Report of Income

All schedules are to be reported on a calendar year-to-date basis in thousands of dollars.

Schedule RI—Income Statement

Dollar Amounts in Thousands		Bil	Mil	Thou	
1. Interest Income:					
a. Interest and fee income on loans:					
(1) In domestic offices:					
(a) Loans secured by real estate	RIAD				1.a.(1)(a)
(b) Loans to depository institutions	RIAD				1.a.(1)(b)
(c) Loans to finance agricultural production and other loans to farmers	RIAD				1.a.(1)(c)
(d) Commercial and industrial loans	RIAD				1.a.(1)(d)
(e) Acceptances of other banks	RIAD				1.a.(1)(e)
(f) Loans to individuals for household, family, and other personal expenditures:					
(1) Credit cards and related plans	RIAD				1.a.(1)(f)(1)
(2) Other	RIAD				1.a.(1)(f)(2)
(g) Loans to foreign governments and official institutions	RIAD				1.a.(1)(g)
(h) Obligations (other than securities) of states and political subdivisions in the U.S.	RIAD				1.a.(1)(h)
(i) All other loans in domestic offices	RIAD				1.a.(1)(i)
(2) In foreign offices, Edge and Agreement subsidiaries, and IBFs	RIAD				1.a.(2)
b. Income from lease financing receivables	RIAD				1.b.
c. Interest income on balances due from depository institutions:					
(1) In domestic offices	RIAD				1.c.(1)
(2) In foreign offices, Edge and Agreement subsidiaries, and IBFs	RIAD				1.c.(2)
d. Interest and dividend income on securities:					
(1) U.S. Treasury securities and U.S. Government agency and corporation obligations	RIAD				1.d.(1)
(2) Securities issued by states and political subdivisions in In the U.S.	RIAD				1.d.(2)
(3) Other domestic securities (debt and equity)	RIAD				1.d.(3)
(4) Foreign securities (debt and equity)	RIAD				1.d.(4)
e. Interest income from assets held in trading accounts	RIAD				1.e.
f. Interest income on federal funds sold and securities purchased under agreements to resell in domestic offices of the bank and of its Edge and Agreement subsidiaries, and in IBFs	RIAD				1.f.
g. Total interest income (sum of items 1.a. through 1.f.)	RIAD				1.g.
2. Interest expense:					
a. Interest on deposits:					
(1) Interest on deposits in domestic offices:					
(a) Interest on time certificates of deposit of $100,000 or more	RIAD				2.a.(1)(a)
(b) Interest on other deposits	RIAD				2.a.(1)(b)
(2) Interest on deposits in foreign offices, Edge and Agreement subsidiaries, and IBFs	RIAD				2.a.(2)
b. Expense of federal funds purchased and securities sold under agreements to repurchase in domestic offices of the bank and of its Edge and Agreement subsidiaries, and in IBFs	RIAD				2.b.

Schedule RI—Continued

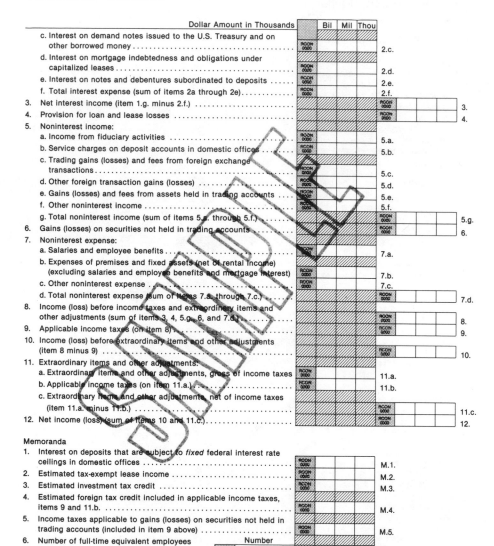

Dollar Amount in Thousands   Bil   Mil   Thou

    c. Interest on demand notes issued to the U.S. Treasury and on other borrowed money . . . . 2.c.

    d. Interest on mortgage indebtedness and obligations under capitalized leases . . . . 2.d.

    e. Interest on notes and debentures subordinated to deposits . . . . . . 2.e.

    f. Total interest expense (sum of items 2a through 2e) . . . . 2.f.

3. Net interest income (item 1.g. minus 2.f.) . . . . 3.

4. Provision for loan and lease losses . . . . 4.

5. Noninterest income:

    a. Income from fiduciary activities . . . . 5.a.

    b. Service charges on deposit accounts in domestic offices . . . . 5.b.

    c. Trading gains (losses) and fees from foreign exchange transactions . . . . 5.c.

    d. Other foreign transaction gains (losses) . . . . 5.d.

    e. Gains (losses) and fees from assets held in trading accounts . . . . 5.e.

    f. Other noninterest income . . . . 5.f.

    g. Total noninterest income (sum of items 5.a. through 5.f.) . . . . 5.g.

6. Gains (losses) on securities not held in trading accounts . . . . 6.

7. Noninterest expense:

    a. Salaries and employee benefits . . . . 7.a.

    b. Expenses of premises and fixed assets (net of rental income) (excluding salaries and employee benefits and mortgage interest) . . . . 7.b.

    c. Other noninterest expense . . . . 7.c.

    d. Total noninterest expense (sum of items 7.a. through 7.c.) . . . . . . 7.d.

8. Income (loss) before income taxes and extraordinary items and other adjustments (sum of items 3, 4, 5.g., 6, and 7.d.) . . . . 8.

9. Applicable income taxes (on item 8) . . . . 9.

10. Income (loss) before extraordinary items and other adjustments (item 8 minus 9) . . . . 10.

11. Extraordinary items and other adjustments:

    a. Extraordinary items and other adjustments, gross of income taxes 11.a.

    b. Applicable income taxes (on item 11.a.) . . . . 11.b.

    c. Extraordinary items and other adjustments, net of income taxes (item 11.a. minus 11.b.) . . . . 11.c.

12. Net income (loss) (sum of items 10 and 11.c.) . . . . 12.

Memoranda

1. Interest on deposits that are subject to *fixed* federal interest rate ceilings in domestic offices . . . . M.1.

2. Estimated tax-exempt lease income . . . . M.2.

3. Estimated investment tax credit . . . . M.3.

4. Estimated foreign tax credit included in applicable income taxes, items 9 and 11.b. . . . . M.4.

5. Income taxes applicable to gains (losses) on securities not held in trading accounts (included in item 9 above) . . . . M.5.

6. Number of full-time equivalent employees on payroll at end of current period . . . .   Number   M.6.

Schedule RI-A—Changes in Equity Capital

Indicate decreases and losses in parentheses.

	Dollar Amounts in Thousands		Bil	Mil	Thou	
1.	Equity capital end of previous calendar year..	RCON 0000				1.
2.	Equity capital adjustments from amended Reports of Income, net.....................	RCON 0000				2.
3.	Amended balance end of previous calendar year (sum of items 1 and 2)	RCON 0000				3.
4.	Net income (loss) (must equal Schedule RI, item 12)...............................	RCON 0000				4.
5.	Sale, conversion, acquisition, or retirement of capital stock, net	RCON 0000				5.
6.	Changes incident to business combinations, net	RCON 0000				6.
7.	Cash dividends declared on preferred stock	RCON 0000	(		)	7.
8.	Cash dividends declared on common stock..	RCON 0000	(		)	8.
9.	Cumulative effect of changes in accounting principles from prior years (see instructions for this schedule)...	RCON 0000				9.
10.	Corrections of material accounting errors from prior years (see instructions for this schedule)	RCON 0000				10.
11.	Net unrealized gain (loss) on marketable equity securities..........................	RCON 0000				11.
12.	Foreign currency translation adjustments	RCON 0000				12.
13.	Other transactions with parent holding company (not included in item 5, 7, or 8 above) ...	RCON 0000				13.
14.	Equity capital end of current period (sum of items 3 through 13) (must equal Schedule RC, item 28)	RCON 0000				14.

Schedule RI-B—Charge-Offs and Recoveries and Changes in Allowance for Loan and Lease Losses

I. Charge-Offs and Recoveries on Loans and Leases

Dollar Amounts in Thousands	(Column A) Charge-Offs			(Column B) Recoveries			
	calendar year-to-date						
	Bil	Mil	Thou	Bil	Mil	Thou	
1. Loans secured by real estate:							
a. To U.S. addressees (domicile)							1.a.
b. To non-U.S. addressees (domicile)							1.b.
2. Loans to depository institutions and acceptances of other banks:							
a. To U.S. banks and other U.S. depository institutions							2.a.
b. To foreign banks							2.b.
3. Loans to finance agricultural production and other loans to farmers							3.
4. Commercial and industrial loans:							
a. To U.S. addressees (domicile)							4.a.
b. To non-U.S. addressees (domicile)							4.b.
5. Loans to individuals for household, family, and other personal expenditures:							
a. Credit cards and related plans							5.a.
b. Other							5.b.
6. Loans to foreign governments and official institutions							6.
7. All other loans							7.
8. Lease financing receivables:							
a. Of U.S. addressees (domicile)							8.a.
b. Of non-U.S. addressees (domicile)							8.b.
9. Total (sum of items 1 through 8)							9.

II. Changes in Allowance for Loan and Lease Losses

Dollar Amounts in Thousands	Bil	Mil	Thou	
1. Balance end of previous calendar year				1.
2. Recoveries (must equal part I, item 9, column B above)				2.
3. Charge-Offs (must equal part I, item 9, column A above)	(		)	3.
4. Provision for loan and lease losses (must equal Schedule RI, item 4)				4.
5. Adjustments (see instructions for this schedule)				5.
6. Balance end of current period (sum of items 1 through 5) (must equal Schedule RC, item 4.b.)				6.

Schedule RI-C is to be reported only with the December Report of Income.

Schedule RI-C—Applicable Income Taxes by Taxing Authority

Dollar Amounts in Thousands	Bil	Mil	Thou	
1. Federal				1.
2. State and local				2.
3. Foreign				3.
4. Total (sum of items 1 through 3) (must equal sum of Schedule RI, items 9 and 11.b.)				4.
5. Deferred portion of item 4				5.

Schedule RI-D—Income from International Operations

For all banks with foreign offices, Edge or Agreement subsidiaries, or IBFs where international operations account for more than 10 percent of total revenues, total assets, or net income.

I. Estimated Income from International Operations

Dollar Amounts in Thousands		Bil	Mil	Thou	
1. Interest income and expense booked at foreign offices, Edge and Agreement subsidiaries, and IBFs:					
a. Interest income booked	RCON 0000				1.a.
b. Interest expense booked	RCON 0000				1.b.
c. Net interest income booked at foreign offices, Edge and Agreement subsidiaries, and IBFs (item 1.a. minus 1.b.)	RCON 0000				1.c.
2. Adjustments for booking location of international operations:					
a. Net interest income attributable to international operations booked at domestic offices	RCON 0000				2.a.
b. Net interest income attributable to domestic business booked at foreign offices	RCON 0000				2.b.
c. Net booking location adjustment (item 2.a. minus 2.b.)	RCON 0000				2.c.
3. Noninterest income and expense attributable to international operations:					
a. Noninterest income attributable to international operations	RCON 0000				3.a.
b. Provision for loan and lease losses attributable to international operations	RCON 0000				3.b.
c. Other noninterest expense attributable to international operations	RCON 0000				3.c.
d. Net noninterest income (expense) attributable to international operations (item 3.a. minus 3.b. and 3.c.)	RCON 0000				3.d.
4. Estimated pretax income attributable to international operations before capital allocation adjustment (sum of items 1.c., 2.c., and 3.d.)	RCON 0000				4.
5. Adjustment to pretax income for internal allocations to international operations to reflect the effects of equity capital on overall bank funding costs	RCON 0000				5.
6. Estimated pretax income attributable to international operations after capital allocation adjustment (item 4 minus 5)	RCON 0000				6.
7. Income taxes attributable to income from international operations as estimated in item 6. .	RCON 0000				7.
8. Estimated net income attributable to international operations (item 6 minus 7)	RCON 0000				8.

Memoranda

		Bil	Mil	Thou	
1. Intracompany interest income included in item 1.a. above	RCON 0000				M.1.
2. Intracompany interest expense included in item 1.b. above	RCON 0000				M.2.

II. Supplementary Details on Income from International Operations Required by the Departments of Commerce and Treasury for Purposes of the U.S. International Accounts and the U.S. National Income and Product Accounts

Dollar Amounts in Thousands		Bil	Mil	Thou	
1. Interest income booked at IBFs	RCON 0000				1.
2. Interest expense booked at IBFs	RCON 0000				2.
3. Noninterest income attributable to international operations booked at domestic offices (excluding IBFs)	RCON 0000				3.
4. Provision for loan and lease losses attributable to international operations booked at domestic offices (excluding IBFs)	RCON 0000				4.
5. Other noninterest expense attributable to international operations booked at domestic offices (excluding IBFs)	RCON 0000				5.

Schedule RI-E—Explanations

Detail all adjustments in Schedules RI-A and RI-B, all extraordinary items and other adjustments, and all significant items of other noninterest income and other noninterest expense in Schedule RI. (See instructions for details.)

Index

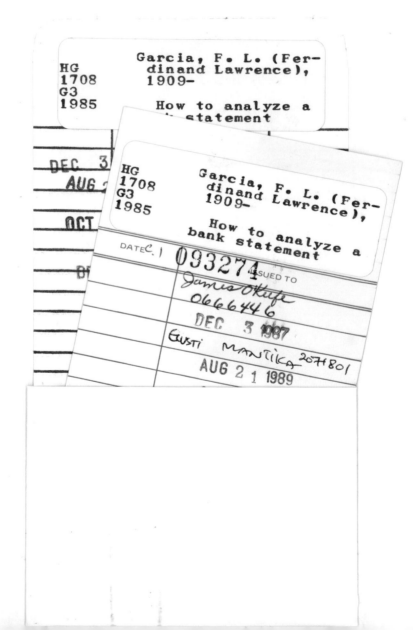